THE MODERN
INQUISITION

THE MODERN INQUISITION

Seven prominent Catholics and their struggles with the Vatican

Paul Collins

THE OVERLOOK PRESS
Woodstock & New York

This edition first published in the United States in 2002 by
The Overlook Press, Peter Mayer Publishers, Inc.
Woodstock & New York

WOODSTOCK:
One Overlook Drive
Woodstock, NY 12498
www.overlookpress.com
[for individual orders, bulk and special sales, contact our Woodstock office]

NEW YORK:
141 Wooster Street
New York, NY 10012

Library of Congress Cataloging-in-Publication Data

Collins, Paul.
The modern inquisition : seven prominent Catholics
and their struggles with the Vatican / Paul Collins.
p. cm.
1. Catholics—History—20th century. 2. Dissenters, Religious—History—20th century.
3. Chatholic Church. Congregatiopro Doctrina Fidei—History—20th Century. I. Title
BX4669 . C69 2002   282—dc21   2002025223

Printed in the United States of America
ISBN 1-58567-270-X
1 3 5 7 9 8 6 4 2

Contents

Preface

This is a book about the inner workings of the Vatican, intellectual freedom, and passionate and deeply held convictions. It also contains the personal stories of seven Catholic sisters and priests who have experienced a unique inquisitorial process: examination of their opinions, writings and even their consciences by the Vatican's Congregation for the Doctrine of the Faith (CDF). But this is not just about their personal stories. What happened to them typifies the tensions and contradictions within the contemporary Catholic Church and exposes the forces that have already alienated from the policies of the Vatican a sizeable majority of thinking Catholics in many parts of the world.

The seven protagonists in this book represent the kind of agenda embraced by most committed Catholics in the Western world, as well as many in Latin America, Asia and Africa. These Catholics are demanding a more decentralised, participative approach to the Church, with much of its decision-making authority being devolved to local communities and national conferences of bishops. The Vatican and the CDF are supported by a small but influential minority of Catholics who want to concentrate all power and authority in the papacy. One of the most potent weapons used to rein in their fellow Catholics is the secret reporting of bishops, priests, sisters and laity to Rome for supposed heresy, deviations or dissent from Catholic belief and practice.

The prominent English Catholic journalist, Clifford Longley, writing in the respected London weekly, the *Tablet*, has compared being turned into the Vatican for investigation by the CDF to what Judas did to Christ when he went to the chief priests to betray him. I certainly felt a sense of betrayal in late January 1998 when I discovered that I had been 'delated' (denounced) to Rome some time in 1997 for so-called 'doctrinal problems' with my book *Papal Power*. It was a rude reminder that the Inquisition's Australian minions are still alive and well.

My personal experience of this process has prompted this book, which contains my own story and those of six other well-known Roman Catholic sisters and priests who have been similarly investigated. In November 1999 I visited Sri Lanka, Germany, the UK and the US to interview all the contributors and to get some understanding of their pastoral and theological approach as well as of the local context.

The first thing that struck me about the people featured in this book was how psychologically well adjusted they are. Articulate, calm and intelligent, all of them have a healthy sense of humour and can laugh at themselves, a key prerequisite in anyone called to a prophetic role. But at a deeper level you perceive in them an inner strength and determination, a passionate commitment to God, to their ministry and to the search for the truth and the inner meaning of Christian existence. You also find a deep love of the Catholic Church and a complete absence of paranoia or any feeling of persecution. Never once did any of them suggest that they had been badly done by, either by the Vatican or by their religious orders, despite a complete clarity about the injustice of the process imposed on them by the CDF and by others in the Church.

In fact, as their stories show, these men and women are among the genuine prophets of the Catholic Church at the present time. While what has happened to them is compelling as personal story-telling, it also points towards the agenda that will guide the Catholic Church into the future. This is because they articulate the issues that most concern the vast majority of faithful Catholics and give expression to their faith-experience.

For the first time in the 450-year history of the Roman Inquisition and its lineal descendant, the CDF, a group of Catholics who have recently undergone examination by the Vatican's inquisitorial procedures talk openly about the experience and the effect the process had on their vocations and careers, and describe in detail how the CDF operates. The interviews clearly reveal a number of things about the CDF. First, it is obvious that ultimately the CDF does not play by any rules, even its own. By any modern standards of jurisprudence its processes are secretive, inquisitorial, often blatantly unfair to the accused and lack any application of the basic principles of human rights. Despite the Church's good record in this area in the broader, secular world, the CDF completely ignores human rights and shows no respect for normally accepted due process in its interactions with the accused. It is willing to invade their inner conscience and demand that even the most intimate and deeply held conscientious views be revealed. Fundamentally, the CDF lives in a time warp: despite attempts to tart it up in modern dress, it is essentially a creature of the sixteenth century whose methods have survived to the present day. Sadly, the evidence also is that the CDF cannot always be trusted to tell the whole truth, or even always to act with integrity, at least from the perspective of modern notions of equity and justice.

Second, it is clear from all the cases reported here that the CDF is not interested in genuine dialogue or real reconciliation. Without the slightest equivocation or doubt, it identifies its own view completely with the 'teaching of the Church', totally oblivious to the fact that its narrow orthodoxy often constricts and sometimes distorts the genuine Catholic tradition. What is quite extraordinary is that at times CDF 'consultors' do not seem to have a sound knowledge of, or even recognise, the basic principles of Catholic theology and ethics. This arises from the narrowness and lack of breadth of their theological approaches and their attempts to constrict the creative possibilities inherent in the Catholic tradition. The CDF constantly demands total conformity to its own view. There is never any question that its view might itself be limited, partial, or even wrong. It is this total lack of theological self-awareness that is most frightening.

Third, the CDF is highly selective in its choice of targets, and the selection of the person to be investigated often arises out of conflicts, jealousies and ambitions in the Catholic community of the country where the dispute starts and in which the accused person lives. People are also pursued because they are seen as 'symbolic' of a movement which troubles the Vatican. For instance, the CDF was concerned by Latin American liberation theology in the 1980s, so Brazilian Franciscan friar Leonardo Boff was targeted. In the 1990s the Vatican trained its sights on Asian theology, and Sri Lankan Father Tissa Balasuriya became the quarry.

The CDF rarely gives up; it pursues people for years. In the process it largely ignores local bishops and leaders of religious orders, except to try to manipulate them to do its will. And, as the cases of Sister Jeannine Gramick and Father Robert Nugent show, even condemnation is not the end of the long process. The Vatican continues to try to muzzle them and to prevent them speaking about the process and its result, despite the fact that they live in a democracy where free speech is guaranteed.

With the exception of the prefect (at the time of writing, Cardinal Josef Ratzinger) and the secretary (at the time of writing, Archbishop Tarcisio Bertone), all officials of the CDF remain strictly anonymous. Consultors, judges, prosecutors and even the 'defence counsel', who are usually drawn from the same group of people, are unknown to the accused, who will probably never meet them. However, the diligent researcher can discover the names of the CDF staff and consultors in the Vatican yearbook, the *Annuario Pontificio*, but this gives no clue as to the officials involved with specific cases. Finally, the CDF is above all right of judicial appeal to the Apostolic Signatura, the Vatican appeals court, specifically because the CDF's acts are always approved by the pope and, as such, are beyond appeal.

Early in the evolution of this book I decided that it would be an 'oral history'; that is, each of the interviewees would speak in their own voice. I have given a historical, biographical and theological context to their stories in order to make the book as accessible as possible. Where the contributor deals with a complex theological or ethical issue, I have intervened editorially to explain the background or to clarify the matter under discussion. The contributors' stories are unique, each a compelling, moving document in its own right. However, these are not purely subjective, inward-looking accounts. In all cases there has been a conscious effort to maintain a sense of both the wider Church community and the broader cultural and secular context.

By speaking publicly, as it were, for the first time, we hope to raise to some extent the veil of Vatican secrecy. We hope, too, that our personal stories will throw some light on a dark and arcane process which only undermines the Church whose truths it purports to uphold. The whole business of examination by the inquisitorial CDF is cloaked in mystery for most people, including the vast majority of Catholics. We hope that our stories will give readers a sense of what it means to be accused by anonymous informers, investigated in secret and 'tried' at arms length, with no recourse to appeal. Our aim is to use these stories as a stimulus to reform not only the Vatican, but also the whole process by which the Catholic Church arrives at the articulation of its belief. It is based on Jesus' premise that it is only 'the truth [that] will make you free' (John 8:32).

This book has been written precisely to break this kind of silence and to begin to reclaim the freedom that belongs to the sons and daughters of God. St Paul tells the Corinthians that freedom and God's Spirit go together: 'Where the Spirit of the Lord is, there is freedom' (II Cor 2:17). He further tells the Christians of Galatia: 'Stand firm, therefore, and do not submit to a yoke of slavery' (Gal 5:1). It is precisely this deep sense that freedom should characterise Christian and Catholic existence that motivates this book.

Books like this require generosity and support from many people. My thanks are due first to the six contributors. All of them are very busy people but they have given of their time, knowledge and expertise without stint. My agent, Mary Cunnane, has supported the book from the beginning and contributed much to it. Friendship is essential to the isolated editor and writer and many people have given me generous support. They know who they are.

Canberra, November 2000

CHAPTER 1

Palazzo del Sant'Uffizio

For several centuries now visitors have marvelled at the sheer size and baroque grandeur of St Peter's Basilica in Rome. But I doubt that many would even have noticed, unless they were really looking for it, a rather bland, dun-coloured, fortress-like building just to the left of the basilica and behind Bernini's glorious colonnade enclosing the piazza of the great church. This plain building faces its own tiny piazza and is just across the road from a clerical outfitter called 'Euroclero', a kind of Kmart for priests who cannot afford clerical haute couture. The bland building is called the Palazzo del Sant'Uffizio and is the modern-day home of the Inquisition. Nowadays, however, it has the less threatening but still rather grandiose title of the Congregation for the Doctrine of the Faith (CDF).

The word 'inquisition' has always had sinister and threatening connotations in English. It is derived from the Latin legal term *inquisitio*, meaning a legal investigation or inquiry. As soon as the word 'inquisition' is mentioned, most people immediately presume that they know what it means. They are usually thinking of the Spanish or the medieval versions, with images of the burning of thousands of witches, Jews, Protestants and other religious dissenters. While there are clear and traceable connections with the

1

medieval inquisitions, the CDF's parent body, the Sacred Congregation of the Roman and Universal Inquisition, or Holy Office, was not founded until 1542, whereas the medieval inquisitions began in southern France in 1232. The sixteenth-century Roman Inquisition's power was primarily limited to the Papal States, which then straddled Italy from east to west and from Ferrara and Bologna in the north to Terracina on the coast just south of Rome. To a lesser extent its authority was recognised by the inquisitions which operated in most of the other states of sixteenth- to eighteenth-century Italy, among them Venice and Naples.

The Roman Inquisition was founded by Pope Paul III (1534–49) in 1542 to counter Protestantism, which had started to penetrate into northern Italy in the late 1530s. At the same time, the *Index of Forbidden Books* was established. This was a list of 'dangerous' books that Catholics were not permitted to read, although for four hundred years the vast majority of Catholics had no idea nor any interest in the books listed in the *Index*. Pope Paul III hoped that by censoring heretical books and prosecuting those suspected of heresy, the Roman Inquisition would be a potent instrument in saving Italy from the Protestant Reformation.

By the mid-eighteenth century the Roman Inquisition had become less influential and was abolished when French Revolutionary forces occupied the Papal States and Rome in the 1790s and early 1800s. After the defeat of Napoleon in 1815, the Inquisition was restored in papal territory, although its impact was minimal. It was the *Index* rather than the Inquisition that prevailed in the nineteenth century. In 1907 the term 'Roman Inquisition' was dropped, and in 1913 the body was renamed the 'Supreme Sacred Congregation of the Holy Office'.

In December 1965, on the second-last day of the Second Vatican Council (Vatican II), it was again renamed as the 'Congregation for the Doctrine of the Faith'. However, despite claims that the present prefect of the CDF, Cardinal Josef Ratzinger, has opened up the Congregation and made it more modern and accountable, the evidence in this book indicates that the name changes were merely cosmetic. The secretive attitudes inherited from the baroque period and the early twentieth century have survived and still flourish in the attitudes and procedures of the CDF.

Today the CDF is a department within the Vatican bureaucracy, charged with protecting Catholic orthodoxy and examining and judging the theological, spiritual and religious writings and opinions expressed by all Catholics. According to Pope John Paul II's 28 June 1988 apostolic constitution on the Roman Curia, *Pastor Bonus*: 'The duty proper to the Congregation for the Doctrine of the Faith is to promote and safeguard the doctrine on faith and morals throughout the Catholic world: for this reason everything which in any way touches on such matters falls within its competence' (Article 48). This means that its ambit is wide indeed and almost limitless, because everything pertaining to faith and belief has a doctrinal or ethical aspect. In the *Regulations for Doctrinal Examination* (29 June 1997) the net seems to be cast even wider: 'In order that faith and morals not be harmed by errors *however disseminated* [my emphasis], it [the CDF] ... has the duty of examining writings and opinions which appear contrary to correct faith or dangerous' (Art. 1). The CDF is also assisted by and linked to two advisory bodies, the Pontifical Biblical Commission and the International Theological Commission, in that its cardinal prefect is also president of both these bodies.

Today's CDF offices look like a baroque fortress, an appearance that is reinforced by thick bars protecting the high windows. Through the narrow entrance you can see a peristyle with a rather lifeless fountain. Perhaps the reason for this fortress-like architecture is that a previous building housing the Roman Inquisition was burned down by the Roman mob in 1559 upon the death of the intransigent and inquisitorial Pope Paul IV (1555–59). However, the late-Renaissance popes obviously valued the Inquisition's work because in 1566 the building of St Peter's Basilica was suspended by the then pope, Pius V, himself an ex-inquisitor, so that construction of the palazzo of the Holy Office could be quickly completed. The present building has been the home of the Inquisition for most of its history since then.

In order to make sense of where the CDF fits into the Vatican bureaucracy, you need to know something about how the central government of the Roman Catholic Church operates. Because the origins of the papacy extend far back in European history, the Church bureaucracy still largely reflects the governmental patterns of the past. The Vatican resembles an absolute monarchy much more than a modern democracy. The pope's primary role is that of spiritual head of the Roman Catholic Church. But he is also the secular ruler of the Vatican City State, a tiny independent enclave of just over 40 hectares (108 acres) situated in the middle of the city of Rome. He is supported in his administration of the Church by a bureaucracy called the Roman Curia, which by contemporary bureaucratic standards is reasonably small and not particularly efficient. In February 2000 there were 2581 people employed in the Curia, comprising 1132 priests and members of religious orders and 1449 lay persons; of the total, 2171 were men and 410 were women. This number does not include those who work for the Vatican City State in jobs such as the maintenance of St Peter's, Vatican security, the museums, Vatican Radio, and the many other jobs involved in running a tiny city state.

In its present form the Roman Curia dates from the early seventeenth century, although, as we shall see, it has been through several attempted reforms since then. Substantially it is divided into congregations, or departments, that are usually presided over by a cardinal prefect, assisted by an archbishop secretary, and supported by a staff that is mainly comprised of priests, with a small minority who are sisters or lay people, almost all of these in minor roles. Italians still make up a majority of the staff, but nowadays the composition of congregational personnel is usually reasonably international. Foreigners are often 'more Roman than the Romans', and the world in which they work remains essentially Italian in style and operation. (For a fascinating and accurate insight into how the whole system works, see Thomas Reese's *Inside the Vatican: The Politics and Organization of the Catholic Church* (1996). John Cornwell's book, *A Thief in the Night* (1989), which deals with the death of Pope John Paul I, also gives you a good sense of the 'feel' of the Vatican.)

While the CDF is the most important of the curial congregations, the central body and real power-house of the Vatican is the Secretariat of State. Its head is the cardinal secretary of state, who functions as a kind of papal prime minister. The present secretary of state is Cardinal Angelo Sodano, appointed in 1991, who spent a decade from 1978 as papal nuncio (ambassador) to Chile where he was friendly with the dictator Augusto Pinochet. The Secretariat of State is divided into two sections: one deals with the internal affairs of the Church, reduplicating much of the work of the curial congregations, the other conducts the Vatican's foreign-relations activities. The Secretariat's nearest equivalent in the British system is a kind of combined cabinet office and foreign office; there is nothing strictly equivalent to it in the US system. The Curia also has other bodies: tribunals, pontifical councils (these have largely come into existence since Vatican II), and offices dedicated to various specific tasks.

But back to the CDF. The names of its staff and general information about their respective positions are all set out in the *Annuario Pontificio*. In 1999 the CDF had a full-time staff of thirty-four. They are reported to complain often about being very overworked; apparently there is a lot of 'heresy' around! Examining the composition of the full-time CDF staff in 1999 reveals that a small majority are Italian. The next-largest group is Germans, followed by English, Spanish and other Europeans; there is only one non-European. Of the eight lay people listed, five are women. Four of these were either *addetti tecnici* (technical staff) or *scrittori* (secretaries/writers), with the significant exception of Dr Marie Hendrickx. She is a Belgian with a doctorate in theology and is one of sixteen staff members who work for CDF secretary, Archbishop Bertone. She is the first and only full-time lay woman on the CDF staff. Perhaps she is trying to humanise the place a little: it is reported that she hosts a daily tea-break for her colleagues.

The administrative head of the CDF is Italian Archbishop Tarcisio Bertone, SDB. Born in 1934, he is a member of the Salesian order, the 'SDB' after his name referring to the Salesians of Don Bosco, a religious order founded in 1859 in Turin, Italy, and numerically one of the largest male religious orders in the Church. He was appointed Archbishop of Vercelli in north-central Italy in

1991, and was transferred to the CDF Secretariat in 1996. Bertone, like his predecessor as secretary, Archbishop Alberto Bovone, is not an expert theologian. He is essentially an administrator.

If Bertone runs the office, the real inquisitorial power lies with the prefect, Cardinal Josef Ratzinger. He chairs the Congregation (the English word 'congregation' comes from the Latin *congregatio* which means 'committee') of cardinals and bishops who run the CDF. Most of them are resident in Rome, but there are always some members of the Congregation from different parts of the world. In 1999, eleven of the CDF congregational cardinals were Rome-based and worked in the Vatican in other senior jobs; they all held down memberships of several congregations. Three cardinal members of the Congregation were from outside Rome: the cardinal-archbishops of Bordeaux, Vienna and Genoa. The other members of the Congregation comprised one eastern patriarch and five diocesan bishops. The bishops were from Dublin (Ireland), Melbourne (Australia), Granada (Spain), Goma (Zaire) and Rottenberg-Stuttgart (Germany). George Pell, Archbishop of Melbourne, who features in my own story, has been a member of the CDF since the early 1990s. He retired at the beginning of 2001.

While serious questions could be raised about the theological standing of virtually all the CDF's staff and consultors, the prefect, Cardinal Josef Ratzinger, is an established theologian with an international reputation. He chairs the meetings of the full Congregation and conveys the CDF's recommendations to the pope. Born in Bavaria in April 1927, Ratzinger was one of the more radical young turks at Vatican II. After Vatican II, Ratzinger taught systematic theology at Münster, Tübingen and Regensburg universities, was a member of the International Theological Commission from 1969 to 1980, and was appointed Archbishop of Munich-Freising and cardinal in 1977 by Pope Paul VI. The white-haired, distinguished-looking Ratzinger has been the head of the CDF since 1982 and, in terms of influence on Pope John Paul II, he is the most powerful cardinal in the Curia. Despite suffering from heart problems, he is sometimes described as the 'grand inquisitor' or the *panzerkardinal*. He is actually a pious, elegant intellectual who is pessimistic about modern culture's abandonment of absolute truth. While he is not an intimate friend of John Paul II, he is without doubt his closest collaborator.

Ratzinger has been accused by some of betraying Vatican II and of being a turncoat in order to gain ecclesiastical promotion. I do not agree with this assessment. In some ways his pessimism about modern culture is the real clue to the consistency of Ratzinger's theological position. What has only been recognised over the last decade and a half is that there was a deep 'fault-line' running through the majority of progressive bishops and thinkers at Vatican II. On the one hand there were those whose emphasis was on a radical opening-up of the Church to modern culture. This is what the man who started Vatican II, Pope John XXIII (1958–63), called *aggiornamento*. Many of the strongest supporters of this emphasis were those who were very much aware of the Church's past interactions with culture, of the many relativities of its teachings, and of the forms and shapes that the structure of the Church had taken in different periods. In other words, they were people whose approach was shaped by an historical awareness.

Generally, such people have a more optimistic approach to modernity and emphasise the role of the Church as part of contemporary culture. While they certainly want the Church to offer a prophetic critique of culture, nevertheless they want to do it from within. Probably most Western-educated Catholics would fit into this category, even if they have not articulated it for themselves. The foundation for this approach was laid by theologians such as the French Dominican, Yves Congar (1904–95), who emphasised the role of laity and the importance of ecumenism, and the Austrian Jesuit, Karl Rahner (1904–84), the greatest Catholic theologian of the twentieth century, whose emphasis on the universal self-communication of God through grace laid the foundations for a much more positive assessment of the world and culture.

In contrast, there are a minority of especially but not exclusively continental-European Catholics, such as Ratzinger and the Swiss theologian, Hans Urs von Balthasar (1905–88), who are much more concerned about a return to the sources of the Catholic tradition, especially in the early Church and patristic period up to the fifth century. Ratzinger, for instance, is an expert on the great theologian, St Augustine (354–430). It is in the early Church that these theologians find the absolute basics of Christian faith. While the interest of this group lies in the past, most of its influential members are theologians rather than trained historians. They share a common pessimism about contemporary culture and tend to see the Church as standing over and against the world. They do not deny the kind of emphasis that Rahner gives to grace, but they do not highlight it. For this group the key issue is always seeking the Truth with a capital 'T'. For them the Church, which already has the Truth, must stand over and against a world of post-modern philosophical, doctrinal and ethical relativities, of consumerist selfishness and sexual permissiveness. They are prepared to see the Church reduced to a much smaller community, so long as its remnant members maintain a coherent commitment to Truth. (There is a good treatment of Ratzinger's theological approach in John L. Allen's *Cardinal Ratzinger: The Vatican's Enforcer of the Faith* (2000).)

Before describing how the CDF operates when dealing with an accused, we should first look briefly at the history of the Congregation to examine if much has really changed in its attitudes and modes of operation over the past 450 years.

When Pope Paul III established the Roman Inquisition in 1542, he was the first pope of the Reformation period to take the internal reform of both the hierarchy and the wider Church seriously. As Cardinal Alessandro Farnese, he was a typically worldly Renaissance prince who rose in the ranks of the Church because his beautiful sister, Giulia, was a mistress of Pope Alexander VI (1492–1503). He had a noblewoman-mistress himself and was father of several illegitimate children. However, he underwent a conversion and became the first great reforming pope of the Counter-Reformation period. But unlike many other reformed characters, he never became a fanatic or rigorist. A wonderful portrait of him by Titian shows him aged and stooped, but with extraordinarily intelligent and keen, worldly eyes, looking at something in the distance. He was also the pope who began the reforming Council of Trent.

The Roman Inquisition was established in response to both the penetration of Protestantism in northern Italy and the spectacular conversions to the reformed faith of a couple of prominent Italian clerics. The now abolished *Index of Forbidden Books* was also established during Paul III's time and worked in tandem with the Inquisition for most of its history. However, it was not until the papacy of Paul IV (1555–59) that the Roman Inquisition really became pervasive in the Papal States particularly, and in Italy generally. Many subsequent popes had been members of the Inquisition as cardinals and, in the reform of the Roman Curia by Sixtus V (1585–90), the Congregation of the Roman and Universal Inquisition, or Holy Office, became the senior and most important congregation of the Curia.

Certainly, the Inquisition was very active in the latter part of the sixteenth century and the earlier part of the seventeenth century. However, the Roman and Italian inquisitions need to be clearly distinguished from the Spanish Inquisition, which was entirely independent and fundamentally an instrument of state policy. The Italian inquisitions also need to be placed within their specific historical context. In the sixteenth and seventeenth centuries, religion was an integral part of the cultural fabric and as such was determined by state authority. A famous Latin adage summed up the situation: *cuius regio eius religio*. In other words, the ruler determined the religion of everyone who lived under his rule. While there were certainly notions of freedom of religion current at the time among both Catholic and Protestant thinkers, these were not recognised by state authority. Surprisingly, there have been very few major studies of the Roman Inquisition and presuppositions about the Spanish Inquisition are generally projected onto it, as well as the inaccurate myths of 'hundreds of thousands of victims'.

Part of the problem has been the vandalising of the curial archives during the Napoleonic period, when most of them were taken from Rome to Paris. Some were returned after the defeat of Napoleon in 1815 almost in their entirety (such as the archives of the Congregation of Propaganda Fide), but unfortunately about half of those of the Roman Inquisition were destroyed, a proportion dispersed (there is a sizeable set of Roman Inquisition material in Trinity College, Dublin), and what was returned to Rome has now become unavailable because it is part of a closed archive – that of the CDF. The American scholar John Tadeschi has devoted much of his life to the Roman Inquisition and much of the current material is drawn from his fascinating *The Prosecution of Heresy: Collected Studies on the Inquisition in Early Modern Italy* (1991). Tadeschi points out that for the diligent researcher there is abundant information available on both the Roman Inquisition and the local Italian inquisitions, such as the Venetian or the Neapolitan.

Dominicans and Franciscans staffed the Inquisition, and tribunals were often held in their religious houses. Jesuit influence waxed and waned with different popes. Tadeschi notes that 'in several respects the Holy Office was a pioneer of judicial reform' and was often more justly administered than many of the contemporary court systems, including the British. The Roman Inquisition was particularly careful on questions concerning witchcraft and never gave way to the communal mania that saw many women judicially murdered in northern Europe, and in Salem and various other places of Puritan North America. In fact, the inquisitors were increasingly sceptical about witchcraft. Between 1560 and 1610, the major concern was 'Lutheranism' and heresy – that is, Protestantism – especially in northern Italy and the Papal States. The activities of the Roman Inquisition declined from the mid-seventeenth century onwards, and in the eighteenth century it did little. One sometimes has the impression that the eighteenth-century Inquisition is reflected reasonably accurately in the caricature of the Venetian grand inquisitor in Gilbert and Sullivan's *The Gondoliers*.

In addition, the pattern of charges against the accused changes after the early seventeenth century, when the emphasis shifts from heresy to 'illicit magic' and superstition – what today we would call 'popular religion'. The Roman Inquisition also issued dispensations from the fasts imposed on Catholics during Lent and Advent, and was very concerned with clerical immorality in the Papal States, especially solicitation in confession.

It is often seen as quite bloodthirsty, and the case of the ex-Dominican philosopher and cosmologist Giordano Bruno (1548–1600) is regularly cited as an example of this. He was burned in Rome's Campo dei Fiori in February 1600. The house-arrest of Galileo Galilei (1564–1642) for the last ten years of his life is also well known. Less famous is the incarceration of the Spanish mystical theorist, Miguel de Molinos (c.1640–97). Although in 1685 he recanted the errors of which he was accused, he was sentenced to lifelong imprisonment on charges of immorality with the women and nuns he directed. His letters, upon which the charges of heresy were based, are still held by the CDF and have never been made publicly available. Despite these famous cases, Tadeschi points out that the sentence of 'perpetual incarceration' usually meant about three years, especially if the accused showed signs of contrition. Certainly, imprisonment by the Roman Inquisition was a much better fate than the stake, mutilation, the galleys or banishment. This is how Tadeschi sums it up (p.151):

> A survey of the thousands of surviving sentences suggests that ... milder forms of punishment prevailed. Most frequently encountered are public humiliation in the form of abjurations read on the cathedral steps on Sundays and feast days before throngs of churchgoers, and salutary penances, fines or services for the benefit of charitable establishments, and a seemingly endless cycle of prayers and devotions to be performed over many months or years ... Only a small percentage of cases concluded with capital punishment.

According to Tadeschi no more than 160 people were burned in Rome between 1542 and 1761, slightly fewer than one per year.

In fact, confession, repentance and contrition were the real aim of the whole inquisitorial process and for the sixteenth and seventeenth centuries the Roman Inquisition would be judged to be reasonably merciful. One thing, however, that has survived in the practice of the CDF is that names of prosecution witnesses before the Holy Office are suppressed. Heresy used to be considered a public, capital crime and the intention was to favour the prosecution in support of the interests of the faith. It was also felt that witnesses needed to be protected from possible revenge by the family and friends of the accused. Inquisitorial officials were bound by a strict vow of secrecy, partly to protect the reputation of the accused and partly to maintain the element of surprise in order to be able to apprehend heretical accomplices more easily.

Perhaps the most stultifying aspect of the whole inquisitorial process on Italian culture, especially in the seventeenth and eighteenth centuries, resulted from the censorship of books. This happened elsewhere in Europe at that time, but the large number of books placed on the *Index* prevented the spread of new ideas into Italy. This was perhaps less true in the eighteenth century. For much of its history the Congregation of the Index was separate from the Roman Inquisition, but the two worked closely in tandem. However, the resulting stultification should not be exaggerated. Books were only condemned after they had been reported to Rome and usually only after they had been translated into Italian or Latin. As Owen Chadwick says: 'No tribe of sharp-nosed secretaries sat down to comb the literature of Europe in fear or hope of finding matter to deplore' (*The Popes and European Revolution* (1981), p. 325). From the beginning there was also a tendency to condemn the *omnia opera* (the complete works) of a suspect author. The Roman bureaucrats did not have time to sort through the often prolific writings of many seventeenth and eighteenth century authors.

In 1789 the French Revolution broke out and by 1799 Pius VI (1775–99) had died as a prisoner of the French Revolutionary forces in Valence. The Papal States were occupied. Many in Europe saw this as the end of the papacy. From the mid-1790s to 1815 the papal government and Curia went through a period of crisis and chaos. The Inquisition, as well as the papal civil government of central Italy, was swept away. The new, revolutionary ideas of liberty and equality were given free reign throughout Europe, even though they were hypocritically ignored by the upstart emperor, Napoleon I.

With the defeat of Napoleon at Waterloo in 1815 and the

restoration of the Papal States, the Roman Inquisition was revived, but while its physical reach was confined to that part of Italy governed by the papacy, its ambit gradually began to spread throughout Europe. As the condemnation of Félicité Robert de Lamennais (1782–1854) and those Catholics who argued that the Church had to embrace the liberal principles of the French Revolution and freedom of conscience showed, the Roman inquisitors were increasingly interested in what was going on in the wider Church rather than just the Papal States. Others condemned by the restored Inquisition were German and Austrian theologians who taught in state universities and who followed the theological ideas of Georg Hermes (1775–1831). Influenced by the great German philosopher, Emmanuel Kant, Hermes argued that theology must begin with a critical doubt that ultimately would become the source of genuine faith. Two of Hermes' books were placed on the *Index* in 1835, but despite this Hermes' former students continued to fill chairs of Catholic theology in the state-run universities of the Rhineland. The Inquisition interfered in German theological disputes without really making any effort to understand either the context or approach of this movement.

Another famous nineteenth-century victim of the *Index* was the priest Antonio Rosmini-Serbati (1797–1855). Two of his books were condemned by the Congregation of the Index in 1849 and an attempt was made to have his *omnia opera* placed on the *Index*. While this failed, long after his death forty propositions from his works were condemned by Pope Leo XIII in 1887.

The palazzo of the Holy Office was briefly occupied during the period of Giuseppe Mazzini's Roman Republic, which followed the 1848 Revolution in Rome, when Pope Pius IX (1846–78) fled to Gaeta. However, the influence of the Inquisition throughout the nineteenth century was still largely exercised through the *Index of Forbidden Books*. Although they remained separate congregations, the Inquisition and the Index worked closely together, and often the same cardinals were members of both congregations.

But with the arrival of the twentieth century, the expansion of the Inquisition's ambit to the universal Church, which had begun in the nineteenth century, was intensified. With the gradual loss of the Papal States to a unified Italy, culminating in the final occupation of Rome in 1870, the interests of the Inquisition were increasingly focused outward to the universal Church. In 1908, as part of Pius X's (1903–14) reorganisation of the Curia, the name of the Roman Inquisition was changed to the 'Sacred Congregation of the Holy Office'. In 1913 it was designated as 'supreme', because it was presided over by the pope, and from then on the pope was seen as its prefect, although it was in fact run by a cardinal secretary. For six years under Pius X the Holy Office vetted all episcopal appointments.

The intellectual crisis of the papacy of Pius X was the so-called heresy of 'modernism'. This was the term used by the pope to describe the attempt by cultured and educated professional Catholics – mainly theologians, philosophers, and biblical and historical scholars – in the late nineteenth and early twentieth centuries to reconcile Catholic theology with modern developments in science, literary and historical criticism, biblical studies, and philosophy. Pius X perceived in this movement a serious threat to the narrow orthodoxy that dominated Rome, and condemned it as a 'synthesis of all heresies' in both the decree *Lamentabili* and in the encyclical *Pascendi Dominici Gregis* (1907). An 'anti-modernist oath' was imposed on all clergy. Many theologians, scripture scholars, philosophers and Church historians were quite mercilessly hounded as 'modernists' or even 'quasi-modernists' by a small integralist group led by Monsignor Umberto Benigni, who worked in the Secretariat of State. The *Index* was also used as a weapon against the modernists. At first the Holy Office apparently seemed to play only a minor role in the papacy's overreaction to 'modernism', possibly because its cardinal prefect between 1908 and 1913 was Mariano Rampolla, the cardinal who represented the more moderate regime of Pius X's predecessor, Leo XIII (1878–1903), and who came within an ace of being elected pope in 1903. However, this changed after the appointment of Cardinal Raphael Merry Del Val, who ran the Holy Office as secretary from 1914 to 1930. In 1917 the Congregation of the Index was abolished and the Holy Office also took complete control of the censorship of books.

In 1917 the *Code of Canon Law* was issued. Prior to this Church law was a complex and often confusing collection of many different types of legal enactments. At the beginning of the century the decision was made to remove the confusion and to draw up a manageable code. However, the process involved re-enforced the illusion that the Church was somehow a kind of monarchical state which was able to enact legislation governing its own subjects. Bishops, theologians and the community were excluded from the process of resolving what was ultimately true Catholic doctrine, and the entire process was handed over to the centralised bureaucracy of the Holy Office, whose aim was to search out and prosecute error with neither guidelines nor legal limitation.

Two particular canons of the new *Code* (cc. 1323 and 1324) increased centralisation and enhanced the power and influence of the Holy Office. Canon 1323 equated the solemn, infallible teaching authority of the Church with the ordinary day-to-day teaching authority of the pope. So there was a sense in which everything the pope said started to take on a 'quasi-infallible' status, and this was used by the Holy Office to enforce its often narrowly orthodox view on the whole Church. Canon 1324 conflated 'heresy' with 'error'. In other words, new theological ideas, minority theological opinion or even mistaken doctrinal views took on the status of a formal denial of a defined doctrine of the Church. As such, they could be condemned by the Holy Office with commensurate harshness and serious canonical penalties.

Both canons enhanced the authority of the pope's day-to-day teaching. As a result, from the 1920s onwards the Holy Office became a kind of interpretative mouthpiece for papal teaching. It constricted the participation of Catholics in ecumenical activities, constantly tried to apply the breaks to ecclesial renewal, censored books, and prevented, for example, the publication of most of the Jesuit thinker Pierre Teilhard de Chardin's output until after his death. It also constrained theologians and had them dismissed or suspended from their teaching posts, excluded millions of Catholics in several countries from the sacraments for politically cooperating with communists, and attempted to prevent all possibility of dissent within Catholicism. It was a bureaucracy completely above appeal or control, save that of the pope.

However, despite the best efforts of the Holy Office, the theological foundations of Vatican II were laid by a group of European theologians in the 1930s and 1940s. And, in a series of encyclicals in the areas of biblical studies, ecclesiology and liturgy, Pius XII (1939–1958) himself had encouraged renewal.

But by 1950 the pope seems to have turned his back on his forward-looking encyclicals of the 1940s. On 12 August 1950 he published the encyclical *Humani Generis*, which fundamentally targeted a movement that had emerged primarily in France and which was known as *la théologie nouvelle*. The emphasis in the 'new theology' movement was on the personal assimilation of the truths of faith, a consciousness and respect for the historical context in which faith is lived, and the importance of relating faith to contemporary philosophy and culture. The *théologie nouvelle* centred around the Dominican faculty of theology in Paris, La Saulchoir, a group of Jesuit scholars, and the theological revues *Nouvelle Révue Théologique* and *Études*. Although Pierre Teilhard de Chardin (1881–1955) was not specifically named, the encyclical also targeted his views about original sin, human origins and evolution, and the reconciliation of religion and science. *Humani Generis* sketched a dark, unreal scenario of the progressive collapse of 'the very foundations of Christian culture'. The only solution it offered was a narrowing and tightening of theological speculation. Any form of dissent from the papal magisterium and the teaching of the Holy Office was identified with error and, as we have already seen, in the *Code of Canon Law* error had now been conflated with heresy. The task of theology was redefined as explaining 'the sacred magisterium as the proximate and universal norm of truth in matters of faith and morals', rather than the profound exploration of the meaning of the Church's teaching and faith in relationship to contemporary culture. It was modernism revisited.

This was the situation in which the Church found itself as it approached Vatican II. While there was profound disquiet and deep distrust in the Curia after John XXIII (1958–63) called the Council, the Holy Office nevertheless set out to control the agenda. Between 1951 and 1959 the cardinal secretary of the Holy Office was the intransigent Giuseppe Pizzardo, who also doubled as the prefect of the Congregation for Seminaries and Universities which he controlled from 1939 to 1968. Joining him was the equally reactionary Cardinal Alfredo Ottaviani, promoted in 1953 from the role of assessor of the Holy Office, a job he had held since 1935, to that of pro-prefect. In 1959 he was appointed secretary of the Congregation by John XXIII.

It was inevitable that with preparation for Vatican II in the hands of prophets of doom like these that the documents presented to the bishops on arrival in Rome in October 1962 would totally reflect the reactionary line taken by the Curia. While it did not happen immediately and Vatican II took some time to find its feet, Ottaviani's theological documents were one by one completely rejected and ordered to be rewritten by committees representing a much broader cross-section of opinion. There is a sense in which Ottaviani was deeply humiliated and with him the whole intransigent group in the Curia. Much of this came to a head during the second session of the Council on 8 November 1963.

There had already been a number of critical comments about the Curia from bishops such as the Melkite Patriarch of Antioch, Maximos IV Saigh. Cardinal Josef Frings of Cologne (whose theological advisor was the then young Father Josef Ratzinger), in a debate about the possible establishment of a senate of bishops in Rome, attacked the Holy Office saying bluntly:

> [Its] methods and behaviour do not conform at all to the modern era and are a cause of scandal to the world. No one should be condemned without having been heard, without knowing what he is accused of, and without having the opportunity to amend what he can be reasonably reproached with.

This was followed by long and loud applause. Furious, Ottaviani counterattacked by saying, 'In attacking the Holy Office, one attacks the pope himself, because he is its prefect.' It was the usual identification of the Curia with the pope, with the unspoken implication that the Curia shared in the pope's infallibility. However, while the Curia lost the battle completely during Vatican II, it was they, as Ottaviani pointed out, who stayed on in Rome after the bishops finally went home in December 1965.

On the second-last day of the Council (7 December 1965), Paul VI (1963–1978) issued the apostolic letter *Integrae Servandae*, changing the name of the 'Supreme Sacred Congregation of the Holy Office' to the rather vapid 'Congregation for the Doctrine of the Faith'. However, the title 'Holy Office' is still often used and no attempt has been made to change the name of the Palazzo del Sant'Uffizio. Quoting the First Letter of John (4:18) that 'love casts out fear', the CDF was told that the safeguarding of faith was better achieved these days by promoting good doctrine, and that erring Catholics were to be brought back to the right path *suaviter* – sweetly or pleasantly. The CDF was to encourage, rather than repress theology and to sponsor the study of disputed questions. When it did judge errors it was to do so according to a set of legal norms. The problem was that no norms were set out in *Integrae Servandae*. On top of that, the changes were to be carried out under the direction of Ottaviani and his henchmen. It was 'like asking the Mafia to reform the Mafia', according to Monsignor Charles Moeller of the Catholic University of Leuven who was brought into the CDF for a brief period to try to reform the office.

As a kind of token gesture, the *Index of Forbidden Books* was swept away on 14 June 1966, as well as the excommunication attached to reading such books. Much of the rest of Ottaviani's career until his retirement in January 1968 was taken up with clawing back the power that had been lost during Vatican II and in the period immediately afterwards. One of his key victories was persuading Paul VI to ignore the report of the advisory committee that the pope himself had set up to study the question of the morality of contraception. Ottaviani died in 1979.

In the apostolic constitution *Regimini Ecclesiae Universae*

(15 August 1967), Paul VI decreed that the pope would no longer preside over the CDF and that it would be run by a cardinal prefect. It is significant that in this apostolic constitution it is clearly stated that an author is to be condemned only 'after having [been] heard ... and having given him an opportunity to defend himself' (Art. 33).

Ottaviani was succeeded at the CDF early in 1968, the year in which the encyclical against contraception, *Humanae Vitae*, was issued, by the genial Serbo-Croat, Cardinal Franjo Seper. Seper's whole ecclesiastical career had been spent in Zagreb as priest, secretary to the archbishop, rector of the seminary, and finally as co-adjutor and then archbishop. Much of this time was spent under dictatorial regimes: the Ante Pavlic regime during World War II and the communist regime of Tito.

In 1968, however, Seper's geniality was no match for the Roman bureaucrats of the CDF when an incident occurred which illustrated that the old attitudes still prevailed. He had only been in office for a couple of months when the brilliant polymath, Monsignor Ivan Illich, was summoned to Rome. Illich was an American citizen of mixed Spanish, German, Croat and Jewish origins, and a priest of New York archdiocese who worked in Cuernavaca in Mexico to prepare missionaries for Latin America. Two minor CDF monsignori, Sergio de Magistris and Giuseppe Casoria, attempted to interrogate him in the back rooms of the Palazzo. He confronted them with *Integrae Servandae* and demanded that all CDF proceedings should be a matter of the public record. He insisted on everything being written down and was sent a set of absurd questions which he simply refused to answer. Among other things, Illich was to be questioned about his 'Marxist affiliations' and his assumed relationships with Che Guevara, and with the radical Colombian priest, Camillo Torres and, of all people, Cardinal Francis Spellman of New York, who could hardly be construed as a 'subversive'! Illich wrote to the pope and published the document, thereby implying that Seper was not in control of his own office. The CDF had made a fool of itself on the eve of *Humanae Vitae*. The two monsignori suffered a temporary setback in their careers but, as is the way of the Vatican when dealing with its own, the pair subsequently became archbishops; Casoria eventually became a cardinal.

After having been requested by Paul VI in *Integrae Servandae* in 1965 to issue a set of norms for doctrinal examination, the CDF finally produced a *Nova agendi ratio in doctrinarum examine* (a new plan of action in doctrinal examination) on 15 January 1971. This was to remain in operation until June 1997. However, despite the new nomenclature and papal requests for a reform of procedure, the CDF retained the approaches and attitudes of its predecessor, the Holy Office. This is vividly illustrated in the cases of Jacques Pohier and August Bernhard Hasler. The CDF was only too happy to ignore its own procedures when it suited it.

In the late 1960s and the early 1970s, the continuing case against Hans Küng seemed to get a new lease of life. At the same time, the German Dominican, Stephan Pfürtner, was judged and condemned without a hearing for his book *Kirche und Sexualität* (1972). The key ethical norm for interpersonal relationships that he proposed was 'love allied to reason', but while that may have been close to the view of his fellow Dominican, St Thomas Aquinas, it caused deep concern in the CDF. Throughout this same period, Bernard Häring, the greatest moral theologian of the twentieth century, who had enormous influence on the renewal of the Church after Vatican II, was constantly under pressure from the CDF. Häring, a man of complete integrity and holiness who died in 1998, had been a medic in the German army at Stalingrad and a POW in the Soviet Union. He later said that his treatment by the CDF was worse than that he had received from the Nazis.

Another who ran into problems at this time was the Swiss historian, August Bernhard Hasler, who had been employed for several years in Rome in the Secretariat for Christian Unity. Having resigned from the Curia, he wrote an article in 1972 attacking the Church's failures in ecumenism, and in 1978 published a two-volume study in German of the First Vatican Council and Pius IX (available in English in a somewhat inadequate summary entitled *How the Pope Became Infallible: Pius IX and the Politics of Persuasion*

(1981)). Among other things he suggested that Pius IX was mentally unstable, and that the First Vatican Council, which defined papal infallibility and primacy, was not free. This deeply upset curial reactionaries. Despite the fact that Hasler was a good priest in excellent standing, the bishop of his diocese, St Gallen, was ordered to laicize him. The bishop refused, and Hasler's sudden death in 1980 at the age of forty-three solved the problem for both Rome and the bishop. Hans Küng had written the introduction to Hasler's book and this was an important issue when his own dealings with the CDF came to a head.

Paul VI died in 1978, and after the short-lived John Paul I followed him, Karol Wojtyla, Archbishop of Crakow, was elected as Pope John Paul II. With his election the task of confronting and silencing those who were perceived as dissenting theologians was intensified. But just before the death of Paul VI, one of the most unjust and outrageous cases perpetrated by the CDF began.

The French Dominican, Jacques Pohier, published a book, *Quand Je Dis Dieu* (When I Speak of God), in October 1977 (he had been a professor at the Dominican house of studies in Paris, La Soulchoir, since 1959). Sales of the book were very small, but in late April 1978 he was informed by the Dominican master general that because of the 'gravity and urgency of the matter' and because of 'clear and certain' errors of faith in the book, which constituted 'an immediate danger for the faithful', the CDF had decided to dispense with all rules and to proceed to an immediate condemnation of *Quand Je Dis Dieu*. Pohier was given one month to retract six specific points regarding Christology, the resurrection of Christ and the resurrection of the body, as well as issues about definitions of faith and infallibility. He replied in less than a month, showing that his positions differed from those attributed to him by the CDF, and that his real views did not differ from the contemporary theological consensus.

The procedure had to be started up twice again because of the deaths of the popes, but in December 1978 the CDF accused him of acting 'in clear violation of the procedure' without ever having informed him of any procedure. Despite his openness and willingness to enter into dialogue with the CDF, he was publicly condemned in April 1979 for the very points that he had already addressed when first accused. It was as though he had said nothing in reply. A series of extraordinary personal sanctions were applied to him: he was forbidden to preach, to celebrate the Eucharist publicly, and was to refrain from all forms of public theological teaching. Despite pressure from many sources, the CDF was adamant. Pohier's priestly life became progressively impossible. He was a trained psychiatrist, so he returned to that calling, but he was effectively driven out of both the Dominican order and the priesthood.

What is interesting about his case, however, is that the secretary of the CDF at the time was another Dominican, the Belgian archbishop (later cardinal) Jérôme Hamer, who seemed to have strong personal and/or theological animosity towards Pohier; he was certainly in a position to push the case against the Frenchman. In affairs like this, personal animosities should never be underestimated. *Odium theologicum* (the hatred which can characterise theological dissensions) is still alive and well. It is likely that Hamer's antagonism may have been because of Pohier's views on the resurrection of the body and on assisted suicide. Pohier has subsequently become a leader in the French movement that is the equivalent of the Voluntary Euthanasia Society. Whatever the cause, his treatment by the CDF was an appalling travesty of justice and utterly outside any established norms of an equitable procedure.

With the election of John Paul II, the CDF seems to have been encouraged to new levels of action against those theologians perceived to be dissident. The action against Hans Küng was revived and the proceedings against the Belgian Dominican Edward Schillebeeckx were also forced to a conclusion. In 1979 Hans Küng had his right to teach as a Catholic theologian withdrawn, and he tells his own story later in the book.

In the same year Schillebeeckx was called to Rome to explain his books on Christology and ministry. He was too well known to be treated like his colleague, Pohier. After long negotiations the case was concluded in June 1981 with the CDF issuing a 'Note' containing what it considered to be a list of clarifications, precisions and rectifications provided by Schillebeeckx. He himself has subsequently said that Rome was not really interested in his Christology. It was his views on ministry in the book *Ministry: Leadership in the Community of Jesus Christ* (1981), and the role of the priesthood that they really focused on. He maintains that the CDF's central interest is actually in practical things, especially when they concern ethics or the structure of the Church, the hierarchy and the priesthood.

Around the same time, the CDF moved on the 1977 book, *Human Sexuality: New Directions in American Catholic Thought* (edited by Anthony Kosnik and Ronald Modras), which had been commissioned by the Catholic Theological Society of America and published by Paulist Press. Obviously North America was increasingly in the CDF's sights because, as his contribution to this book describes, Charles Curran's troubles with the CDF also began during this period and were to drag on for most of the 1980s.

With the arrival of Josef Ratzinger in November 1981, the CDF began to focus increasingly on Latin American liberation theology. This story goes back to the 1968 Conference of the Latin American Bishops (CELAM), held in Medellin, Colombia. Medellin was attended by Paul VI, and the majority of bishops present placed the blame for the social and economic injustices of the continent squarely on those with 'the greater share of wealth, culture and power ... [those who] jealously retained their privileges, thus provoking explosive revolutions of despair'. Medellin thus placed the Church hierarchy in direct confrontation with the wealthy power-brokers, the economic interests of US corporations, and the military strongmen of the national security states. Even before Medellin, *comunidades de base* – grassroots communities of Christians – were flourishing. These groups of poor people reflected on their experiences of oppression in the context of the Bible. In fact, liberation theology is the product of the experiences of these grassroots communities. The founder of the movement, Peruvian Father Gustavo Gutierrez, says that this type of theology can only emerge after those who develop it have made a serious commitment to the poor themselves and are willing to experience life from the bottom. Inevitably, this involved the Church in politics and in confrontation with military governments and the rich. It also meant opposition to economic policies of globalisation and the Thatcherite economic rationalism that was then being applied ruthlessly in Latin America.

Priests and religious who stood with the poor were sometimes murdered. Those churchmen with vested interests, or those who belonged to highly conservative organisations such as Opus Dei, or those who opted to be the chaplains to the rich and to the emerging middle class, were deeply affronted. Their integrity was either implicitly or explicitly questioned by liberation theology.

However, it was not all about politics and clerical sensibilities. It is important to comprehend the process of liberation theology, because then it is understandable why it is so profoundly opposed by Ratzinger and John Paul II. Liberation theology is not so much a specific theological interpretation of revelation, as a way of actually *doing* theology. The living experience of the poor is its absolute starting point. This is in contrast to the traditional way of doing theology which begins with dogma or Church teaching. Liberation theology turns the process upside down and proceeds from the lived experience of those at the bottom of the social scale and then moves through belief, reflection and prayer to worship and ministry. Theology follows and is based on praxis. Thus liberation theology is the systematic reflection on the belief that emerges from the lived experience of the poor. In contrast, in the European way of doing theology, it is the dogma proposed by the Church that is fundamental, and belief and reflection flow through Church teaching. Thus liberation theology is subversive of hierarchical approaches to faith and the Church, and it reflects the different cultures that characterise Third World countries. I do not think we should underestimate the importance of the contrast between continental-European ways of doing theology and those that, despite setbacks, are still growing in the developing world. For the ideas developed in Latin America in the 1970s quickly spread and inspired Catholics in other parts of the Third World, particularly Asia.

By no means all of the bishops at Medellin embraced this theological approach. The most powerful enemy of liberation theology was the staunchly conservative Archbishop (now Cardinal) Alfonso Lopez Trujillo who, in 1974, took over the secretariat of CELAM. Supporting Lopez Trujillo was the Belgian Jesuit, Roger Vekemans. Based in Bogota it was Vekemans who coordinated opposition to liberation theology by making connections between the Colombian and German hierarchies and right-wing elements in Rome. Lopez Trujillo organised the CELAM conference at Pueblo in Mexico in 1979. This was attended by the newly elected John Paul II. At Pueblo, while the pope stressed the Church's commitment to 'human advancement, development, justice, and the rights of the individual', he also emphasised that the Church does not need to fall back on 'ideological systems in order to love, defend and collaborate in the liberation of man'. For 'ideological systems' read 'Marxism'. While never mentioning liberation theology, he said that some reduced the Kingdom of God to secular notions and created a false dichotomy between the people and the poor on the one hand, and the official Church with its 'sacred magisterium' on the other. The theme that liberation theologians used 'Marxist [sociological] analysis' was now to recur constantly, and it was used as a way of caricaturing what liberationists were doing and tarring them with a secular revolutionary brush.

It is significant that Lopez Trujillo was made Archbishop of Medellin in 1979 and a cardinal in 1983. In 1991 he moved to Rome to head the Pontifical Council on the Family. His influence on John Paul II is considerable.

The CDF also began investigations of individual liberation theologians: Gutierrez was accused of advocating a 'people's Church' in conflict with the hierarchy, and of reducing the 'vertical' dimensions of the Gospel to 'mere' personal relationships. Nothing much came of this investigation because the CDF tactic was to try to get the Peruvian bishops to condemn him. These bishops could not agree among themselves; in fact, at that stage, many of them supported Gutierrez. As a result the whole composition of the

Peruvian hierarchy was gradually changed by the Vatican, with progressive bishops being replaced by reactionaries.

The Brazilian Franciscan friar, Leonardo Boff, was then targeted. This served as a shot across the bows of the progressive Brazilian Bishops' Conference. Not only was it the largest episcopal conference in Latin America, but many of its bishops were supporters of liberation theology. Boff, who had done his doctoral studies under Ratzinger, had offended the Roman authorities with his book *Church, Charism and Power* (1981; English trans., 1985), which detailed many abuses of power in Church history. In early 1984 Ratzinger informed the Latin American bishops that liberation theology was 'in the final analysis unacceptable'. When Boff was summoned to Rome he was accompanied by his fellow Brazilian Franciscans, cardinals Aloisio Lorscheider and Paulo Arns, which pitted Ratzinger against two fellow-members of the College of Cardinals. In August 1984 the CDF issued an 'Instruction' on 'certain aspects' of liberation theology. It admits the obvious: that Latin America has experienced 'shocking inequality ... crushing poverty ... and the seizure of the vast majority of wealth by an oligarchy of powers bereft of social consciousness'. But it falls back on accusing liberation theology of using 'concepts borrowed from various currents of Marxist thought ... [and of] containing errors which directly threaten the truths of faith regarding the eternal destiny of individual persons'.

The CDF's attack on 'Communism' and 'Marxism' caused some embarrassment for Cardinal Agostino Casaroli, the secretary of state, who at that time was trying to improve relationships with the Soviet bloc, and he took the extraordinary step of distancing himself from the document. Boff was 'silenced' for a year after this Instruction was issued. But even after that he was still subjected to a whole series of petty restrictions imposed on him by Rome through the Franciscan order.

What is significant in this controversy over liberation theology is that it highlights the deeper struggle that was (and is) going on for the very soul of the Church. Fundamentally, this struggle is all about history. For Boff, the Church, like Jesus, is rooted in the historical process and is only truly incarnated in and through particular cultural realities. It is in the poverty and exploitation of the Third World, especially Brazil, where Boff finds the Church to be most truly itself. For him theology is also caught up in the historical process and it is only through reflection on living experience, on the 'stuff' of history, that the Church can discover God's will for itself.

For Ratzinger, the Church transcends history. It is not the Jesus of history who provides the CDF prefect's primary theological focus. It is the risen and ascended Christ who stands in splendour outside the world-process, both as saviour and as judge, who is the fundamental focus of Ratzinger. The contemporary source of this view can be found in the work of the Swiss theologian, Hans Urs von Balthasar. Ratzinger worried that the attempts of Boff and his colleagues to read back through the resurrection to the radical prophet of Galilee endangered Christ's eschatological significance, his relevance for all times and places. So, as Ratzinger sees it, this was (and is) not just a squabble over who has political control in the Church. It is about the very meaning of Catholicism. But this does not mean politics are not important. Liberation theology's opponents constantly accuse people such as Boff of politicising the Church by constantly identifying God with the poor. If God has a preferential option for the poor, then the rich and powerful have placed themselves outside God's ambience. Thus the structures that they erect to protect their interests are evil and must be overthrown. Once you say that, your attitude is certainly political, if not revolutionary.

Unfortunately, liberation theology has been to a considerable extent marginalised by this struggle. Slowly the episcopates of Latin America have been transformed by the appointment of conservative bishops, and the grassroots communities driven to the edge of the Church. Peru, for instance, now has a number of Opus Dei bishops, including Juan Luis Cipriani, recently appointed Archbishop of Lima, a close confidant of the now defunct Fujimori regime. The religious tragedy of Catholic Latin America continues with the conversion of Catholics, especially those who have attained middle-class status, to the American Protestant fundamentalist sects. However, the significance of liberation theology cannot be underestimated and its influence continues; it has articulated a whole other way of doing theology.

In the 1990s, the CDF turned its attention to Asian theology, as the piece in this book by Father Tissa Balasuriya demonstrates. But Balasuriya has not been alone. In 1998 another Asian Catholic was investigated: the Indian Jesuit, Anthony De Mello (1931–87). De Mello, whose writing takes the form of brief stories in the Buddhist and Taoist tradition, is still very popular and widely read. Ten years after his death, the CDF has accused him of a 'progressive distancing from the essential contents of the Christian faith'. In the place of Christ he is accused of substituting 'an intuition of God without form or image, to the point of speaking of God as a pure void'. Strangely, the CDF does not seem to have noticed that this is very close to the language used by the great Catholic mystics when they speak of God. Among them are the fifth-century mystical writer called the Pseudo-Dionysius, and the sixteenth-century Spanish Carmelite, St John of the Cross, who is a doctor of the Church. But the crux of the CDF criticisms is that De Mello equates Jesus with the other great religious leaders, such as the Buddha, and of seeing institutional Christianity, as well as other systems of religion, as 'major obstacles to the discovery of truth'. Similar ideas have been developed by Raimundo Panikkar who believes that Christ is not the exhaustive fount of all truth. The Sri Lankan Jesuit, Aloysius Pieris, holds that radical involvement with the poor and oppressed is what creates theology.

At about the same time the CDF also began an investigation of the influential French Jesuit, Jacques Dupuis, who teaches at the Gregorian University in Rome. Dupuis' work is premised on the fact that in this age of wider ecumenism, Catholicism now accepts the fact that non-Christians can be saved outside the Church. He is moving on from the question of *whether* salvation is possible for members of other religious traditions, to *how* these traditions mediate salvation to their members. Dupuis also talks about the need for Christianity to listen to and learn from the other great religions. The CDF specifically targeted his book *Toward a Christian Theology of Religious Pluralism* (English trans., 1999).

Cardinal Franz König, the former Archbishop of Vienna, quickly came to Dupuis' defence in an article in the *Tablet* (16 January 1999). König puts his finger on the essential problem. He says that mistrust and disapproval are being spread about Dupuis, and that the CDF 'may well suspect him of directly or indirectly violating the Church's teaching'. König suggests that the Congregation's problem may really arise from the fact that 'the members of the CDF, most of whom are Westerners, are, of course, very much afraid that interreligious dialogue will reduce all religions to equal rank. But that is the wrong approach for dialogue with the Eastern religions. It is reminiscent of colonialism, and smacks of arrogance ... The Indian way of thinking is very different, and we must learn to understand other sorts of spiritual life.' Ratzinger replied to König's article with a letter to the *Tablet* denying 'colonialism and arrogance' in the CDF, and asserting that it is moving with 'maximum discretion'. The case continues. Just as this book was being prepared for publication Ratzinger published his letter *Dominus Jesus* (5 September 2000), which argues that while the other great religious traditions can point the way to a salvific path through the 'mysterious grace of Christ', they are nevertheless 'gravely deficient'. Christians alone 'have the fullness of means of salvation'. Clearly, the CDF is still determined to bring Asian theology to heel.

While the relationship between the CDF and speculative theology over the years has been a fraught one, under Ratzinger it has certainly attempted to participate in the development of theology. In 1999, for instance, the CDF participated in a major conference on the history of the Inquisition at which a subtle and unreal distinction was made between 'the Church' on the one hand and 'the children of the Church' on the other. 'The Church' had no need to repent or be sorry because it had never been in error, but 'the children of the Church' could repent of their sins and errors, such as persecuting people for their religious beliefs, or for being Jews or Muslims. The Italian Jewish historian, Carlo Ginsburg, an expert on the history of the Inquisition, rightly said that this was an evasion of responsibility. It was unreal to ask the dead to forgive. Rather, he wanted an admission of shame from the Church for what it had done.

I describe the distinction between the 'Church' and its 'children' as 'unreal' because the Church *is* its sons and daughters. It is not some ethereal reality, untouched by history and culture. While it certainly has its 'triumphant' aspect in the sense that it is identified with the risen Christ, it is also rooted in historical processes and cannot be divorced from them. The thing that you eventually find wearying in all of this is the constant evasion, the perpetual self-justification, the inability to assume responsibility and simply say 'sorry', not just for the personal sins of the Church's 'children' but for the systemic and real failure of the institutional Church itself. The Church is nothing other than the historical community of Catholics in union with the risen Christ.

While one might praise the CDF for at least participating in this historical symposium, its recent track record is not good in relationship to systematic theology. In fact, as the CDF document, *Instruction on the Ecclesial Vocation of the Theologian* (24 May 1990), makes clear, Rome's view of the role of theology is restrictive; it could even be interpreted as destructive. The *Instruction* admits that theology always occurs within a cultural context and it certainly recommends the value of 'freedom of research'. But this freedom is immediately limited not only when the papal magisterium speaks in a definitive way, but even when it does not act definitively. The CDF maintains that everything the magisterium says 'has a validity beyond its argumentation', which seems to suggest that logic and fact have no real role in papal teaching. The *Instruction* denies that there is such a thing as a theological magisterium, and makes the papacy alone the sole judge of theological truth. In practice the theologian is reduced to being an apologist for the magisterium. The problem with these assertions is that they are at best a restriction of the genuine Catholic theological tradition and at worst a distortion of it.

This approach to theology was further highlighted and imposed in the apostolic letter *Ad Tuendam Fidem* (30 June 1998), which was published with a detailed commentary by Ratzinger himself. The purpose of the letter was to define in the narrowest possible sense the limits of dissent, and to force Catholics to accept all levels of Church teaching, almost as though they were equal. Thus the question of the ordination of women or the validity of a saint's canonisation was in effect placed on the same level as the divinity of Christ and the presence of Christ in the Eucharist. Otherwise Catholics were told that they risked being 'out of communion' with the Church.

A 'Profession of Faith' has been imposed which has to be taken by all priestly and episcopal office-holders in the Church, and by everyone teaching theology professionally. Its aim is to make sure that all persons in any type of influential position, both ordained and lay, conform to the narrow orthodoxy articulated in the letter. The first clause of the oath covers everything defined in the Word of God and in divine revelation. The second focuses on doctrines on faith and morals definitively put forward by the Church. The third covers the teachings of pope and bishops even when they are not intended to be definitive. It is the second category which has caused the most comment. In explanation, Archbishop Tarcisio Bertone has said that this category includes 'all those teachings in the dogmatic or moral area which are necessary for faithfully keeping and expounding the deposit of faith, even if they have not been proposed by the magisterium as formally revealed'; that is, they are not formally defined as infallible. Bertone is saying that de facto they actually *are* infallible. This is a whole new category of doctrine which the CDF seems to have almost single-handedly invented, or if not invented at least expanded far beyond what was previously accepted.

The CDF not only 'invents' doctrine. It also acts as a detective agency and a court. It is to these CDF processes that I will now turn.

CHAPTER 2

How Accusations Become Trials

The Roman Inquisition has followed various procedures in the course of its history. In the period from the sixteenth to the eighteenth centuries Holy Office procedures were secret and the accused had very few rights. The death penalty, life imprisonment, public humiliation and social ostracism were the consequences of a guilty verdict. But the actual processes of the Roman Inquisition were clear and were usually observed.

Certainly theologians today are not facing the possibility of torture and other such draconian penalties, but they often do face a kind of internal exile in which their reputations are impugned and they are often not able to teach or work within the fields for which they were trained. For some, like Pierre Teilhard de Chardin, this internal exile lasted for most of their lives. Both the Holy Office and the Jesuit Generalate had files on Teilhard's views, especially on original sin, from as early as 1924. He was never able to publish his most creative work in his own lifetime and, right at the moment when he was admitted to the *Légion d'Honneur* (June 1947) by the French government, the Holy Office told the Jesuit General, John Baptist Janssens, that his work might well be put on the *Index*. He spent the last years of his life in 'exile' in New York, where he died and is buried. Nowadays the pressure of the CDF on the accused is psychological. Everything is done behind their back, so they are simply not able to check on whether the procedures are observed.

As we saw in Chapter 1, Paul VI had asked the newly constituted CDF in 1965 in *Integrae Servandae* to produce a set of norms governing its legal procedure. Nothing was produced until 1971, when a set of regulations was issued. There was no further structural change until John Paul II issued the apostolic constitution, *Pastor Bonus* (28 June 1988). This was an attempt to complete the reform and 'rationalise' the structures of the Curia that had been begun by Paul VI in *Regimini Ecclesiae Universae*. But in fact the changes John Paul II made to the Curia were minor. The same inertia that had blocked Paul VI was still at work in the Vatican in 1988. However, despite the fact that *Pastor Bonus* said that all the dicasteries of the Curia were equal, the CDF still maintains a unique status.

Since its role is to safeguard faith and morals, it not only exercises a power of jurisdiction, it also claims it shares in the teaching role of the pope. 'The documents issued by this congregation [the CDF] expressly approved by the pope participate in the ordinary magisterium of the successor of Peter' (*Instruction on the Ecclesial Vocation of the Theologian*, 18). Because of its central role, all of the other dicasteries of the Curia are obliged to refer all matters touching on faith and morals to the CDF, and to abide by its judgment. For this reason the *Regulations* according to which it operates are important.

On 29 June 1997 the CDF issued a new set of *Regulations for Doctrinal Examination*. The reason given was that new regulations 'were needed that might respond even better to the needs of the present day'. According to the CDF consultor, Velasio De Paolis, this was motivated by 'a desire to engage to a greater extent the responsibility of Ordinaries [i.e. bishops and religious superiors] in the task of safeguarding doctrine, especially the author's Ordinary, and to ensure with greater breadth and effectiveness both the defence of the patrimony of the faith and the possibility for the author to defend himself'.

It is hard to see how the new *Regulations* offer the author any better form of defence. The evidence is that the CDF simply uses the accused's religious superior or bishop as a conduit for information. In some ways the new *Regulations* are not as good as the 1971 set, but they do achieve clarity as to how the process works. Ideally, these *Regulations* set out the way in which the CDF will operate in all subsequent cases, although again it remains to be seen if they will actually be followed. The *Regulations* also reflect nothing of the positive approach called for by *Integrae Servandae*, and the care for justice and sensitivity for those being investigated is totally lacking. They are simply a set of cold, objective norms that treat the accused as a non-person, issued by the very authority that will act as investigator, judge and jury. Reading them, you are struck with the completely un–Christ-like feel that they reflect.

The *Regulations* begin by pointing out that it is the primary responsibility of local bishops and national episcopal conferences 'to exercise vigilance' and make sure that the people of God 'receive the Gospel message in its purity and entirety'. But the *Regulations* stipulate that the 'the Holy See can always intervene and, as a rule, does so when the influence of a publication exceeds the boundaries of an individual Episcopal Conference, or when the danger to the faith is particularly grave' (Art. 2). So how does the process actually work?

While there is no discussion of this in the 1997 *Regulations*, it begins when a theologian, teacher, or member of a religious order, or priest, or even occasionally a bishop, is delated to the CDF. Most of those against whom action is taken by the CDF are members of religious orders or priests. This is because they are more vulnerable, being directly employed by the Church and vocationally very dependent upon it. Lay people are much less likely to be targeted, unless they are somehow employed by the Church and are thus vulnerable.

The technical term is that someone is 'delated' to the CDF. Delation is an uncommon word in English. It is derived from the Latin legal term *delatio*, which in turn is derived from the verb *defero* which, among a range of meanings, can have the legal connotation of indicting, impeaching, accusing or complaining about someone. It can even mean 'to bring down' in the sense of hunting and killing an animal, or cutting another person down to size. Delations can come from several sources, usually from within the accused's own country. Often reports come from a local bishop or bishops who, for various reasons both doctrinal and political, decide to report a local Catholic to the CDF. Denunciations can occasionally come from papal nuncios, the ambassadors of the Holy See to various counties. But it is more likely that the nuncio will be the conduit through which a delation goes to Rome. Nuncios and bishops, of course, are likely to get a quicker hearing because of their position in the Church. Balasuriya, Gramick and Nugent, and I are examples of people delated by local bishops. In the case of Gramick and Nugent, the bishop was Cardinal James Hickey of Washington, DC, who pursued them and their ministry relentlessly right from the time of his appointment as Archbishop of Washington in 1980.

Delations can also come from reactionary Catholic vigilante groups which, the CDF itself says, are mostly in the US and France. These groups constantly bombard Rome with accusations about 'progressive' and 'dissident' theologians, priests, bishops, sisters or others they deem to be 'unorthodox', or with whose positions they disagree. These people are almost always unsophisticated theologically, are often ignorant of basic Catholic teaching, are extreme and fixated in their views, and are largely unrepresentative of the majority of Catholics. For instance, the great and somewhat conservative US Catholic biblical scholar, Raymond Brown, who died in 1999, and whose commentary on St John's Gospel and books on the infancy and passion narratives are recognised by scholars and readers alike as classics, was often reported and denounced as 'unorthodox' and 'heretical' by people with absolutely no expertise whatsoever in scriptural studies. Lavinia Byrne (see Chapter 6) is not sure who delated her 1994 book *Woman at the Altar* to the CDF, but she believes 'it was the work of right-wing Catholic women in England who target women "dissidents" and bombard the Vatican with complaining letters'. It is astounding how much influence these groups have in Rome and how much notice is taken of them. It indicates first the narrow unreality of many in the contemporary Curia about the real conditions of modern ministry. It also shows that a considerable number of Vatican officials are ideologically aligned with these extremists.

The route the extremists take to the Curia might not be primarily through the CDF, but through another congregation or office or influential individual. One channel that has been mentioned recently is the Congregation for Divine Worship and the Discipline of the Sacraments, presided over by the Chilean cardinal, Jorge Arturo Medina Estevez, a supporter and intimate of the former strongman of Chile, Augusto Pinochet. (It was Medina Estevez and the secretary of state, Angelo Sodano, who in an extraordinarily inept move attempted to influence the British government to release Pinochet when he was under house-arrest in the UK awaiting extradition proceedings on charges of torture and murder filed in Spain.) Sometimes pressure will build from within the Vatican itself and from local bishops because of perceived problems with particular theological approaches, such as in the 1980s when criticism of Latin American liberation theology came to a head. In the case of Tissa Balasuriya, with his emphasis on Asian theology, inculturation and dialogue with the other great religious traditions, what began with a local bishop attacking him in Sri Lanka was quickly taken up by the CDF because in the 1990s concern with Asian theology was very much on its agenda as well. The CDF is also focusing much more attention on popular writers whose books are widely read by Catholics, and on those such as Lavinia Byrne and myself, who are often in the general media.

The process begins when the delations lead to a CDF file being opened on the accused. This can contain letters of complaint, newspaper clippings, books and other writings – everything 'relevant' to the case. The complaints are considered at the weekly Wednesday meeting, called the *congresso*, of CDF staff. The *congresso* is usually presided over by Ratzinger, or the secretary of the Congregation, Bertone. The meeting assesses whether the delated work or writing or speech contains or promotes 'doctrinal error', and makes an estimation of the 'gravity' of the situation. The other criteria mentioned are the 'prominence, seriousness, dissemination, influence and danger of harm to the faithful' of the presumed errors. The *Regulations* state that, 'After a preliminary evaluation of the gravity of the question, the *congresso* decides whether or not to undertake a study by the office' (Art. 3).

It is worth noting that there is no presumption of innocence as there is in the common law and in most civilised legal traditions. Here the old canonical view that 'error has no rights' clearly prevails. It is also important to spell out precisely what happens here: a group of anonymous bureaucrats, none of whom, except Ratzinger, has any demonstrated expertise in theology or ministry, let alone any established reputations as serious theologians, are 'evaluating the gravity of the question'. They often decide whether a professional theologian with established publications and a well-deserved reputation, or a person with a long track record in their particular ministry, should have their work submitted for judgment by an equally anonymous consultor who is also demonstrably a person of very limited theological and ministerial vision or competence.

If the *congresso* decides that the danger from the delated work is 'very grave' and 'clearly and certainly erroneous' teaching involving 'grave harm to the faithful', it follows an 'extraordinary procedure' which can lead quickly to public censure, as happened in the case of Jacques Pohier, or even excommunication (Arts. 23-7). But how does the CDF establish that a particular theological view is 'clearly and certainly erroneous'? No norms or ways of measuring what is 'very grave' are set out nor is this term even defined. This is all simply left to the judgment of the CDF bureaucrats. The process begins when the *congresso* appoints a committee which is asked to determine promptly 'the erroneous or dangerous propositions'. Here again, there is a presumption of guilt. The committee submits the extracted propositions to the ordinary session of the cardinals of the CDF. If the ordinary session judges that they 'are in fact erroneous and dangerous', having informed the pope, it contacts the accused 'through his Ordinary, with the request that they be corrected within two canonical months'. If the cardinals of the CDF are unsatisfied with the accused's response, discipline of the most draconian sort can follow immediately.

But in most cases, if the *congresso* thinks that there is a 'case to answer' which does not involve teaching that is 'clearly and certainly erroneous' and which does not constitute an immediate 'grave harm to the faithful', they can decide to pursue an 'office study' (Arts 4–6). If they decide to do this, the work is farmed out to 'one or more [CDF] consultors or other experts in the particular area', who undertake a detailed review of the matter. The biggest problem here is that the *congresso* and consultor alone determine what is 'clearly and certainly erroneous', and what will cause 'grave harm to the faithful'. Precisely how the office bureaucrats and consultor attain this remarkable level of judgment is not spelled out; again it is just presumed. Surely such a procedure demands much wider consultation, discussion with the accused and the advice of his or her peers, as well as an attempt to understand the perceived problems within the cultural context from which they emerge.

In addition, the term 'office study' is really a misnomer. Most of the work is done by the consultor, who usually works part-time for the CDF. He (there are no 'shes' listed among the twenty-five part-time consultors in the 1999 *Annuario Pontificio*) will normally be a Rome-based priest with some theological or legal training who assesses the whole matter for 'doctrinal error' or lack of 'doctrinal clarity'. The large majority of these reviewers, who have spent most of their careers in Rome, are lecturers in the parochial world of the Roman ecclesiastical seminaries and universities. They would not be consultors if they did not adhere strictly to the narrow orthodoxy that prevails in Rome. A number of them have other important positions in the Vatican.

For instance, the Dominican, Father Georges Cottier, as well as being a CDF consultor, is also the Theologian to the Papal Household. He is a consultor to the Pontifical Council *Cor Unum* (which distributes papal aid money) and to the Pontifical Council for Culture. He is a member of the Committee for Jubilee 2000, and a member of the Pontifical Academy of Science. Another CDF consultor with a plurality of appointments is the Carmelite, Father Jesus Castellano Cervera. As well as working for the CDF, he is also a consultor for the Congregation for Evangelisation of Peoples, the Congregation of the Clergy, the Congregation for Institutes of Consecrated Life and Societies of Apostolic Life (this congregation supervises religious orders), the Pontifical Council for Laity and the Office of Pontifical Ceremonies. He is president of the Carmelite Pontifical Theological Faculty and Institute of Spirituality.

The outcome of the consultor's review of the accused's work is presented to the *congresso*. After further consideration, the superior of the accused (i.e. the local bishop or the head of the religious order) is informed of the charges. In the case of a religious, the CDF asks the superior to draw the Congregation's concerns about his or her orthodoxy to the attention of the accused, who is, in turn, asked to reply in writing via the superior. In the case of a diocesan priest, the CDF usually writes directly to the person concerned and informs the bishop. This is almost always the first the accused involved will ever hear of the proceedings against them, which by then may have been under way for many months, involving a considerable number of people.

From then on, all dialogue passes through the accused person's superior, conducted completely in writing. It is meant to be kept strictly secret on the grounds that this protects the accused person's reputation. In fact, it renders them more vulnerable. As I argue in my own story, the safest procedure is to 'go public' fairly quickly so that the CDF has to think seriously about its own reputation and public image before it acts or uses arbitrary measures.

The accused is required 'to provide the needed clarifications for submission to the judgment of the Congregation'; that is, they have to explain and justify themselves on the specific points nominated by the CDF consultor. The answer has to be provided within three months. The accused's responses are then judged again by the *congresso*. If at this point the CDF wants to get out of or drop the case, the accused person will be asked to write an article in some theological journal or magazine, either repudiating or 'clarifying' their views. In effect, this means accepting not only the CDF's opinion on the matter, but often being obliged to quote the CDF's actual words. The article must be submitted to the CDF for censorship before publication. It is very rare at this early stage for there to be a meeting between the accused and the officials of the CDF, who constantly hide behind the mask of anonymity. The original delator is never named and remains unknown to the accused person. The accused cannot nominate a defence counsel, and certainly cannot be in attendance when their case is discussed by the CDF *congresso*. Usually there will be long delays, often up to a year or more, between letters from the CDF. The whole process seems designed to wear down the accused.

If the CDF bureaucrats in the *congresso* decide that the consultor's report indicates that the publication or opinion 'appears to contain grave doctrinal error', the 'office study' quickly transmutes into an 'Ordinary Procedure for Examination' (Arts 8–22). Presumably this happens also when the office study does not come to a successful conclusion from the point of view of the CDF; for example, if the accused refuses to write a 'retractation', does not submit it for prior censorship or does not set things out with precisely the right wording. The ordinary procedure for examination is a full-blown trial, except that it is only at a very late stage in the process that the accused may be involved.

This is how the ordinary procedure for examination works. The *Regulations* (Arts 8–22) distinguish two stages: 'an internal phase of preliminary investigation' and 'an external phase involving the presentation of objections to the author and subsequent dialogue'. Phase one, which is essentially a secret, internal phase of investigation, begins when the *congresso* designates 'two or more experts ... to give their opinions, and evaluate whether it [the work or opinion] is in conformity with the doctrine of the Church'. At the same time the *congresso* appoints a *relator pro auctore* (defence counsel), 'who has the task of illustrating, in a spirit of truth, the positive aspects of the teaching and the merits of the author, of cooperating in the authentic interpretation of his thought within the overall theological context, and of expressing judgment regarding the influence of the author's opinions'. In other words the accused can neither nominate nor even know the name of their *relator pro auctore*, who will also probably be a Roman theologian totally unknown to them personally and ideologically aligned with the consultors, who have the double role of both prosecutors and judges. The consultors, *relator* and the accused's superior meet in a kind of closed pre-trial meeting known as a *consulta* (consultation). The accused, of course, is not permitted to attend and may not even know that it is happening. The only person who is acquainted with the accused and who can participate in the consultation is his superior (I do not know what happens when a woman is the accused and her superior is also a woman, as in the case of Lavinia Byrne). But the superior is bound to secrecy anyway, so he or she presumably cannot let the accused know what happened at the consultation.

At the end of the consultation, the consultors alone vote on the outcome of the examination. The *relator* and superior must leave the room during the vote. The result of the vote, along with the entire file and minutes, are sent to the ordinary meeting of the CDF – the assembly of cardinals and bishops who are members of the Congregation. Those who live outside Rome presumably are not able to attend all of these ordinary meetings. The ordinary meeting decides whether to present 'objections to the author, and if so, on which points'. At this juncture the pope is informed, as well as 'competent dicasteries of the Holy See'. It is quite clear from the *Regulations* that all of this can happen without the knowledge of the accused.

It is only in the second stage that the accused can participate, but even then only at a distance.

> The list of erroneous or dangerous propositions at issue, together with an explanatory argumentation and documentation necessary for the defence, are communicated through the Ordinary [i.e. author's superior] to the author and his advisor, whom the author has the right to nominate, with the approval of his Ordinary, to assist him. The author must present a written response within three canonical months. It is appropriate that,

together with the author's response, the Ordinary also forwards his own opinion to the Congregation.

The accused has still not been able to put his or her case in person. The consultors will have been able to express opinions about his views, as too will the author's Ordinary, who may or may not be a supporter of the accused. Yet the accused will never see any of this material. It is only at this final stage that 'the possibility is also foreseen of a personal meeting between the author, assisted by his advisor (who takes an active part in the discussion) and delegates of the Congregation'. What influence this meeting is to have on proceedings is not detailed. The evidence indicates that the meeting, while polite, usually achieves little or nothing. Because the consultor has already acted as judge and jury, there is little or no chance that the decision will be changed.

After this, all the material goes back to the *congresso* where it started. If the examination of the *congresso* 'reveals truly new doctrinal elements requiring further evaluation', the whole business goes back to another consultation, at which further 'experts' can be called, and the accused becomes involved in a whole new round of answering questions. The process could and often does drag on for years.

However, if the *congresso* is satisfied, everything is sent on to an ordinary session of the CDF, where the cardinals decide if 'the question has been resolved positively and that the response is sufficient'. Otherwise 'adequate measures are then taken, also for the good of the faithful [*sic*]'. What are these 'adequate measures'? They are detailed in the *Regulations* in a final section headed 'disciplinary measures' (Arts 28–9): 'If the author has not corrected the indicated errors in a satisfactory way and with adequate publicity', and the CDF decides that the accused has committed the offence of heresy, apostasy or schism, he or she is excommunicated *latae sententiae*, that is, automatically. There is no possible right of appeal in the canonical legal system against such an excommunication, as the story of Tissa Balasuriya makes clear (see Chapter 4). If the 'errors' of the accused 'do not involve *latae sententiae* penalties', the CDF can impose various other penalties such as the forced withdrawal of books from sale, or even the destruction of those still in print, suspension from the priesthood, expulsion from religious life, the imposition of various periods of silence, dismissal from a teaching job, and variations and combinations of these and other ecclesiastical penalties.

Commenting on these CDF *Regulations* the respected Jesuit canonist at Washington's Georgetown University, Ladislas Örsy, asks, 'Are Church Investigation Procedures Really Just?' (see *Doctrine and Life* 48 (1998), pp 453–65). He examines the *Regulations* in the light of the Church's concern with human rights and of the widespread concern for fair legal processes. Örsy finds the CDF *Regulations* to be defective in a number of ways.

First, there is no precise definition of the offence. Second, the *Regulations* do not distinguish at all between judge, prosecutor and investigator. The CDF carries out all roles and often the same person acts in the various roles. Third, the accused is given little opportunity to plead his or her case. Fourth, there is no presumption of innocence. Fifth, there is no right of appeal. And, finally, the secrecy provisions mean that justice is not seen to be done, especially when the penalty is automatic excommunication. 'To rush into imposing an extreme sentence (perhaps even without ever having listened to the author) can hardly be a sign and symbol of justice' (p. 464).

Örsy calls for the creation of a climate of trust and argues that if the CDF thinks that norms are needed to prevent doctrinal deviations, 'norms are even more needed to secure legitimate freedom for creative thinking' in the Church. In other words, theologians and those who attempt to communicate the faith need some form of protection from arbitrary investigation and judgment. His conclusion is that overall the *Regulations* 'are not signs or symbols of justice. They have their roots in past ages which did not have the same vision of the dignity of the human person and the same respect for honest conscience that is demanded the world over today' (p. 465).

Given that this is a book of stories about people who have dealt intimately with the CDF, it is inevitable that personalities will be mentioned and assessed. Judgments will be made, some of them blunt and severe. This is not just the result of pique. It emerges from a conviction that the time has come to declare one's position and to tell the truth. This is exactly what the people in this book do.

I cannot, of course, speak for any of the other contributors, but it is my personal view that the moment has arrived for the CDF to be abolished. I repeat what I said in *Papal Power*:

> It is a creature of the counter-reformation and has no place in the contemporary Church. It has proved on several occasions to be essentially irreformable. Nowadays it is ... a manifestation of an exaggerated and over-centralised papalism. Its present personnel demonstrably have little or no pastoral experience nor, with the exception of the cardinal prefect, do they have well-established reputations as theologians. No doubt its personnel are well-intentioned, but their view of the wider Church is not just ignorant; it is blinkered and myopic. As a result it is difficult to see what positive contribution the CDF makes to the contemporary Church. Its purposes could be served more effectively by the peer pressure of other theologians and by the authority of local conferences of bishops. Rome should be involved only as a last resort.

Yet Rome seems obsessed with control. In a personal letter reflecting on his own experience of the Holy Office, the great French Dominican ecclesiologist Cardinal Yves Congar (1904–95) says that the Vatican wants the whole Christian world 'to think nothing, to say nothing, except what they propose'. He continues: 'It is clear to me that Rome has never looked for and even now does not look for anything but the affirmation of its own authority. Everything else interests it only as matter for the exercise of this authority ... the whole history of Rome is about insisting on its own authority and the destruction of everything that cannot be reduced to submission.' The full text of the letter appears in the

March 2000 edition of *La Vie Spirituelle* and the translation in the *National Catholic Reporter*, 2 June 2000.

The primary focus of this book is the obsession with power, which seems to be the most potent motivating force in the Vatican and the CDF. But the most scandalous thing is that inquisitorial procedures of any type have a place in a Church that claims to follow Jesus, a man totally opposed to the religious hypocrisy and the legalism of the scribes and pharisees.

While Jesus deeply respected the Jewish tradition, he had absolutely no patience with the type of legalism that is used to oppress people. He identified it with religious hypocrisy, and it is extraordinary how often this word is used in St Matthew's and St Mark's Gospels. 'Woe to you scribes and pharisees hypocrites!' (Matthew 23:13). Pharisaism is a characteristic of all religions. The terrible danger that Catholicism faces is that if it does not deal decisively with the legalists and literalists at the very top of its hierarchy, it will render itself irrelevant to the vast majority of people of goodwill. But the flip side of crisis is opportunity. As it enters the new millennium, there is a chance for the Catholic Church to leave behind its inquisitorial past and take a whole new approach.

CHAPTER 3

Loyal Dissent and Freedom: Charles Curran

While they may not specifically know his name, Charles Edward Curran has had a pervasive and profound influence on the way most contemporary Catholics, particularly those from the English-speaking world, form their consciences and act on moral, and especially interpersonal issues. Curran is a warm, generous, friendly person with a raucous laugh and a great ability to enliven a theological point with a funny story. Despite a prodigious published output, he is still amazingly generous with his time; his own bishop, Matthew Clark of Rochester, says of him: 'He lives simply and has a remarkable ability to combine a life of serious scholarship with generous availability to a variety of persons.' Also, unlike many academics, he enjoys teaching.

Perhaps precisely because of his influence, popularity and American nationality, the CDF began a major investigation of Curran in 1979. The US was the homeland of so-called 'situational ethics', which the French still superciliously refer to as 'Anglo-Saxon morality', and American Catholic moralists are often unjustly tarred with this brush. So Rome decided it could make an example of Curran. After a protracted process, on 25 July 1986 Ratzinger wrote to the chancellor of the Catholic University of America in Washington, DC, where Curran was employed as a tenured professor, to inform him that Curran was neither 'suitable nor eligible to exercise the function of a professor of Catholic theology'; the chancellor was instructed to take the 'appropriate action'. The chancellor at the time was the Archbishop of Washington, Cardinal James Hickey. On 2 June 1988, the Board of Trustees at the university declared that Curran could not teach Catholic theology at that institution. This led to a civil case, which finally came to an end on 28 February 1989, in which the judge found in favour of the Catholic University of America. After brief stints as a visiting professor at Cornell and the University of Southern California, Curran became Elizabeth Scurlock University Professor of Human Values at Southern Methodist University in Dallas, Texas, in 1991.

Richard McCormick says that 'the Curran affair ranks as among the most significant developments in moral theology in the past 50 years' (Theological Studies, 50 (1989), p. 17). *At the heart of the Curran case is the theological question of the right to dissent from authoritative but non-infallible papal teaching. Throughout the 1980s and 1990s the CDF has attempted increasingly to constrict the role of theologians to that of apologists for the papal magisterium, and to blur the distinction between infallible and non-infallible teaching. Curran has strongly defended the right of Catholics to dissent from non-infallible teaching.*

At another level, the Curran case has widespread ramifications for other moralists. Curran criticised the physicalism in some papal teaching in moral matters; for example, contraception, sterilisation, homosexuality, and the principle of double effect. The problem with physicalism comes from identifying the moral act with the physical structure of the act. Contraception, for example, according to the official teaching is wrong because it interferes with the physical act of marital relations. However, outside the area of sexuality, Catholic teaching does not identify the human moral act with the physical structure of the act. Killing is a physical act, but not all killing is wrong. It is murder that is morally wrong. One must distinguish between physical or non-moral evil and truly moral evil. In this light many theologians such as Franz Böckle, Josef Fuchs and Richard McCormick developed a theory of proportionalism: one can directly do physical or non-moral evil (e.g. interfere with the physical structure of the marital act) if there is a proportionate reason. In the 1960s and early 1970s, Curran frequently

wrote about these controversial issues in sexual ethics. Hence it is not
surprising that he was targeted by the CDF.

'Charlie', as he is generally known, begins by describing his family
background and training.

I was born in Rochester, New York on 30 March 1934. There
were four children in the family and I was the third. Both my
parents were of second-generation Irish background, and both of
them had been born in New York City. My father had gone over
to Ireland as a child, but we never had strong ties with the Irish. As
I got older I remember asking my father why this was, and he said,
'When I was eighteen and my father died, I kicked all those damn
Irish out of the house at midnight and would not have a wake, and
they have not talked to me since, and I've never talked to them.' So
we had no feeling that we were Irish; we were just Americans. My
mother was actually half-German.

My parents had moved to Rochester in 1926 because my father
got a job there. He was an insurance adjuster; the company he
worked for insured the workers of public utilities. I was educated
in the local Catholic school system. I went to the preparatory
seminary in 1947, immediately after grammar school. It was a
different kind of seminary because in both the preparatory
seminary and in college we lived at home. It was a six-and-six
arrangement: you lived at home for the first six years, and then you
lived in when you went to the major seminary.

The first Bishop of Rochester, Bernard McQuaid, was a strongly
intellectual Irishman who had come up from Newark in 1868. He
died in 1909. He started the seminary of St Bernard's and he even
got permission from Rome to give pontifical degrees there. This
was withdrawn in 1930. He was conservative in one sense; he and
Archbishop Michael Corrigan of New York were seen as the
conservatives of their time, in contrast to liberal bishops such as
Archbishop John Ireland, Archbishop of St Paul, and Cardinal James
Gibbons in Baltimore. But McQuaid also had a broader side to
him. It was his view that in the seminary you had to be trained to
be both a priest and a gentleman, and he decided that there would

be no reading during meals so that students could learn to converse as gentlemen. However, the successors of McQuaid had gone the other way; in fact St Bernard's came to be called 'the rock'!

I was only there for two years of philosophy, and then I was sent to Rome. In Rome I lived at the North American College for four years, and was ordained in Rome in 1958, the year that John XXIII was elected. I was in St Peter's Square the night the new pope was elected and quite frankly I was rather disappointed in him. Pius XII gave the impression of a saintly ascetic but John appeared to be a roly-poly peasant. How could such a person ever be a good pope? How wrong I was! During my last year in Rome my bishop, James E. Kearney, wrote to me to say that he wanted me to stay on in Rome and get a doctorate in moral theology in order to teach at the Rochester Seminary.

The three decades from 1930 to 1960 were the high point of Jesuit theological influence on the papacy and the Vatican. Not only did Jesuits act as confessor (Augustin Bea) and secretary (Robert Leiber) to Pope Pius XII, but they were also deeply influential as advisors to the Holy Office. One of the most influential of them was the German, Franz X. Hürth. Jesuits were also often the ghostwriters of papal speeches and encyclicals. For example, the Belgian Jesuit, Arthur Vermeersch, was one of the substantial authors of Pius XI's encyclical Casti Connubii *(1930), and the Dutchman, Sebastian Tromp, later Curran's teacher of apologetics, had a significant influence on Pius XII's* Mystici Corporis *(1943).* Casti Connubii *strongly reiterated the condemnation of contraception; Vermeersch was deeply concerned with the decline in Belgium's population, which he attributed to a 'contraceptive attitude'. One of the important periodicals of the time published by the 'Greg', as the Gregorian University was affectionately known by its students, was the* Periodica de re Morali, Canonica, Liturgica, *usually known simply as* Periodica. *It was here that influential Jesuits often discussed and argued the moral and ethical issues that the pope would soon take up. Curran got to know Hürth who was a leading Jesuit moralist.*

In 1959 I began work on a doctorate at the Gregorian University.

I did my doctorate with a rather quiet American Jesuit, Frank Furlong, and my topic was 'The Prevention of Conception After Rape'. I already knew most of the Jesuits teaching moral theology at the Gregorian, especially Franz X. Hürth and Josef Fuchs. Hürth and I had a funny relationship. At that time he was working for the Holy Office, and I could speak Latin very well. He was a very close advisor to Pius XII on moral matters. There was one famous occasion in 1949 when he had a commentary in the 15 September edition of *Periodica* on the pope's address of 29 September! It was Pius XII's condemnation of artificial insemination, and so we had a very good idea who had written it. Hürth had been brought to Rome by Vermeersch and the two of them worked together on *Casti Connubii*. There is a fascinating sidelight on the encyclical: the Latin version had mistranslated what Hürth had written for the encyclical, and there was a correction in the next fascicle of the *Acta Apostolicae Sedis* (the official Vatican journal and documentary source). It concerned sterilisation. The original text had said that not only was punitive sterilisation wrong, but any form of sterilisation. Hürth taught that sterilisation as a punishment might be morally acceptable. What happened was that the original text was corrected to reflect Hürth's views. It is the only time I know when an encyclical has actually been corrected. The new text said 'Leaving aside the case of punitive sterilisation ...'. Hürth did not want that condemned because he believed in it as a possibility.

As I said, I knew Latin very well and Hürth and I often chatted in Latin. One day Furlong asked me to do him a favour. He said that he had got it on good authority that the Holy Office was going to condemn the so-called 'Doyle cervical spoon'. This had been invented by a very conservative Catholic doctor in Boston. The device was put in the vagina to protect the semen against vaginal secretions and acids which could affect the semen; the aim was to help infertile couples. Furlong was afraid that the spoon was going to be condemned. So he said to me, 'Find out what Hürth thinks about it.' So I went up to see Hürth. By this time he was old, but he liked to chat so I said to him in Latin, 'I want to raise a question about this Doyle cervical spoon.' He replied, '*Ah Pater, habeo problema magnum de hac re'* ('Father, I've got a big problem about this'). We went back and forth on the issue, and then he said, *'In hoc casu, datur inseminatio in machinam Americanam'* ('In this case insemination occurs in an American device'). So I put some arguments to him, and the conversation went for about twenty minutes, and then he smiled and said, *'Tamen, non mihi pertinet. Est problema Americanum'* ('This is not my concern. It's an American problem'), which was his way of telling me that the Holy Office was not going to condemn the Doyle spoon. So I went back to Furlong and said, 'Don't worry. The Holy Office is not going to condemn it.' In a sense, if it was not so tragic it would be very funny; these clerics worrying about such matters. At this time the whole discussion of sexuality was on the level of mechanics rather than relationship.

My thesis was largely a review of the literature, but what helped me immensely later on was that in the process of doing it I came to realise the poor biology upon which our sexual teaching was based. This, of course, was not just confined to the Church. I even came across the fact that some students of Antoni Van Leeuwenhoek, the perfecter of the microscope, won a gold medal from a Parisian academic society for 'discovering' the *homunculus* in the semen under the microscope. In the Middle Ages Aquinas also held that the semen was full of 'little humans'. The tragedy was that so much of our Catholic sexual ethics was based on this primitive and incorrect biology. By definition the presumption was that the seed was all you needed and it simply required a womb; the basic word in Latin for womb was *nidus*, a nest. Interestingly, up until fairly recently the whole of science shared this biological primitivism. It helped me to realise that many of the problems in our sexual ethics had come from this poor biology.

In those days the Gregorian only required five courses, plus the dissertation for the doctorate for those who like myself already had the licentiate. This had been a tradition for some time. One day the rector of the North American College asked me to do some research for him. An American nun writing a biography of Bishop John Lancaster Spalding had written to him about a problem. She claimed that Spalding had three doctorates from Rome: in canon law, philosophy and theology. But he had only lived in the city for two months. Spalding had stayed at the French College so a friend and I went down there to check. My friend kidded me on the way down: 'Well, he got three doctorates in two months. Now it takes a little longer and you have to pay a little more money!' In other words, Roman doctorates are not worth very much.

Influenced by the writings of Bernard Häring, especially his *The Law of Christ*, I also did some work at the Alfonsiana [the Redemptorist university in Rome] and ended up getting a doctorate there as well. So that's how I wound up with two doctorates in two years. However, again this latter doctorate was significant for me because my topic was 'Ignorance of the Natural Law in St Alphonsus Liguori'. What St Alphonsus Liguori [1696–1787] did against the rigorists and Jansenists was to admit the possibility of invincible ignorance of the natural law. This meant that his moral theology emphasised much more the subjective state of the person rather than the objective law. This was to become very helpful for me. While he was still a manualist at heart he did promote this move toward the subjective in moral decision-making. Our problem in the Church today is actually a new Jansenism or rigorism. Vatican authorities today do not want to recognise explicitly the lack of subjective responsibility nor to admit the possibility of the lesser of two evils, which to his credit Alphonsus was always ready to accept. We are moving again in an absolutist direction. It was also at the Alfonsiana that I first met F. X. Murphy.

Born in New York, Francis Xavier Murphy entered the Redemptorists (CSsR) and was ordained in 1940. He got a PhD in Church history at the Catholic University of America. He then served as a US Air Force chaplain for about ten years throughout the world. In Paris he got to know a number of people in the papal diplomatic service, including the nuncios, archbishops Paolo Marella and Giovanni Benelli, as well as George Patrick Dwyer, Archbishop of Birmingham, and John Carmel Heenan, who became Cardinal Archbishop of Westminster.

Murphy then came to the Alfonsiana to teach patristics. Curran says that Murphy was not fluent in Latin, but he did have important connections. 'F. X. is an Irish leprechaun, an astute politician and an entrepreneur.' These and many other Roman connections provided the information for the book Letters from Vatican City *(1963) written under the pseudonym, Xavier Rynne. Murphy kept up the subterfuge that he was not Xavier Rynne because he could say more as Rynne than Murphy. He went on to write three more books about Vatican II (*The Second Session, The Third Session *and* The Fourth Session*) which remain one of the best records of what actually happened.*

After getting the two doctorates I came back to Rochester to teach in St Bernard's Seminary. This was in June of 1961. Before I came back I had a long lunch with F. X. Murphy. He said, 'Charlie, they are going to eat you up in that seminary, you're too liberal for them and you are going to be in trouble. My advice is: when you go back, start teaching in Latin. They always pride themselves on doing something like that in Rochester. That will be the first thing they'll notice, and then after that you can say whatever the hell you like.' So that's what I did: I taught for two months in Latin, and it was quite some time before they began to notice how progressive my views really were. Murphy also told me many interesting things about the Curia and the people who worked there. So when the articles started to come out in *The New Yorker* by 'Xavier Rynne' about the Council, I wrote him a note and said that I knew it was he because some of the stuff we talked about in Rome was in the book. I also told him, 'I know what your mother's maiden name is.' He ultimately confessed to being Xavier Rynne when he wanted to go to Rome to cover the 1985 so-called 'extraordinary synod'.

The semester in Latin at the seminary was followed by my beginning to teach in English. I also refused to follow the traditional moral theology manual. Ironically, I never really wanted to teach in the seminary even though I was there for four years. If I had wanted that I would have become a Jesuit. I really wanted to be a parish priest. Eventually there were complaints about some of the things I said, and a man named Hugo Maria Kellner got on to me. He was a German refugee with a PhD who worked at Eastman Kodak in Rochester as a chemist. He was very conservative, and he used to mimeograph diatribes which he sent to all the US bishops and to members of the Roman Curia. I was helping out in the parish where he lived in Caledonia, New York. On the basis of my preaching and writing – he also picked up a couple of things I had written in *Commonweal* – he decided to go after me as a 'heretic'. Another person he pursued was Gerard Emmett Carter, who had been director of religious education in Montreal archdiocese and who had just become the Bishop of London, Ontario. Carter was to go on to be Cardinal Archbishop of Toronto. There were also complaints about me from the Bishop of Syracuse, New York, who sent his seminarians to St Bernard's. It was around this time that I had begun arguing that we needed a change on contraception.

In the meantime I had been offered teaching jobs at Notre Dame University, Fordham and Catholic University [CU] in Washington, DC. I sent all of these invitations into the bishop's office. In the summers of 1964 and 1965 I had taught at Catholic University. On return from Washington on 1 August 1965, I was informed that, because of my progressive views, I would no longer be teaching in the seminary. Bishop Lawrence Casey, the auxiliary who really ran the diocese, called me in and said that since Catholic University had been after me, they would write a letter and say that I was free to go to CU now. I said I would rather stay in the diocese and work as an associate pastor. He said, 'No, you go to CU.' So I took the job.

The head of theology at the time was Father Walter Schmitz, and he was trying to get younger people onto the faculty. At that time the image of theology at CU was terrible. Monsignor Joseph Clifford Fenton, 'Butch' Fenton as he was known, had just left the faculty and was still the editor of the *American Ecclesiastical Review*. He was a character and almost loutish in his manner. He would refer to progressive Continental theologians like Karl Rahner and say, 'Now listen, kid: no goddamn German theologian is going to destroy the Church of Our Lord and Saviour, Jesus Christ.' Fenton was a great friend of Cardinal Ottaviani, and during the first two sessions of Vatican II he strenuously defended the old regime. By the end of the second session Fenton was becoming an embarrassment to the university. He was a priest of the diocese of Springfield, Massachusetts, and Cardinal Francis Spellman of New York got him to agree to take a parish appointment in Chicopee Falls, Massachusetts, had him appointed a protonotary apostolic (the highest rank of a monsignor), and gave him a big dinner at the Grand Hotel. Fenton is reported to have said, 'The next morning I woke up and realised I was a goddamned stupid son of a bitch to have allowed Spellman to have persuaded me to do that.'

As soon as I was appointed to CU Hugo Kellner wrote a letter to every member of the faculty saying, 'You have now accepted this heretic on your staff.' In the meantime I had been arguing about the contraception issue which was then being debated, and I got a few mentions in the newspapers. On occasion I was called in by the vice-rector, but in 1966 my contract was renewed, and in 1967 the faculty and academic senate voted my promotion to associate professor. However, at the April 1967 meeting of the Board of Trustees, the trustees voted to fire me. (All of the archbishops of the US were automatically trustees, as well as some bishops and some 'tame' members of the laity.) I was called in by the rector. Being a rather suspicious character, I had a recorder in my attaché case which a friend had fixed up for me. The rector told me that the Board of Trustees at their recent meeting had agreed not to renew my contract but that no reason was given. I protested and said that I would fight it and go to the press. He finally got me to agree to think about it for twenty-four hours. A day later some of my friends and colleagues announced that I had been fired and called a meeting. Five hundred people attended. The next day the faculty of theology voted to go on strike. The day after the whole faculty of the university also voted overwhelmingly to go on strike. We closed the whole university down for a week.

It was headlines in all the newspapers. The *New York Times* carried it as front page news for several days. We were not sure if the trustees were going to back down, but in the end Archbishop (later Cardinal) Patrick O'Boyle of Washington, who was the chancellor, came out to meet the faculty. Basically they were going to have the trustees vote again, but the faculty said, 'No, Curran has to be reinstated on the spot, *today*.' The key archbishops who wanted me out were John Krol from Philadelphia, Philip Hannan from New Orleans, and O'Boyle. I am sure that Rome knew about the whole affair, and definitely had a hand in it. My protocol number at the Holy Office is 48/66 which means that the file was opened in 1966, and this was 1967. At the time we actually got significant support from Archbishop (later Cardinal) Lawrence Shehan of Baltimore and Cardinal Richard Cushing of Boston.

The Cushing story is an interesting one: a reporter from CBS in Washington had called the Boston archbishop's house in Brighton, and got Cushing himself on the phone. By that time Cushing had had a drink or two and the CBS reporter later told me he had 'had to clean up the interview a bit' before putting it to air. Substantially Cushing said: 'I don't know a goddamn thing about running universities, but why can't the poor guy teach. I don't go to their meetings, I don't know what they're talking about, but why can't they leave the poor guy alone.' The Boston chancery later tried to deny it, largely because they probably did not know that Cushing had actually said it. However, once Shehan and Cushing came out in our favour it was a sign that the trustees were backing down.

So even before *Humanae Vitae* I was pushed into a leadership role I should never have had. I was thirty-three years old at the time, but all of this gave me a kind of stature and position that I was not really prepared for. Linked with this was the fact that most of the older US moralists could not make the transition that was implicit in Vatican II. They offered no leadership, so there was a void that pushed me into the position of the public leader of progressive American theologians.

The year 1968 was a pivotal one in the period after Vatican II because it was the year of Humanae Vitae, *Pope Paul VI's encyclical condemning contraception.* Humanae Vitae *was to become a dividing line in more ways than one. In the years leading up to it there was much debate in the Church over the issue of the contraceptive pill, which had only come on the market in 1959–60. One of the key figures in the development of the pill was Dr John Rock (1890–1984), a Boston Catholic doctor and a professor at Harvard University. In 1962 in his book* The Time Has Come: A Catholic Doctor's Proposal to End the Battle for Birth Control, *he argued that the pill operated in the same way as the body's own endocrine system, and that placed it well within the bounds of a 'natural' process, which had already been permitted by the papacy. For Rock the pill was really a variation on the rhythm method. But it was not until late 1963 that a few Catholic theologians began to challenge the traditional teaching against contraception.*

John XXIII had secretly established a commission to advise him about birth control, and Paul VI continued it. He had withdrawn the topic from the purview of the Council and handed it over to the Birth Control Commission. In 1966 reports were leaked to the press claiming to be the majority report favouring change and the minority report against it. There is good evidence that Paul VI was attracted by the majority report in favour of change. However, in the period between 1966 and 1968 intense pressure was brought to bear on the pope by Cardinal Ottaviani and Archbishop Pietro Parente of the Holy Office, the American Jesuit John C. Ford, and the Franciscan, Ermenegildo Lio. Ford's whole argument was based on the threat to papal authority implied in any change in Church teaching: 'Therefore one must very cautiously enquire whether the change which is proposed would not bring with it an undermining of the teaching and the moral authority of the hierarchy.' It was this view that ultimately prevailed. (For the whole story of the Birth Control Commission see Robert Blair Kaiser, The Politics of Sex and Religion *(1985)). Curran takes up the story.*

But the Catholic University strike was just the overture to *Humanae Vitae*, which Rome published on Tuesday, 29 July 1968. That summer I was in upstate New York studying German. I got a call from *Time* magazine on the previous Sunday night saying that they had a copy of the encyclical and that it condemned contraception. I called people in Washington and got a flight back immediately. I was given a copy of the encyclical about five o'clock on the Monday night and about twelve of us academic theologians from CU met and discussed it. So the assertion that we had not read it before we came out against it was utterly false. By 9 pm we had agreed on a public statement. The encyclical was in the papers the next morning. During that evening CBS had taken footage of us as we discussed the encyclical. We then called around to see how many signatures we could get for our statement. We got eighty-eight signatures from scholars by the next morning. On Tuesday morning the Washington Priests Association, which was already having trouble with O'Boyle, scheduled a press conference for 10 am at the Mayflower Hotel. We took over their press conference and announced that eighty-eight Catholic scholars had signed a letter of dissent. This was all over the news by the next day. This type of so-called 'organised public dissent' was unheard of; it had never happened in the US Catholic Church before. However, it still annoys me that people say we had not read the encyclical; you could not have written what we wrote if you had not read it. The next day I got as many of the lay members of the Papal Birth Control Commission as I could to come to Washington, and we held another press conference.

In the statement we pointed out the positives in the encyclical, but we said that we thought that the actual decision was wrong, and we argued as to why one could remain a good Roman Catholic and disagree in theory and in practice with the papal teaching. Our arguments were that you could dissent from a non-infallible papal teaching, which is what the encyclical was, and that it reduced the human moral act to its physical components, and that it lacked a personalist context. We were also critical of the natural law arguments embedded in *Humanae Vitae*. We wanted to keep our disagreement very respectful, but also very strong.

The CU Board of Trustees met in September and Cardinal James McIntyre of Los Angeles wanted to fire 'Father Curran and his followers' on the spot. But the trustees had learned something from the strike the year before, so they instituted an academic inquiry to see if we had violated our responsibilities as Catholic theologians. At the same time a good friend of mine on the faculty, Bob Hunt, a systematic theologian, decided he was going to leave the active priestly ministry. He told the family over the summer vacation about his intentions, as well as describing the fracas over *Humanae Vitae* and the inquiry. His brother John was a partner with a Wall Street firm, Cravath, Swaine & Moore. John assumed that I was the bête noire in this whole affair and that I had influenced his poor, unwilling little brother to go along with this whole thing.

However, he told Bob he would defend us before the academic inquiry; this was really his way of keeping his little brother in the priesthood. John told Bob he should never have disagreed with the pope, that he should not leave the priesthood, and that it was clear that I was to blame! John had been the successful son in the secular world, and had become one of the first Catholics to be a partner in a prestigious 'Wasp' Wall Street firm. Bob was the success in the Church and had become a professor at CU. So John was going to do his best to maintain the family status quo by defending us, and in the process keep his brother in the priesthood. My first meetings with John were the frostiest I have ever experienced. But before long John realised that this dissent was not as crazy as he had thought. He and I became very good friends. He not only defended us pro bono in 1969, but he had Cravath be my lawyers in my subsequent suit against Catholic University in 1988.

The first issue that came up at the academic inquiry was the question of dissent. By this stage we had established with the trustees the fact that even in the traditional textbooks of Catholic theology dissent was seen as legitimate. The issue of dissent from non-infallible teaching arose after the definition of papal infallibility. From then onwards you had to distinguish infallible teaching from non-infallible teaching. In the debates leading to the definition of infallibility reference was made to the times when the popes had changed decisions about non-defined teaching. Even older textbook authors like the Spaniard Salaverri says that a teaching can be wrong, but you have to hold to it unless and until the Church teaches the contrary. But he does allow that a teaching can be wrong. Others, like the Austrian, Diekmann, say that ordinarily the Holy Spirit protects the Church from error through the teaching of the pope and the hierarchy, but it could happen on occasion that the teaching office could be wrong and the Holy Spirit would then raise up people in the Church who would disagree. [See Joseph Komonchak's article in Curran (ed.): *Contraception, Authority and Dissent* (1969)].

So because we had already argued that dissent was possible, they changed the charge to 'the manner and mode' of the dissent. They were referring to our public, organised, quick response to the encyclical. There were twenty of us at CU involved in this case. John Hunt and Terry Connolly, an associate of the firm who was also a CU alumnus, argued the case for us. In the end we gathered so much detail we were able to publish our brief as two books: the first was theological and was edited by Bob Hunt and myself, *Dissent in and for the Church: Theologians and Humanae Vitae* [1970]; the second was the practical, legal side of the case [John F. Hunt and Terrence R. Connolly et al., *The Responsibility of Dissent: The Church and Academic Freedom*, (1970)]. The hearing went through various stages: establishing a process (I represented the School of Theology at this time and so was part of developing the process that was used); the establishment of a hearing committee (a professor of engineering was appointed chair of the committee, a decent man who handled the whole thing very well), and then the actual hearings. In April 1969 a report came in exonerating us.

One negative aspect of the whole thing was that the bishop who officially represented the trustees at the hearings was the then Auxiliary Bishop of St Paul, James Patrick Shannon. Some months later, in January 1970, he was to resign as a bishop and leave the active ministry entirely, precisely over the question of contraception. But at the hearings he was terrible to us; he gave us no quarter and vigorously defended the trustees. He admits all this in his book *The Reluctant Dissenter* [1998], and in fact he sent me a copy when the book was published. John Hunt could not stand him at the time and he often said, 'Give me O'Boyle any day. At least you know where he stands, and he is not pulling shenanigans the way that Shannon is!'

The committee and academic senate accepted the report, but the trustees never fully embraced it. They also never forgot what had happened, and from that time on I was a marked man. This was even more true among the activists of the Catholic right as well as arch-conservative newspapers like the St Paul-based, the *Wanderer*. These reactionary Catholics frequently urged people to write letters to Rome to dismiss me from the university. The organisation Catholics United for the Faith (CUFF) was founded right after *Humanae Vitae*, and I increasingly became one of the targets of these people as well. During the committee hearings we had a right to all Catholic University's past documents, and one of the amusing things that came out of this was that I caught out John Patrick Cody, the then Cardinal Archbishop of Chicago, in a deliberate lie. At the time of the previous attempt to dismiss me from CU, I had met Cody at a clerical party in Washington. Cody saw me, came over and said, 'That's terrible what they're doing to you. If I had been there at the trustee meeting, that never would have happened.' A year later during the committee hearings I discovered from the past documents to which we had access that John Patrick Cody actually seconded the motion to sack me in 1967!

At this point Charlie and I went off on a tangent about the origins of the Wanderer. *It is typical of his approach that he has a thorough understanding of the history of reactionary Catholicism and of the people most opposed to him. He told me that the* Wanderer *began in St Paul, Minnesota, and was one of many German-language newspapers in the nineteenth-century German–American Catholic community. German identity and culture in the immigrant situation in the US was also strengthened through the* Central-Verein, *a national federation of German–American benevolent societies. A key issue for German immigrants was how to keep the second generation loyal to both German culture and Catholicism. They often achieved this through their opposition to capitalism, and by their anti-Irish and anti-Protestant stances. However, this does not mean that they were supportive of trade unions. Rather they looked backwards towards the Middle Ages and towards corporatism and the guild system. They were also pioneers in the liturgical movement. The* Wanderer *was originally intimately associated with all of this. Unfortunately, the paper eventually devoted itself to the negation of 'all the terrible modern things' that were happening in the*

Church after Vatican II. In the 1970s the Wanderer *and other Catholic reactionaries argued that much of the abandonment of traditional Catholic ethics was due to the influence of Charles Curran.*

Things settled down to some extent at CU in the period after Humanae Vitae. *Pope Paul VI never mentioned the encyclical again, and there was still a sense of optimism present in the Church. Renewal still seemed a possibility. This was also the period when proportionalists began to apply the theory in earnest to the practicalities of moral life. Curran's specialisation was sexual ethics.*

Because of the public leadership role I had in the university strike and in the dissent over *Humanae Vitae,* I tried throughout the 1970s to keep much of my writing to a scholarly level and I published most of my books with the more academic Notre Dame University Press. While many of us in this period were disappointed with Pope Paul VI and the latter part of his papacy was not a particularly open period, there were still possibilities and a degree of optimism remained.

This was also the period when a whole group of moralists continued to rethink Catholic sexual teaching. Basically, what we were trying to do at this time was to deal theoretically with Catholic sexual ethics and its underpinning theological problems. I was the one of the first to use the word 'physicalism' to describe the Catholic approach to sexuality. The basic problem was that we identified the human, moral act with the physical structure of that act. As a result, the physical structure became normative. For example, we Catholics have never said that all killing is wrong; killing is a physical act. The moral act is murder. False speech is a physical reality; but not every false word is a lie. It is the deliberate lie that is the moral act. While we recognised this in other moral spheres, what happened with regard to Catholic sexual teaching was that we completely identified the human, moral act with the physical structure of the act; physicalism became morally normative.

The other problem with the Catholic tradition of sexual morality was that the faculty had become divorced from the person involved and the person, in turn, was divorced from their relationships with other persons. The usual Catholic position was that the nature and purpose of the faculty was procreation and love-union. But in doing this we had forgotten to say that the faculty should never have been absolutised in itself, but that it should be seen in relationship to the person, and the person in relationship with other persons. Thus many of us began to argue that for the good of the person, or for the good of the relationship, you can interfere with the sexual faculty.

I also began to think about some of the historical sources of the old-style Catholic attitudes to sexuality. Clearly one of these was the poor biology which I had become aware of while doing my doctoral dissertation. Second, I realised that another problem for Catholic sexual ethics was to be found in Thomistic ethics. St Thomas Aquinas distinguished three purposive levels of existence: the first and most basic, which all living things share, is the desire to keep themselves in existence. The second level, which is shared by both animals and humans, is the desire to procreate and educate offspring. The highest level, which is proper to us as human beings, is the desire to worship God and to live together in community. Aquinas defined humankind as a rational animal. The noun here was 'animal'. This came to be understood as a layer of animality complete and independent in itself, and a layer of rationality simply placed over the top of it. In this understanding physical and animal processes became sacrosanct; they had to be observed and you could not interfere with them even for the sake of the rational. This provided a faulty basis for traditional Catholic sexual teaching.

While Curran was trying to move beyond the absolutising of the physical, he did not want to fall into the problems inherent in a consequentialist or utilitarian approach to moral reasoning. Consequentialism is the absolutising of the results or consequences of a human act as morally normative. Fundamentally, consequentialism says that the moral species of an act is determined by its results. Certainly, in the Catholic moral tradition, the consequences of an act are an intimate part of the determination as to whether that act was moral. However, when it is absolutised it becomes a dangerous oversimplification. Curran says:

I wanted to avoid consequentialism because I think it is a simplistic reduction of everything to results. It opens the door to the notion of the greatest good for the greatest number, and it ultimately does not give enough importance to the dignity and rights of the individual. In the consequentialist understanding you can sacrifice an individual for the good of the community.

So I tried to find a path between Catholic physicalism and consequentialism. My view is that there is a distinction between physical and moral evil, and that you can commit a physical evil if there is a proportionate reason. So if your lower leg is gangrenous, you can cut it off to save the whole body. Cutting off the leg is not a moral evil; it is a physical evil. You can do that if there is a proportionate reason.

Let us take contraception in this context. You can begin by saying that contraception is a physical evil. But it can be done for a proportionate reason. But the problem is that most people nowadays would even have difficulty calling an act of intercourse between a loving couple a 'physical evil'. So I tend to call contraception an 'imperfection' rather than an 'evil'. Part of the problem is that people often think that theories come first; they are there to be applied to particular cases and thus come up with a moral answer. I would argue that theory comes afterwards to explain already existing teachings. I do have some problems with proportionalism, but I don't have a better theory at the present time. It basically arose out of trying to deal with the flawed inheritance of Catholic sexual ethics, and specifically the fallout from *Humanae Vitae*.

With thoughts such as these it is inevitable that the CDF would be after Curran. They had begun a file on him in 1966, and with the advent of John Paul II inquisitorial processes increased in intensity. First there was the CDF's dreadful treatment of Jacques Pohier, then there was the Edward Schillebeeckx case and then Hans Küng. Curran was the first American tackled publicly by the CDF.

My troubles with the CDF began on 2 August 1979. They came via a letter that Cardinal William Wakefield Baum of Washington, the chancellor of the university, passed on to me. The letter had been signed by Cardinal Franjo Seper, the then prefect of the CDF, on 13 July 1979. In essence, the sixteen pages of Observations contained in the letter outlined the CDF's concerns primarily with my views on the possibility of dissent in the Church, and my views on sexuality, specifically contraception, sterilisation, homosexuality and divorce. It was the worst kind of critique: I had never denied that I dissented from non-infallible teaching, but they would cite passages out of context and conclude that my arguments did not add up.

However, I took the letter very seriously. I wrote back to them on 26 October 1979 sending twenty-one pages of response dealing with the primary question of dissent from non-infallible teaching. What I said substantially was that there was no possibility of dialogue on the basis of what they had written to me. I formulated five questions and I suggested that we use these as a basis for discussion. I told them that I would say how I answered the questions, and I requested that they tell me how they would answer them, or how they disagreed with me. Then, on that basis, we could come up with some kind of conclusion. The questions were:

1. Does the teaching of the ordinary, non-infallible, authoritative, hierarchical magisterium constitute the only factor, or the always decisive factor in the magisterial activity of the Church?
2. Does there exist the possibility or even the right of public dissent on the part of a theologian who is convinced that there are serious reasons?
3. Is *silentium obsequiosum* the only legitimate response for a theologian who is convinced that a teaching is wrong?
4. Can the ordinary faithful make a prudent decision to act against the teaching?
5. In the course of history have there been errors in the teaching of the ordinary, non-infallible magisterium which have been subsequently corrected?

Of course, they would not respond to my questions. I knew then they were not going to take any form of dialogue seriously.

There was a kind of interesting overture to this. In February 1979 I was scheduled to give a talk at the Catholic Campus Ministry at Louisiana State University in Baton Rouge. Even before I got there I had a call to tell me that there was trouble with the bishop and the talk had to be moved off Catholic property. On the day of the talk there was a snow storm and I was actually lucky to get there. In the meantime, the then bishop, Joseph Sullivan of Baton Rouge, held a press conference where he said that I was 'heretical', that 'I was not in accord with Catholic teaching', and he released to the media an article out of the *Wanderer* which compared my position to that of the official Church. In response to Sullivan's action, Archbishop Jérôme Hamer, OP, then secretary of the CDF, wrote to him thanking him for pointing out my erroneous positions on moral issues. What really angered me was that the protocol number on Hamer's letter to Sullivan was my protocol number – 48/66! So on 29 August 1979 I wrote to Rome to protest. I said:

> Your Sacred Congregation has already violated its own principles by publicly condemning me. As a result any fair-minded person could readily conclude that I cannot receive a fair hearing from the same Congregation. I refer specifically to the letter of J. Hamer (copy enclosed) to Bishop Joseph V. Sullivan of Baton Rouge, dated April 24, 1979, with the same protocol number as the letter you sent to me. This letter was published in two national Catholic newspapers as well as in others, and copies were sent to many priests in the US.

I received no reply to this protest.

In my 26 October reply to the CDF's letter of 13 July, I also pointed out that nowhere did they mention my most substantial writing on dissent, the book *Dissent in and for the Church*. I told them that they should have a look at that book. In August I also wrote to several European moralists, including Franz Böckle in Bonn, and

Josef Fuchs and Bernard Häring in Rome. Now, Fuchs is a real fox; he is very knowledgeable about what is going on in the Vatican but has been a leader in the revision of Catholic moral theology since 1950. He was also my teacher at the 'Greg' and has been a friend and supporter, especially in my problems with the Vatican. Prior to my first hearing from the CDF, he had sent me an aerogram which was filled with one long sentence in Italian. He told me that he had been able to observe 'from a distance' that it might be that there were some people in Rome who were 'somewhat interested' in me. In November I went to Rome to talk to Fuchs, Häring and others, and I asked Fuchs, 'What the hell was that letter about?' I also showed him the August letter that I sent back to the CDF. 'Ah,' he said, 'do you know why they did not cite that book of yours on dissent? It is because you never gave me a copy, and its not in our library. What I was referring to in the letter was that the librarian of the "Greg" came to me and said: "You have some of Curran's books out of the library and you have some yourself. The Holy Office would like them." You never sent me a copy of that book. That is why the Holy Office does not have it. My letter was an oblique warning that they were on to you.'

There was intervening correspondence with the CDF where I objected to the process saying that it was unfair, and then fifteen months later, on 9 February 1981, another letter arrived from them. The CDF addressed these letters to me, but they actually came through the Archbishop of Washington. They told me that they had examined the book *Dissent in and for the Church* and that their earlier observations still remained pertinent. Then, on 10 May 1983, Ratzinger sent another letter with a further eight pages of Observations, and he asked me if I wished to revise my dissenting positions. From that time on I took it as a matter of course that I would take as long to respond to them as they took to respond to me. I responded on 10 August 1984. As a result things were dragged out. To be honest, at the very beginning I did not think that they were really serious, or that much would come of it. There were other people in other parts of the world saying many of the same things as I was saying. Also I thought they would have to move, just like CU, from the dissent itself to the manner and mode of the dissent. But basically that did not happen. I had not really gone public even at this time, although *Le Monde* had carried an article saying I was being investigated. The London *Tablet* picked up this story, and I said that I 'was in correspondence with the Vatican'. At that time I felt it was not helpful for me to go public.

But as time went on things became worse and I started to realise that it was not going to go away. For instance, in the summer of 1984, Pope John Paul II started giving his famous addresses at papal audiences to pilgrims in Rome on the theme of sexuality in Genesis. After his talk one Wednesday, there was an official press conference given by the then Monsignor Carlo Caffarra [since 1995, the Archbishop of Ferrara]. He said that unfortunately there were four theologians in the world who were responsible for the lack of acceptance of *Humanae Vitae*. They were Hans Küng, Franz Böckle, Marc Oraison and myself. Oraison was dead by this time, but I suddenly realised that Rome was serious. I wrote to Häring and Fuchs, and they both agreed.

After that, in the fall of 1984, came Ratzinger's famous interview, which was originally published in the Italian magazine *Jesu*. There it was called 'The Crisis of Faith in the World'. [It was later published as a book entitled *The Ratzinger Report* (1985).] Ratzinger said that each part of the world has a different problem: in Europe it was supposedly indifference to religion, in Africa inculturation, in South America it was liberation theology. 'Across the Atlantic' it was ethics. He said that scripture and systematic theology in North America was derivative from Europe, but that the specifically American contribution was ethics. But, he argued, unfortunately the American ethos is so opposed to the Catholic ethos that Catholic ethicists 'across the Atlantic' felt they either had to dissent from Church teaching or from the American ethos, and unfortunately too many of them choose to dissent from the Church. I was pretty sure then that the dye was cast.

Throughout the period 1983 to 1985 letters went back and forth, and finally on 17 September 1985 Ratzinger wrote 'concluding the inquiry' and asking for a final reply, saying that 'one who holds such positions cannot be called a Catholic theologian'. Right through the whole affair the core issue was that of dissent. In my very first response to them I focused on dissent, and simply did not respond to specifics about sexuality. Fundamentally, I argued that responsible dissent from the non-infallible magisterium is legitimate. Basically, the CDF has responded that there can be no dissent from the non-infallible magisterium. But the problem is that they never argue their position; they simply state it. They never engage in any form of dialogue. I have been sometimes asked who the consultor was who wrote the observations, and I have a fairly good idea that it was the Spanish Jesuit, Marcellino Zalba. The reason why I think it was him is because references to my writings began appearing regularly at this time in footnotes in his articles.

It was at this time that I started negotiations with Hickey, who by now had become Archbishop of Washington and university chancellor, and Cardinal Joseph Bernardin of Chicago, the chairman of the Board of Trustees at CU. Ultimately I had four meetings with the two of them, trying to work out what we could do. Joe Bernardin loved nothing better than a compromise, so I made the offer to them not to teach sexual morality. I told them honestly that I had not taught it for fifteen years anyway. The CDF could declare the errors that it perceived in my works. In return I would maintain my position on the faculty of CU and I would remain a Catholic theologian in good standing. If that offer was satisfactory to Rome, then the problem for Catholic University and the Church in the US would be removed. We went back and forth on this deal, and I had hoped that it would be Bernardin who would take it to Rome, because he would at least have his heart in it. But it was actually Hickey who took it to Rome in January of 1986. He saw both the pope and Ratzinger. I am not sure about this, but my guess is that he saw the pope first and realised the compromise was not going to be accepted. I have a feeling that he might not have even mentioned the compromise to Ratzinger, or if he did, it was the briefest of mentions. In fact, there was a rumour that Ratzinger had said that the hardest case he ever had to handle was my case, but in the end 'it was taken out of his hands'.

Hickey returned to Washington and said the compromise would not work, but that Ratzinger was willing to have an informal meeting with me. I said that I would go, so I flew to Rome for a meeting on 8 March 1986 with Ratzinger. Häring came to the meeting with me in the Palazzo del Sant'Uffizio. He was recognised throughout the world as the leading proponent of renewed moral theology before and after Vatican II. He was the most influential person in my own theological development, was my teacher, and was a constant source of support for me. He, too, had had his problems with the CDF. Ratzinger was accompanied by Archbishop Alberto Bovone, Monsignor Tom Herron, the English-language secretary, and the Canadian Jesuit moralist from the Gregorian, who insisted he was only there as a translator, Father Édouard Hamel. Ratzinger was friendly, cordial and courteous in a formal kind of way. We went for about two hours, but there was no real dialogue of any type; just talking back and forth. Before we went in Häring had advised me strongly not to get angry, but as soon as proceedings opened he began with a blistering attack on them with all guns firing. He denounced the Holy Office and all their mistakes over the years. Ratzinger heard him out, and then gave him the back of his hand and said, 'Are you through now, Father Häring?' Ratzinger said that he did not want to speak in English and that he would speak in Latin. I said that was okay with me. I used a little Latin with him, and then we went into Italian. He said, 'Oh, you know Italian?' I said, 'Yes, I lived in Rome for a number of years.' This obviously surprised him; he clearly did not know that I had studied in Rome for six years.

He was always polite and he maintained a kind of fixed smile on his face; he had a role to play and there was no way he was going to enter into genuine dialogue. The two testy parts were when I said to him, 'You are a respected German theologian, and are on a first name basis with six German moralists whom I could name, and you know as well as I do that they are saying the same things as I am saying.' He replied, 'Well, if you would want to delate these people, we will open a dossier on them.' I replied, 'I'm not here to do your dirty work.'

The other testy time was when poor Bovone, a product of the worst of the Roman system, was drawn into the conversation. He had sat there for over an hour and said nothing, and then finally Ratzinger turned to him and said, 'Archbishop Bovone is a canonist and he will explain to you the canon law involved here.' Bovone began speaking in Italian and he said, 'You are supposed to teach in the name of the Church, and if you are not teaching what the Church teaches you should resign. It's just like me. I work for His Eminence here. If I disagree with His Eminence I should resign and go back to my diocese and be just a parish priest.' I got angry and said, 'That's the trouble with you people. *Just* a parish priest! Don't you realise that is the most important thing you can be in the Church?' Ratzinger said, 'You misunderstood him.' I said, 'I did *not* misunderstand him!' Thank God Bovone died. If he had ever been pope I would have been in hell!

At the end Häring said, 'What about the compromise?' Ratzinger replied, 'What compromise?' Häring started talking, and Bovone quickly said, 'Oh, you remember, Eminence.' It was then that I realised that Hickey had never put the compromise to him. So Häring and I then explained the compromise. Ratzinger did not make any comment one way or another. Nothing came of it.

I was already planning a press conference when I got back to the US, but I did not want them to say that I was the first one to go to the media. So while we were having coffee at the end, I said that people knew we were meeting and I thought that it was appropriate that we issue a joint statement to the media. Surprisingly, Ratzinger agreed to it. It appeared in *Osservatore Romano* and in other ecclesiastical outlets. But I was covered for not going to the press first. When I returned to the US I had a press conference on the second day back. I announced publicly for the first time that I was under investigation. Among other things I said: 'I have never been told who my accusers are. I have been given no opportunity of counsel ... The Congregation itself has performed the roles of both accuser and judge.' Ratzinger's later specious response to this was: 'Your own works have been your "accusers", and they alone.'

I sent a final reply to Ratzinger on 1 April 1986 and I said that I could not change my positions. I told him:

> I respond expeditiously to your request for a final written reply so that you can bring this reply and the results of our informal meeting to the Cardinals of the Congregation as soon as possible ... I remain disappointed with the dialogue that has ensued between the Congregation and myself on this matter. Good theology and justice demand that the Congregation explicitly state what are the norms governing the legitimacy of the possibility of dissent from such non-infallible teaching, and then indicate how I have violated those norms. In January I proposed five questions; you never gave a response to them. Later I expressed my willingness to accept the criteria for dissent proposed by the US Bishops in 1968, but again the Congregation was unwilling to accept those norms ... In conscience I cannot and do not change the theological positions I have taken.

Ratzinger's final letter was given to me by Hickey at his residence at 4 pm on 18 August 1986. The letter was dated 25 July. In it Ratzinger stated that I was no longer 'suitable nor eligible to exercise the function of a professor of Catholic theology'. Hickey admitted that he had given it to the press earlier that afternoon before he had given it to me; he wanted to beat me to the media. Hickey, as chancellor, had also received another letter from the CDF instructing him to take 'appropriate action' now that I was neither 'suitable nor eligible' to function as a professor of Catholic theology.

A long process followed involving a faculty committee which eventually decided that: 'If the canonical mission is withdrawn, the rightful autonomy of the University, and the tenure rights of Professor Curran as understood in the American academic tradition, must be safeguarded. The withdrawal of the canonical mission cannot be allowed to abrogate Professor Curran's right to teach in the field of his academic competence ... namely ... in the area of moral theology and/or ethics.' In other words, the university could only take away my canonical mission provided I was still able to teach in the area of my specialisation. This pleased neither Hickey nor the Board of Trustees. As a result there were a number of offers and counter-offers to teach various subjects in different faculties, but finally on 2 June 1988 the Board of Trustees bit the bullet and said that it accepted 'the declaration of the Holy See as binding upon the University as a matter of canon law and religious conviction'. Therefore, I was not able to teach theology at all at CU. I would have been able to teach something else, but I replied that I could only really teach in the area of my expertise. When the board made that decision I decided to take them to court, arguing that I had academic freedom at CU and that no external body could make a decision that would take away my job.

Fortunately, in this case I again had the services of the Wall St firm Cravath, Swaine & Moore. My friend John Hunt had always said that if anything happened he would always take care of me. At this time John himself was ill, so the lead was taken by another member of the firm, Paul Saunders. Paul is a litigator, and he, John and three associates worked on the case. They always said they were going to send me a bill, but they never did. The cost of it would have been probably close to one million dollars.

The details of the court case are not immediately relevant to the story of Curran's dealings with the CDF. A detailed description can be found in Larry Witham's Curran v. the Catholic University: A Study of Authority and Freedom in Conflict *(1991, pp 139–278), a book that sets out to be balanced and ends up simply acerbic. But the civil case does illustrate the problems inherent in arguing complex issues about academic freedom and Church authority before the state courts. Curran maintained that the Catholic University had violated his contract because it guaranteed academic freedom. He had been denied this because of the unwarranted intervention of the CDF.*

The case was heard in the Superior Court in the District of Columbia. Curran himself says that: 'If there were no laws against drugs and prostitution, there would not be a Superior Court of the

District of Columbia. It's all they ever hear.' As a result, two of the top ten law firms in the US (the university was defended by the prestigious Washington firm of Williams & Connolly) ended up arguing the case before a court that specialised in drugs and prostitution. The judge was a Frederick H. Weisberg. The premier American Catholic Church historian, John Tracy Ellis, told Curran that he was sure it was the first time that two cardinals had testified in a civil lawsuit. He was referring to the testimony of Bernardin and Hickey. The case was held in Washington in December of 1988.

The university argued that the 'Curran affair' was an internal Church matter and that the case should be thrown out on the grounds of the separation of Church and state. Weisberg refused this, but Curran eventually lost because the judge handled the matter largely as a contract case. Curran's lawyers argued that CU had sent documents to the university accrediting association (the Middle States Association of Colleges and Schools) in which CU had emphasised its care to protect academic freedom, and it asserted that nothing could take it away. But Weisberg ruled that these were not official documents of the university; the only official documents were those that had been actually passed by the Board of Trustees. He held that there was nothing in those documents that would guarantee that there would be academic freedom in a case of conflict with the Vatican. In other words he found that there was no academic freedom at Catholic University. In the end Curran lost the case because the judge admitted that the university does have a special relationship to the Holy See, and therefore they had to accept the Vatican's decisions. He further said that there was nothing in Curran's contract, nor that of any other faculty member at CU, that guaranteed academic freedom. As Curran himself says the result was that: 'He not only decided against me, but he also cast a pall over the whole university by saying that they don't have academic freedom.' The judgment was handed down on 28 February 1989.

But the fall-out from the Curran case was much wider. A good summary of the broad-based and remarkable response is to be found in Richard McCormick's 'Notes on Moral Theology: 1986' in Theological Studies, *48 (1987), pp 87–105. As McCormick notes: 'By far the majority of the commentary has been critical of the Vatican decision.' McCormick concludes, 'During thirty years in the field of moral theology I have never seen so many priests – and so many laypersons – so deeply angry and utterly alienated.' Curran himself wrote a book about the affair as it was happening,* Faithful Dissent *(1986). This book includes all of the documentation involved in his dealings with the Vatican.*

Again we come back to the core of the issue between the CDF and Curran: 'The central issue involved in the controversy between the CDF and myself is the possibility of public theological dissent from some non-infallible teaching which is quite remote from the core of faith, heavily dependent on support from human reason, and involved in such complexity and specificity that logically one cannot claim absolute certainty' (Curran in Origins *16 (1986), pp 181–82). The position taken by the CDF and Ratzinger has led a number of theologians, including the ecclesiologist, Francis Sullivan, to comment on the 'novelty' of the Congregation's position. Sullivan says: 'I don't know of any previous case that has raised the issue of dissent in a way that tends to threaten the critical function of theologians with regard to the non-definitive teaching of the magisterium. I find this quite extraordinary, if what is meant is that infallible and non-infallible Church teachings are equally beyond criticism. This is new.'*

The situation in the Church has certainly not improved since Curran lost his canonical mission in 1986. In fact, if anything, it has worsened. Looking back Curran reflects on the future of the Church and the sources of his personal hope.

First of all my theology and my personal experience says that the Church is much more than hierarchy; the Church is the people of God. There were a tremendous number of people in the Catholic community who supported me throughout the whole affair, who have been faithful and loyal friends since. At the time there were various groups formed such as the Friends of Curran, and the Friends of American Catholic Theology. Over twenty thousand people signed petitions for me and Catholics from right across the spectrum supported me. For me the Church has been a very positive experience. Second, there is also the historical aspect.

Anyone with a sense of Church history knows that these things happen. I always love the story of St Alphonsus Liguori, the patron saint of moral theologians: Alphonsus was living in Naples and ecclesiastical censorship was under the control of the rigorist and moralistic Jansenistic theologians, who were supported by the Bourbon government of the Kingdom of the Two Sicilies. The publisher of Alphonsus' theology books was Remondini in Venice, and in order to get around the censor and the customs in Naples, at one time he had to go out in a row boat into the Naples harbour to meet the boat coming from Venice to get his books off before they were confiscated.

Also the whole history of Vatican II reminds us that the theologians who were under suspicion in the 1940s and 1950s were the ones who were ultimately vindicated by the Council. Spiritually, one person sows and another reaps. That is simply our spiritual tradition. I am convinced that the Church will eventually have to move in the way that contemporary moral theology suggests. In fact, the large majority of faithful Catholics have already moved that way. They have made up their own minds about a whole range of moral issues. Ironically, it is often theologians like myself who are trying to save the Church hierarchs from their own narrowness, their unwillingness to admit that they were wrong and their arbitrary use of authority, which has made it so difficult for so many sincere people to remain in the Church. In terms of my own spirituality, I am happy to live with the hope that things have to change, will change and, in one sense, are already changing. However, in the long run, if the hierarchical Church continues to put so great an emphasis on arbitrary authority the Catholic community will simply descend into ever deeper problems.

I have always maintained that the Roman Catholic Church was never more centralised and authoritarian than in the years immediately preceding Vatican II and now again in the years following it. Unfortunately, part of the problem is exacerbated by modern communications, mobility and transportation. Many American Catholics, for example, are amazed to discover that the first English Catholics in Maryland celebrated the liturgy in the vernacular. This was a new country, they were months away from Rome by boat, and if they tried to get there they might make it, and then again they might not. So they had to make their own decisions. Those early American Catholics were right; the local Church should make those kinds of decisions. But now we are merely a cell phone call away from the Vatican. There is also a way in which the media keeps this going. They focus so much on the pope. As a result, the idea is conveyed that the pope is a monarch and everybody's pastor and bishop rolled into one. That is not right; the pope is the Bishop of Rome. So we not only have to fight centralisation on theological grounds; we have to fight it in terms of modern media and communications, which is aiding and abetting the centralisation of the Catholic Church.

What does the future hold? In the short term I think we are going to have all sorts of problems. In the long term I am not sure if I am optimistic that we are going to get it right, but I do have hope. But hope is not based on what you can see. If you can see something, it is not hope, as St Paul reminds us. I have hope because of the promise that Jesus made to the community of his disciples to be always with us. In addition I am very worried about the other alternatives. It seems to me that the greatest danger to our society is that of secularism and materialism. In the US it expresses itself in terms of total individualism.

If there is one thing that Christianity stands for it is community, and as such it provides a real antidote to an individualism in which people are concerned only about themselves, their own wellbeing and financial security, and not much else. I am very glad when Pope John Paul II reminds us of the dangers of consumerism and materialism. That is a role that the pope should play. I once said, probably a little too frivolously, to someone in the media: 'I agree with the pope on many issues. The pope is very good, except when he speaks about women, sex and the Church.'

What also worries me is the fact that unfortunately the mainstream liberal Protestant churches in the US are having great problems and are in decline. Certainly, the fundamentalist churches are growing, but not the mainstream Protestants, who are decreasing in numbers and influence. I think that is terrible. It reminds us, however, that the authority issues which we have discussed are *not* the most important issues. We have to get over the hump of the issue of authority in order to be able to confront these other more important issues: the meaning of human existence, the global economy, and the role of the civil community, to mention just a few. Here the Catholic Church has got something to offer: we have always insisted that we are a community, that we have obligations to each other, and that we are not isolated monads. I guess that is another reason why I try to make the Church work. In a certain sense my theology of the Church is in many ways old fashioned. God did not make a covenant with individuals; God made a covenant with people. You belong to God by belonging to a community. Therefore, you have to be willing to put up with all the types of nonsense and difficulties embedded in community relationships.

This same thing applies in the broader civil community. Here in the US we are increasingly facing the issue of whether we are even able to say 'we the people'. Can we say, for instance, that we are the people of Dallas? Dallas is divided racially, economically and culturally. Can we admit that there is such a thing as 'the people'? It is hard to say that of Dallas, or of Texas, and it even harder to say that of the US, and very difficult to say it of the world. But Christianity and Catholicism can still offer a sense of belonging to the people and to the community. In my own troubles with the Church I have always argued that you need some form of unity. If you belong to a community, it has to stand for something. The difficulty in Catholicism is that we have substituted uniformity for unity. In civil society we face the same problem: how can we have unity in the face of the tremendous pluralism and diversity that characterises our world?

A good example is the problem of homosexuality in the Anglican communion. It was precisely the new, conservative churches of Africa that blocked any change on this at the last Lambeth Conference. There is not one mainstream Protestant Church that is not going through this same problem. How do you maintain community, but at the same time maintain the right of dissent? I have always appreciated the famous axiom that probably owes its origin to the great Protestant reformer, Philip Melanchthon: *In necessariis, unitas; in dubiis, libertas; in omnibus, caritas* (In necessary things, unity; in doubtful things, freedom; in all things, charity). At times one has to make some personal sacrifices for the sake of maintaining the community. I think it is profoundly important that there are signs that some communities can work, because that is so important in the midst of the rampant individualism that characterises our culture at present. If we can't do it in the Church where we believe in forgiveness, in a transcendent God, and that we are brothers and sisters of one another, secular society is never going to be able to do it.

In the long run I see a great need for the possibility for the Church to model genuine community. It could play a marvellous role, and it is so tragic and unfortunate that we are bogged down in these sad disputes about authority versus freedom.

CHAPTER 4

Excommunication and Liberation:
Tissa Balasuriya

To the outsider Sri Lanka seems like a country at war with itself. Yet paradoxically, away from the areas of conflict in the Jaffna Peninsula and the north and east of the country, the island is apparently remarkably peaceful and, despite omnipresent military checkpoints, people are open and friendly. But even this is deceptive, as continuing political violence and assassination attempts on the president and other political leaders during election campaigns have shown. Neither the Sri Lankan government nor the Liberation Tigers of Tamil Elam shows any signs of compromise, despite intermittent efforts by various parties to bring about a truce and eventual peace. The roots of the civil conflict are incorrectly assumed by outsiders to be between the majority Sinhalese and the minority Tamils, who are thought to have been brought into Sri Lanka from south India by the British colonial authorities to work the tea plantations. But the reality is much more complex, and Tamils have been on the island for over a thousand years.

Civilization in Sri Lanka goes back a long way. The Sinhalese people came to Ceylon from the northern or north-eastern shores of the Bay of Bengal, four to five centuries before the Christian era. Originally, they only occupied the Jaffna Peninsula and the northern plain of the island, and they were well established in their capital Anuradhapura in the central north, when Buddhism first came from India in 307BC. A large majority of Sinhalese are Buddhist.

The word 'Tamil' is the generic term for the Dravidian peoples of south India. While there had been both constant trade and warfare between the Sinhalese kingdom in Ceylon and Tamil south India for hundreds of years, in 992–93AD a major Tamil invasion occurred which led to the eventual abandonment of Anuradhapura and the retreat of the Sinhalese kingdom, first to Polonnaruwa, and then finally to Kandy in the central highlands, which nowadays is the Buddhist centre of the island. By the sixteenth century the island was divided into seven separate kingdoms. In 1505 the Portuguese arrived and rapaciously dominated much of the western coast of the island for a hundred years. This is when the first Christian conversions occurred. From the beginning of the seventeenth century the Dutch were the predominant colonial power although, like the Portuguese, they never really penetrated far into the centre of the island. In 1795–6 the British defeated the Dutch and took over control of the coastal areas. By devious means they finally captured the kingdom of Kandy, and in 1815 brought the whole island under their colonial control. Sri Lanka attained independence in 1948.

In 1999 the population of Sri Lanka was 18.3 million. Seventy-four per cent were Sinhalese, 13 per cent Sri Lankan Tamils, 5 per cent Indian Tamils brought in by the British for the tea plantations, with mixed-race Burghers making up most of the rest of the population. In terms of religion, the Buddhists are the largest group with 69 per cent, Hindus comprise 15 per cent, Muslims make up 7.5 per cent and Christians 7 per cent. The vast majority of the Christians are Catholics, who number 1.2 million, people of both Sinhalese and Tamil background having converted to Catholicism. While tolerant of all other religions, local Catholic converts were persecuted under the Dutch, and then began to prosper again under the British. As in India, the Church emphasised education. A very high percentage of the clergy are indigenous.

Numerically, the largest religious order of priests in the country are the Oblates of Mary Immaculate (OMI), and this is the congregation to which Father Tissa Balasuriya belongs. Founded in 1816 in France as a missionary and educational order, the Oblates came to Sri Lanka in 1847 and have had a considerable influence on local Catholicism.

In many ways the current civil struggle in Sri Lanka is fundamentally *about democratic pluralism and the ability of different cultures and religions to live together in peace. Throughout his long life Father Tissa Balasuriya has stood for pluralism, tolerance and social justice, and has worked to strengthen contacts between people of different beliefs and values. 'Father Bala', as he is popularly known, has supported the poor and oppressed against the powerful, and more recently he has been very critical of the way Western multinational corporations exploit developing countries like Sri Lanka. As well as calling for dialogue within his own society, he also works in a practical way for refugees from the ongoing civil war in the north of the island.*

At the deepest level, Tissa Balasuriya has struggled to integrate his Catholic faith with Sri Lankan culture. For much of his life he has questioned the old missionary approach – salvation through conversion and conformity to a form of Catholicism that is essentially European and Roman. In other words, Catholicism expressed as a form of ecclesiastical colonialism. This dispute goes back to the days of Vatican II, when Balasuriya and a number of others, including Oblate Father Michael Rodrigo, who studied with him in Rome, tried to get the Church to be more open to the world and to adopt the fundamental change of attitude that was implicit in the whole approach of the Council. Rodrigo was murdered in 1988 while celebrating mass in a remote area because of his opposition to those who exploited the rural poor. Other Sri Lankan Catholics have been working along similar lines. The Jesuit Aloysius Pieris has worked with base communities that include members of all religious faiths who are experiencing oppression and poverty. He says that 'spirituality is not the practical conclusion of theology, but radical involvement with the poor and the oppressed, and [it is this which] creates theology'. Another group that works along similar lines is the Satoyada community in Kandy led by another Jesuit, Father Paul Casperz.

However, many of the bishops, including the first indigenous Archbishop of Colombo, Cardinal Thomas Cooray, found it hard to adjust to the conciliar reforms and to a non-Roman approach to theology and ministry. The Church establishment has remained essentially conservative and is close to right-wing elements in the country, including the military. It is this conflict about missionary method and cultural integration that is at the core of the attack that Bishop Malcolm Ranjith and others launched on

Balasuriya in 1992. This was quickly taken up by the CDF, which in the second half of the 1990s had become increasingly concerned with 'Asian theology'. Intolerant of pluralism, the CDF views Balasuriya as a 'relativist' who equates all religions and philosophies and who reduces Christian spirituality to 'social action'.

But Balasuriya has been involved with the issue of cultural integration for a long time. In his book Jesus Christ and Human Liberation *he describes the image of Jesus traditionally presented by Western missionaries to Asian converts. There Jesus is someone sent by God to save humankind from the effects of original and personal sin. He became man in obedience to God in order to make reparation for our sins through his death. His act of obedience in embracing the human condition and dying on the cross redeemed all humanity. Salvation for the individual was mediated by the Church. There was no other form of salvation. Thus the great religious traditions, such as Buddhism, were insufficient for salvation.*

The very process of conversion meant that new converts were to a considerable extent cut off from their culture and forced to adopt a religion that was Roman and Western. In the traditional missionary approach, the emphasis on the personal unworthiness of the convert and obedience was important. This was precisely what the colonial power demanded in the civil sphere from the 'natives'. There was no conscious collusion, of course, but both Church and state were working from the same set of presuppositions. However, as Balasuriya points out, the Gospels could have been used to present a very different image of Jesus: one who cared for the poor and oppressed and worked for human liberation. But the Jesus presented to Asian converts was passive and obedient. In contrast, Balasuriya presents a Jesus who is active and liberating, a fully 'conscious human being capable of suffering, being angry and even tempted'.

The missionaries also presented a 'watered-down' image of Mary. In place of the strong woman concerned with social justice and liberation described in the first chapter of St Luke's Gospel (Luke 1:51–53), Mary was presented as passive, domesticated and obedient. Sri Lankan Catholicism, like much of the popular Catholicism of Asia, is deeply devotional, and Mary and the saints play an important 'mediating' role. The social radicalism of the Mary who praises God for showing 'the

83

strength of his arm' and 'scattering the proud-hearted', for bringing 'down the powerful from their thrones' and lifting up the lowly, for filling 'the hungry with good things' and sending 'the rich away empty', is replaced by the passive Blessed Virgin, the 'purest of creatures', the Mary who is both 'sweet mother [and] sweet maid'. In Mary and Human Liberation *Balasuriya's describes her as 'a loving mother and sister of all; a woman among women, a human being among us; one who faced the difficulties of being united to Jesus for a better humanity'.*

There is a sense in which Balasuriya's challenge is as much politico-social as it is theological. As such it is seen as deeply subversive by many in the Church establishment, especially in a country that is as deeply divided as Sri Lanka.

The CDF process against Balasuriya led eventually in 1998 to the radical and draconian penalty of excommunication. He is the only theologian to have been so drastically treated since Vatican II. The only other well-known example of excommunication of a theologian in the twentieth century is that of the Italian priest Ernesto Buonaiuti, who was accused of 'modernism'. Yet Balasuriya's consistency and strength of character, as well as worldwide public pressure, forced the CDF to compromise and abandon the excommunication a year later. In the process it has made Balasuriya one of the best-known priests and theologians in the world. He lives and works at the Centre for Society and Religion (CSR), a four-storey building taking up one side of a large compound in inner-city Colombo, which also houses a very busy Catholic church and shrine, and a residence for the Oblates of Mary Immaculate.

When you first meet 'Father Bala' at home, he seems serious and almost withdrawn. But very quickly an exquisite courtesy emerges and a ready smile takes over, which is often highlighted by an impish laugh. He is generous with his time and open and provocative in expressing his views. At seventy-six you would expect him to be slowing up, but he seems to be going faster now than ever before and there seems to be no end to his energy and creativity. He is very much a man of the people: when travelling he either walks or catches the bus. His cloister is both the world and his own culture, in which he is very much at home. No doubt it reflects his family background in the local village. Balasuriya begins by telling something of his background and training.

I was born on 29 August 1924 in the village of Kahatagasdigiliya, close to the ancient capital of Anuradhapura. Catholicism runs in my family. My father was in the medical profession, with two years' medical training. He was a medical officer in charge of dispensaries, mainly in rural areas, and between 1924 and 1930 worked in the North Central Province. Throughout his life my father was also a coconut planter, and on his retirement from government service he set up a desiccated-coconut mill in his home village of Andiambalama, north of Colombo. After my excommunication, it was on this farm, bequeathed to me by my parents, that we began a home for disadvantaged children.

My father was later transferred to the village of Dankotuwa, near the central west coast, and I was educated there for a short time in a Sinhalese school. Then I went to the Catholic Marystella College in Negombo, just north of Colombo, as a boarder at the age of six and a half, and was there for eight years with the Marist Brothers. In 1938 I gained the Junior School Certificate and then went to St Patrick's College, Jaffna, which was run by the Oblate Fathers. There I lived in a Tamil environment, passing the matriculation in 1940. I then moved to St Joseph's College in Colombo.

From there I went to the University of Ceylon where, from 1942 to 1945, I studied economics and political science. While I was at university I read the lives of the saints and was a member of the Legion of Mary. Founded in 1921 in Ireland, the Legion of Mary has a strong Marian emphasis in its spirituality, but it encouraged apostolic activity as a way of giving expression to spiritual commitment. So it was a kind of combination of social and political action with theological and religious convictions that later led me to move in the direction I did as a priest.

After university I went to the Oblate novitiate, I think because I experienced a kind of inner call that was indefinable, yet irresistible. For me the priesthood was also a way of serving society and of bearing witness to Jesus Christ. I had been part of the Catholic Student Movement at university, which in those days was more open and searching, even if still rather conservative. So for me the priesthood was a combination of a desire for both spirituality and social change. When I decided to enter the seminary, I went to see the French Archbishop of Colombo, who was an Oblate of Mary Immaculate – he was the last foreign archbishop – and I said I wanted to be a priest but that I had not yet decided which group to join, either the Oblates or the diocesan clergy. He said: 'Oh well, it doesn't really matter. Whether you join the Oblates or the diocese, you'll still be under me!'

The notion of a French archbishop brings up the question of whether Catholicism is viewed as a 'foreign' religion in Sri Lanka. In the past, Catholicism was seen as such, but that is not so much the case now because the Church has changed the liturgy into the local languages, and we have tried to adapt our music and even our thinking to Sri Lankan culture. The Portuguese refused to ordain locals, so most of the clergy and all of the bishops were foreign. The Oblates came to Sri Lanka in 1847, and from that time onwards we have ordained Sri Lankan priests. However, it was not until about 1940 that the first indigenous bishops were appointed; the first Sri Lankan archbishop came in 1947 with independence. Now all the bishops are local. But, as my own experience has shown, we are still a long way from solving the theological problem of integrating Catholicism into our culture.

Looking back on why I joined the Oblates, I think it was the vow of poverty I took as a member of a religious order which made the real difference. A vow of poverty implied that I had to do something practical for the Sri Lankan poor. I also knew several Oblate priests and they attracted me. I did my novitiate and one year of philosophy in Colombo, and then went to the Gregorian University in Rome where I did two more years of philosophy and four years of theology between 1947 and 1953. In those difficult years after World War II we never went home and had to study in Latin and speak Italian and French. I was probably in Rome at the same time as Cardinal Josef Ratzinger and Father Hans Küng. After ordination in Rome, I returned to Sri Lanka in 1953.

Father Peter Pillai, who had already influenced me a lot, met me at the ship and took me back to St Joseph's College where he was rector. He had been concerned with social justice and workers' rights for quite some time. He was an intellectual who had studied mathematics and physics in Cambridge, had read G. K. Chesterton and Hilaire Belloc, and was influenced to some extent by Joseph Cardijn and his Young Christian Workers' movement. Chesterton and Belloc were English Catholics who, while right-wing and conservative, encouraged Catholic engagement with culture and society. Father, later Cardinal, Joseph Cardijn was a Belgian priest who, in the 1920s and 1930s, encouraged Catholic action and helped young lay Catholics to integrate their work in the world with their faith. He founded the Young Christian Workers, or 'Jocists' as they are sometimes called, a movement which developed a spirituality of reflective action that has had considerable influence on modern Catholicism. Pillai had also studied in Rome, and had come under the influence of the social thinking of popes Leo XIII and Pius XI. European trends towards socialism influenced him, although he was very unfavourable to anything that smacked of communism. He had studied Hinduism, and the work of Gandhi and the freedom movements of Asia and Africa had impacted on him.

I taught with Pillai at St Joseph's College, and in 1954 we began to develop what was to become Aquinas University College, an institution similar to an American liberal arts college. I was registrar there and taught economics and theology. In those days we only had the University of Ceylon, and we developed Aquinas as an alternative for those who, because of restricted numbers, could not get into the university, or who could not afford it. At Aquinas we had afternoon and evening classes for those who were working. However, there was strong opposition among many of the elite to the idea of a private Catholic college. Nevertheless, we attracted large numbers of students, many of whom were later to become very influential in Sri Lankan society.

Before going to Rome I had been influenced by the movement for independence from the British. We did not have to struggle for freedom as the Indians did. We had universal suffrage from 1931 onwards and were granted independence in 1947. But the tragedy was that we did not have to struggle and never developed political leaders like Mahatma Gandhi and Jawaharlal Nehru. As result of their own experiences fighting for independence, both these men were far more committed to a struggle for liberation and the service of the people than our Sri Lankan political leaders. At the same time, the leadership of the Catholic Church was very insecure about independence and the democratic process. The bishops were concerned as to how the Buddhist majority would treat Christians.

So I developed in the context of a forward-looking Catholicism, combined with social radicalism and an openness to other thinking and religions. Sri Lanka today sees itself as a 'socialist' country, a view very much influenced by a parallel secular group to us socially involved Catholics. This secular group was formed in Britain by the Marxism of the 1930s and the thought of Harold Laski, the Fabian Socialists and the 1917 Russian Revolution. When they returned to Sri Lanka they founded the socialist and Marxist parties, and had a major influence on the independence movement. After 1947 this same group began the transformation of our society in a socialist direction through the parliamentary system, in the process establishing social services and free education. In 1950s and 1960s non-communist socialist thinking influenced most Sri Lankan intellectuals. It was a period when the solution to the country's problems seemed to be through state enterprise. In 1972, when we became a republic, the word 'socialism' was brought into the constitution. After 1977 right-wing politicians opted for liberal capitalism, and opened the country up to the transnational corporations. But they kept the word 'socialism' in the constitution.

From 1962 to 1964, I was abroad. This was the time of Vatican II. Between 1962 and 1963 I studied at the Agricultural Economics Institute at Oxford, headed by the Australian, Colin Clark. Since Father Pillai wanted me to take over Aquinas College, a further secular degree from Oxford would have been useful. However, I quickly realised I did not agree with the capitalistic and Western economics that underpinned Clark's approach. Also, I knew I was not really interested in getting a degree. I wanted instead to look critically at the Thomism in the philosophy and theology in which I had been trained, in order to try to find a new way of viewing life. I had a deep concern for social justice and the values of socialism because I realised that this was the trend that would really help poor people. I also came to see that the whole academic system was basically in favour of those who dominated society. After Oxford, I went to the Institut Catholique in Paris between 1963 and 1964.

Even when I was a student in Rome in the early 1950s I could not quite accept the Western missionary approach. The notion underlying this was that through increasing numbers of conversions, the other great religions like Buddhism would slowly disappear and that Christianity would be triumphant. However, when I returned to Sri Lanka in 1953 the Church was on the defensive. I saw that there was a dissonance between the Western–Aristotelian-Thomistic-Roman synthesis, and the aspirations of Asian people for liberation. In 1961 the Sri Lankan government nationalised the private schools, including 2500 Catholic schools. That showed us how little sympathy there was among ordinary people for these schools. Many people felt that they had been used for proselytism, as well as giving the Catholic community a social advantage. The Church establishment increasingly found itself allied with the political right wing, and in opposition to the more socialistic approach. So, as a result, a group of us Catholics began to rethink our whole approach to theology and social action.

By 1964 I was writing in favour of openness to other religions. In a sense, I and others had already moved beyond Vatican II, although that was the source of much of our hope. By the time the Council finished in 1965 I was rector of Aquinas College, where we held seminars in English and Sinhalese to introduce the ideas of the Council to the local Church and to change the mind-set of Catholics. In 1968–69 there was a National Synod of the Catholic Church. What became clear then was that the main leadership of the Church was not prepared for change of any sort, neither in terms of openness to other religions, nor in a willingness to take a more socialistic approach. These people were formed in the old mind-set that the primary function of the Catholic Church was 'to save souls', and that social action neglected Church ministry and could involve the abandonment of spiritual values.

By the late 1960s it was clear that serious change was not going to come from within the Church, despite the fact that a few Church leaders such as Bishop Leo Nanayakkara, of Kandy, and my Oblate colleague, Father Michael Rodrigo, were involved in social change. So some of us decided to move outside present Church structures: I resigned from Aquinas College and went out to live alone in a village area in order to see what would happen, and then to work out which direction I should take. Bishop Leo left Kandy for the newly established and poor, remote diocese of Badulla in the south of the island. Slowly the idea of a centre for research and action in social justice grew in our minds, and in July 1971 we decided to form the Centre for Society and Religion in Colombo.

At that time most bishops neither approved nor disapproved of the centre, so long as we did not challenge the system too publicly. My religious congregation permitted the situation to develop, so long as they were not held responsible if the venture failed. From 1969 to 1979 I was chaplain to the Catholic Students Federation and chaplain for Asia for the International Movement of Catholic Students. That gave me some other work and involvement abroad, putting me in contact with people from different parts of Asia and giving me a broad knowledge of what was happening in the Asian Church.

The origin of my problems with Church authority is rooted in the fundamental theological issue of salvation. Many Christians in Asia are increasingly unable to think of salvation exclusively in terms of the Church, or as only mediated by Jesus Christ. We have come to realise that such a view would imply that the vast majority of the people of Asia were not saved. The point has slowly dawned on us that this is not acceptable. Vatican II pointed to some openings concerning the salvation of non-Christians, but even in the 1970s the leadership of the Church in Rome was retreating into itself. The more I studied the issue of salvation, the more I was impressed with the serious inadequacy of the Church's doctrinal thinking. It gradually became clear to me that what we have presented for a thousand years as dogma and doctrine is not really from Jesus Christ. Certainly Catholicism and Vatican II have clearly said that the Church is not the sole means of salvation. The real problem is that the Church usually denies this in practice and acts as though you need to be baptised in order to be saved. The whole missionary thrust through sermons and teaching is that, even today, salvation is to be found only in the Church and in Jesus Christ. Thus we are fitting God and people into our own categories and perspectives.

As far back as the late 1970s questions were raised about my books *Jesus Christ and Human Liberation* [1976] and *The Eucharist and Human Liberation* [1977]. But my real problems with Church authority began with my book *Mary and Human Liberation*, published in June 1990. This book was written during a period of insurrection in Sri Lanka, when a lot of people were killed, including my friend and colleague, Father Michael Rodrigo. The book centred on the role of Marian devotion. But this inevitably touches on a number of fundamental doctrines, including that of original sin.

By 1990 I had realised that the idea of original sin was basic to the concept of salvation, and that once you posit the idea that original sin infects everyone, some form of universal redemption is required. This was interpreted by medieval theologians such as St Anselm and others in the past, to mean that there had to be a divine redeemer. If there is a divine redeemer, the theory of merit and grace follows, with the Church as the medium for this grace. Once you enter into this complex of ideas, you are dealing with the substance of Christian dogma as traditionally presented, and you are dealing with one of the central underpinnings for the justification of missionary work. The Vatican saw this clearly. Their critique of my writing is not so much about the role of Mary as about my treatment of these fundamental doctrines. But since Mary is important for Catholic peoples' devotion, especially in Asian countries such as Sri Lanka, it is very easy to present me as somebody against Mary. My book was essentially a simple one, which suggested that we need to change the accent of Marian devotion. It also implicitly questioned the fundamental traditional understanding of the Bible and the myths developed around the concept of original sin that resulted in the exclusion of the rest of humanity from salvation, except through Jesus Christ and the Church. All of that was implied in *Mary and Human Liberation*.

The origins of the investigation of Balasuriya's writings are to be found in the tensions inherent in the post-Vatican II history of the Sri Lankan Church, and there is no doubt that he has been one of the main standard bearers for a whole new understanding of the role and function of a minority Church in a largely Buddhist nation. In a number of places recently, including Sri Lanka, more conservative and ambitious younger bishops have been emboldened to go on the attack against those theologians who are well known and construed as 'progressives'. In the case of Balasuriya the bishop was Albert Malcolm Ranjith Patabendige Don, born in 1947, ordained priest in 1975 and bishop in 1991, and appointed Bishop of Ratnapura in 1995.

The book that focused Ranjith's attack was Balasuriya's Mary and Human Liberation. *Marian devotion is very strong among Asian Catholics and it tends to express itself in forms of piety that emphasise the Blessed Virgin's mediating role between God and believers. For Balasuriya the study of Mariology leads straight to Christology and the role and function of Christ as the sole mediator. It also raises the question of the role of women in the Church and in society, and, by implication, the question of the ordination of women. This issue appears almost out of the blue in the personal profession of faith that the CDF later demanded that Balasuriya sign. However, it is connected with the way Balasuriya discusses the role of women. But it was specifically the Christological issues in the book upon which Balasuriya's opponents first focused.*

Mary and Human Liberation was first read by a Sri Lankan bishop who proposed that it should be examined doctrinally for theological errors. The first I heard of this was on 22 December 1992 when I received a letter from the Archbishop of Colombo, Archbishop Nicholas Fernando, saying that an ad hoc committee of the Bishops' Conference had made a study of my book, and that they wanted to discuss it with me. On 7 January 1993 we met at the Bishops' Conference office in Colombo. The ad hoc theological commission consisted of bishops Malcolm Ranjith of Ratnapura and Vianny Fernando of Kandy, and theologians fathers Dalston Forbes, OMI, and Emmanuel Fernando. I went to the meeting with the Oblate provincial, Father Camillus Fernando.

After some small talk, Bishop Ranjith began reading rather quickly from a written document that he then gave to the commission members, and which was later given to me at my request. When Ranjith finished reading, he said that disciplinary action should be taken against me and that I should be prevented from spreading heretical views. He also claimed that what he had read were the conclusions of the whole commission. However, it became obvious later that the other members of the commission had not even seen the document in advance, although it was claimed that all four of them accepted it. So it would seem that the problem started with Bishop Ranjith and that the others were basically hedging their bets. In other words, from the very beginning there was ecclesiastical 'hanky-panky'! This may not be theological language, but it reflects the reality of what happened.

When there is a question of dogma, most people in the Church hedge and try to argue that authority is right. Both elements were there in my case right from the start. One person, Bishop Ranjith, took a strong position, and the others were incapable of a just response because they began equivocating. That is a significant phenomenon in Church investigations: the burden of proof is always placed on the accused and the advantage of innocent correctness is accorded to the status quo. This is not the normal way that justice operates in civil society. My feeling throughout the process was that false accusations had been made which were difficult to overcome, and that everyone was protecting themselves. As a consequence I had to develop faith in my own conscience. I took down careful notes at the meeting, and when I got home I wrote them up. I was able to show that Bishop Ranjith's document contained misrepresentations and distortions of the text of *Mary and Human Liberation*, largely through selective quotation. This pattern of distortion became a common phenomenon throughout the whole process. My refrain became, 'I have not said what you say I have said.' All along I demanded a fair inquiry by competent persons. Actually, I was not only asking for theological expertise but for competence in the English language. I wanted someone who would present my writings accurately. Often a word, like 'however' would be taken out of a quotation, and it changed the whole context and sense of what I was saying.

I responded to the Bishops' Conference committee along these lines, but did not receive an answer. Suddenly, at very short notice, I was summoned to another meeting at Kandy, 190 kilometres from Colombo, on 20 April 1994, and was told without any discussion that the bishops would soon make a public statement on the book. On 5 June they published a statement in the *Catholic Messenger* saying that the book contained 'four glaring errors' and recommended Catholics not read it. They then accused me of 'going public', and cited as an example the fact that I had asked some nuns to pray for me, in a private letter! My public reply to their statement was never published in the *Catholic Messenger*. However, I did send the Bishops' Conference a detailed 53-page response on 27 March 1995. Again, I have never received any reply to this, except that in the *Catholic Messenger* of 19 January 1997 this response was described as 'inadequate'.

The other interesting thing is that I subsequently learned that the ad hoc theological commission had not met in advance to agree on Ranjith's text. Eventually, I was informed that one commission member, Father Dalston Forbes, OMI, a theologian well known for his orthodoxy and a former rector of the national seminary, had argued that Ranjith's theology was 'weak', that there had been no prior discussion of the text, and that he did not agree with a number of the assertions in it. Forbes eventually disowned Ranjith's text.

In the meantime there had obviously been some 'movement of the Spirit', because on 27 July 1994 I received a letter from my superior-general in Rome, Father Marcello Zago, OMI, telling me that the CDF had 'discussed the question of your book in their meeting of 22 June and decided to initiate the procedures foreseen in such cases; that is, that the author be requested to withdraw the opinions which are erroneous and contrary to the faith'. Specifically, the CDF said that 'the book contains statements (existence and nature of original sin, divinity of Christ, need for redemption, Christ as the only saviour, the nature and mission of the Church, mariology) which are manifestly incompatible with the faith of the Church'. The superior-general was asked 'to take the necessary measures as he shall see fit, which include eventually the request for a public withdrawal, and within a reasonable time he shall let the Congregation know the author's answer'. Then came the threat: 'Should the author not withdraw these opinions, then the Congregation would proceed to issue an official condemnation of these opinions as being contrary to the Catholic faith.' Accompanying this letter was an anonymous set of Observations on *Mary and Human Liberation*.

On 14 March 1995 I sent a long response of fifty-five single-spaced A4-sized pages to the CDF's Observations. But since I was told by those who knew Rome well that the people in the CDF would never read all of this, I also prepared an 'executive summary' for them. The entire exercise took me seven months of careful work. In my response, I put side by side what the CDF consultor claimed I said and what I actually said. My problem was with the CDF's methodology. I showed fifty-eight specific instances where the consultor's Observations contained unproved generalisations, misunderstandings, misrepresentations, distortions and falsifications. They were really unhappy about this, but there were so many mistakes that I had to protest.

The Observations had first been sent to me in Italian, and I asked for an English translation. They sent me this, including in the footnotes quotations from the text of *Mary and Human Liberation*. Then it suddenly dawned on me: This is not what I wrote. Their translation did not correspond to the English text of my book, and I was able to show that in the process of translating English into Italian and then back again, they had actually injected heresy into what I had said. It was such a blatant example of mistranslation and misunderstanding that a class in a Buddhist university here in Sri Lanka took it as an example of the way in which texts can be manipulated and totally misunderstood in the process of translation.

It was also a very good example of the way the system operates, because nobody listens when you protest, nobody in authority is held accountable; the accused alone must explain themselves. In my response to the Observations I asked Cardinal Ratzinger 'to inquire into these grave misrepresentations and render justice to me by taking due action against such misrepresentations, distortions and falsifications'. I have had no response to this because everyone else involved in the process is presumed to be right. They also hide behind the mask of anonymity. This lack of accountability leads to basic miscarriages of justice which must be reformed for the sake of the Church. Dealing with these arbitrary methods is one of the key issues facing those who want to reform the CDF.

Right through this period the superior-general of the Oblates, Father Zago, kept telling me that I should conform and accept the decision of the Church authorities. He advised me that submission was 'good for my spiritual development'. That remained his line until after my eventual excommunication, when he saw that I was not budging and that something had to be done. The local Oblates were divided: a few thought I had been treated unjustly, a few thought Rome was right, and most of the others did not seem to understand what it was all about. They tended to adopt the 'spiritual' line: 'God's will has to be accepted' and 'It is better to obey than to discuss all these issues'. I was told, 'You will never succeed with Rome.'

In fact, it was interesting to reflect on people's response to the whole affair. It really revealed the different types of personalities that make up the Church. The majority of people have goodwill but they surrender their intelligence to authority. They say that anyone going against authority or contesting a situation is wrong. Others say there must be something wrong with you personally. They try to find all types of reasons: 'You are not a theologian, you are an economist. You don't know what you are talking about.' Some are more sympathetic and say: 'What has happened to this poor old fellow after fifty-one years in priesthood? He must be disappointed, or disloyal to the pope, or have hang-ups!' Still others claim, 'He is too confrontationist', or 'proud', 'arrogant' or 'conceited'. They say, 'His replies are too long', or 'Too negative', or they ask, 'Why is he going public?' Others say you are 'all emotional', 'obstinate', 'breaking the promises of ordination', 'ambitious', or 'not sufficiently supernatural'. It is a strange type of situation; you simply cannot win.

Then there are those who give you advice:'The Church is right; therefore, you must accept.' Or they tell you: 'The Church is human, you must accept that you are criticised or misunderstood.' You get these suggestions in various combinations:'Live in peace as an old man and look after your health.' Or:'Go to a retreat house and spend four months there.' I was warned:'You should not upset the simple faithful.' I was advised:'You can think these kinds of things, but you should not publish them.' I was asked:'How many people will lose their faith? And you will be responsible for them going to hell.' 'What will the Buddhists think?', or 'the Marxists?' I was often told: 'The pope is the ultimate authority. You must submit.' Then there was the 'club argument'. It goes :'If you are in the club you must accept the rules of the club. If you don't accept, you can leave. You can always found your own Church.' Finally, I was told:'Just sign the Profession of Faith and get it over and done with. You don't have to believe it.'

Throughout this period I carried on a considerable correspondence, much of it with the superior-general. Eight months after my detailed reply of 14 March 1995, I received a letter from the CDF, dated 20 November 1995. It was very brief and to the point. My detailed response of March 1995 was simply described as 'unsatisfactory'. No further details were given as to how or why it was unsatisfactory. This letter was forwarded to me by Father Zago just before Christmas 1995.

In order for me to prove my faith the CDF told Father Zago that they had 'decided to request that [I] pronounce *coram testibus* [in the presence of witnesses] a Profession of Faith' which the CDF had prepared specifically for me. They told the general: 'If the religious decides to accept this procedure, the method of repairing the damage done to the faithful will later be decided. If he decides otherwise, besides the disciplinary provisions [of] Canon 1364, consideration will be given to an eventual public declaration by this Congregation that Fr. Balasuriya is no longer a Catholic theologian.'

Canon 1364 threatens excommunication *latae sententiae*, a penalty reserved for apostates, heretics, schismatics and those who profane the Eucharist. The term *latae sententiae* means that the penalty is automatic, because the action is considered so reprehensible. Everyone, including the local bishops, was now excluded from having any participation in my situation. The CDF had taken over completely. When this threat of excommunication was made I found it unthinkable. There had been no excommunication of a theologian for half a century. I asked myself how they could come to this extreme action, when all they had said was that my response was 'unsatisfactory'. I felt this was a complete travesty of justice.

The personal Profession of Faith was sent to me unauthenticated, unsigned, with no heading, no address and no indication of its source, except that there were Vatican stamps on the envelope. On three occasions I demanded confirmation that this was indeed their document, and asked that someone sign it on behalf of the CDF. Since I received no response I can only conclude that no one in the CDF was willing to take responsibility for it. Of course, the Profession of Faith and the threat of excommunication were merely a substitute for a fair inquiry. As I said at the time, it 'seemed an unreasonable and unnecessary device for resolving the problem, a device which is far removed from the spirit of intellectual investigation and fraternal correction. It is a punitive act assuming that the judgment of the CDF on my book is correct.'

The whole thing seemed designed to force me into a corner, almost to give me a heart attack! In this situation I was faced with the question of personal stamina, because they trap you by a combination of forces, psychological, spiritual, theological, social, political and economic, the purpose of which is to bring you down. The old Inquisition brought the coercive power of Church and state to bear on an individual. Now they use a combination of other more subtle forces, as well as the media. In fact, it was through the BBC that I first heard about my own excommunication!

There were a number of theological problems with the CDF's Profession of Faith. First, many Catholics who saw it had difficulty with the demand that an act of faith be made under immediate threat of excommunication. As the Indian theologian, Father Samuel Rayan, SJ, pointed out, a Profession of Faith is a celebration, a joyful act of freedom which people choose to make. It cannot be imposed. If it is imposed it ceases to be an act of faith.

Second, to preclude my argument that original sin is symbolic, and that it primarily refers to the sinful pathos of the human condition and the proneness that we all have towards evil and the collective sinfulness of society and the human environment, the CDF demanded that I profess under oath that: 'Every man is born in sin. Therefore I hold that original sin is transmitted with human nature by propagation, not by imitation, and that it is in all men, proper to each; it cannot be taken away by the powers of human nature.' But if this is the case, the idea that God loves us into existence is wrong, the very act of human generation is vitiated by sin, and the notion that we are born into a redeemed world is completely deceptive.

Third, I was asked to swear that: 'I firmly accept and hold that the Church has no authority whatsoever to confer priestly ordination on women.' But, as has been pointed out by many theologians, this is still under discussion in the universal church. As Father Rayan said: 'Dogmas cannot be fabricated overnight by any bureau by a naked use of power, bulldozing Christian conscience. To impose this as a matter of faith is an insult to Christian faith and an affront to human dignity.'

Fourth, the CDF's Profession of Faith does not positively affirm the possibility of salvation outside the Catholic Church, as does Vatican II and the *Credo of the People of God* of Pope Paul VI. If the Church were to insist on this CDF Profession of Faith as binding on all, it would be a real setback for inter-religious relations and a lessening of inter-religious communion.

So what I did was to make the *Credo of the People of God* of Paul VI. The key differences between Paul VI's Profession of Faith and the one drafted specifically for me by the CDF is that theirs *subtracted* the clause on salvation outside the Church, and *added* the clause forbidding women's ordination. To Paul VI's profession, I added the following: 'I, Fr Tissa Balasuriya, OMI, make and sign this

Profession of Faith of Pope Paul VI in the context of theological development and Church practice since Vatican II and the freedom and responsibility of Christians and theological searchers under canon law.' I signed it on 14 May 1996, and it was forwarded to Rome.

I heard no more until 7 December 1996, when I was summoned to the residence of the papal nuncio, Archbishop Oswaldo Padilla. I wanted to take a theologian with me, but I was told just to come with my provincial [Father Camillus Fernando]. The nuncio read out to me the Notification of Excommunication. It was about 7:15 pm. He said: 'Here and now you must sign this Profession of Faith, or else tomorrow, 8 December [the Feast of the Immaculate Conception], you will be excommunicated.' I refused to sign, even though the provincial suggested that I do so. No copy of the notification of excommunication was given to me. I was informed that the CDF considered that my additional clause about theological development to the *Credo of the People of God* 'rendered the declaration defective since it diminished the universal and permanent value of the definitions of the magisterium'. My claim was that the clause was not a condition, but only a note of context. Anyway, such interpretations were irrelevant since the excommunication was already signed with effect the next day.

Fortunately, the previous day I had heard from a source in Rome that the notification was coming. So I had written a letter appealing directly to the pope. I gave it to the nuncio and asked him to forward it to the pope. He told me to post it myself. I said: 'No. You are here to represent him. I want you to send it.' The point of my appeal to the pope was that there had been no formal, impartial inquiry to establish the orthodoxy or otherwise of my theological positions. I added that natural justice and the law of the Church require that a judgment on a matter as serious as apostasy, heresy or schism, referred to in Canon 1364, cannot be made without a formal juridical procedure in which the accused enjoys 'the right to know his accusers and also the right to a proper defence', and in which the accusers are not also the judges. I also pointed out that it was not only a question of justice to me; the administrative and judicial integrity of the Church was also at stake. My view was that if I appealed, the excommunication would be stayed.

On 27 December I received a letter from the secretary of state, Cardinal Angelo Sodano, saying that the pope was well aware of the whole process, and that he had approved of the excommunication. Despite this, I have always questioned whether the pope had seen the documentation. It is clear to me that he views *Mary and Human Liberation* as presented by the CDF, not by me. I have no idea as to how much time was spent by the pope considering my case, but I really cannot believe that he would do such a thing without thorough study. Of course the Curia uses the system and the pope. They operate in the name of the pope – and of God. We must challenge that.

On 5 January 1997 the notification of excommunication (dated 8 December 1996) was published in the Vatican newspaper *Osservatore Romano*. This information was reported by the foreign media and that was when I heard about my excommunication on the BBC. Again I felt a travesty of justice had been committed, so I decided to appeal on 13 January 1997 to the Apostolic Signatura. This is the highest tribunal of appeal in the Church's judicial system. Its role is to examine procedural issues that arise in other tribunals and administrative systems. Only approved advocates can practise before it. At first the Signatura seemed almost enthusiastic to take up the case. They sent me a list of lawyers accredited to appear before them. I had just chosen an Austrian woman lawyer and had begun negotiations with her, when they suddenly refused to hear the case because the excommunication had been approved personally by the pope. It was at this point that I totally lost confidence in the process. It was not possible to have any honourable dealings with this type of legal system.

I had tried to convince Church authorities at all levels that what they were saying about my book was not accurate and that they were misreporting what I wrote. They always had the initiative and insisted on remaining anonymous. They were not subject to any form of appeal. They claimed to speak on behalf of the truth and wisdom of God. Yet they did not allow even the local hierarchy to try to come to a compromise solution. The ultimate disappointment for me was that the appeal to the Holy Father was totally frustrated by a statement that the pope had approved of all the CDF decisions. If the pope had really read the book and considered all the issues involved, I honestly believe he would have never acted in the way he is said to have done. A terrible problem of conscience arises. One cannot accept the blunders and untruths perpetrated constantly by Church authorities. They were imposing not only social and ecclesiastical ostracism, but also implicitly threatening eternal damnation.

I then had to make a decision – between trust in God and Jesus and fidelity to my conscience, and acceptance of the right of the authorities to impose sanctions which are binding. As I told the BBC television program 'Absolute Truth', this all turned out to be 'a terrible engine of oppression that must be changed'. It is necessary to remedy this situation for the sake of the Church herself, for the sake of the pope and papacy. I saw how much the pope was used as a spiritual bogeyman to oppress people and cow them. I had to make a decision that, come what may, I would not give in to terror tactics. I had long struggled against injustice in civil society, and I had faced death threats from those who opposed our efforts for justice and human rights in Sri Lanka. Now it was a question of facing the threat of being cut off from the Christian community and all the services and activities of the Church to which I had given my life. As a result of the excommunication I could not participate in any Church ceremonies such as weddings or funerals, let alone mass or any other liturgical service. On the one hand, I felt like I was being treated as a spiritual leper by people with whom I had lived my life. On the other, I had affirmation, support and solidarity from people from near and far.

Even today there is no remedy against the false accusations and abuse of theological authority and biased judicial process, as well as against the one-sided, prejudiced presentation of the case given in the Church media. For instance, in Sri Lanka the Catholic newspaper, the *Catholic Messenger*, attacked me every week for four and a half months, and when the excommunication was eventually lifted, they did not have the graciousness to say even one word acknowledging what had happened and withdrawing the false charges that they had run for so long. This newspaper is published by the archdiocese of Colombo. It also serialised what was to become a booklet attacking me entitled *Mary and Human Liberation – the Other Side*. This shows how much some Catholics are indoctrinated to think they are completely right when they toe the party line in the Church.

Many people have asked me what it was that finally persuaded Rome to participate in bringing about a reconciliation and lifting the excommunication a year later. Was it the worldwide outcry and the extensive media coverage that followed the excommunication, or was it the work of the Oblates, or what? I think it was a number of things. Certainly, the Oblate general house in Rome initiated the process. They had received a lot of critical letters. It is an interesting juxtaposition that I was excommunicated in January 1997 and in April 1998 Father Zago was made an archbishop and Secretary for the Congregation for Evangelization of Peoples in the Roman Curia! So perhaps this was a kind of clearing of the way; because it would be difficult for him to be an archbishop in Rome if he had a member causing so much trouble that he was excommunicated.

There was also a consciousness and conviction among senior people in Rome that they were wrong and had handled the whole thing badly. There was no way that they could escape from my calls for an independent tribunal, even a secular one, to come to grips with the fact that I had not said what the CDF had accused me of saying. I also think that they realised that they could not avoid the problems involved with the doctrine of original sin, salvation outside the Church and women's ordination. Also, the threat to take the Archbishop of Colombo to the civil court for defamation over the pamphlet *Mary and Human Liberation – the Other Side* put pressure on Church authorities to resolve the issue.

Eventually, the Vatican agreed that a process of reconciliation might occur, but insisted that I make some form of Profession of Faith, express regret, and that I submit future works for Church approval. So the Oblates set up a week-long process in Sri Lanka to explore the possibility of reconciliation. We did get an agreement on the very last morning of the process, but even then it was touch and go. We were able to work out a formula of reconciliation that left some room for ambiguity, which everyone accepted. A reconciliation liturgy was celebrated on 15 January 1998 when the excommunication was removed. I agreed again to sign the *Credo of the People of God* of Paul VI. As a basis for reconciliation we all accepted 'that the meaning of dogmatic formulas remains always true and unchangeable, though capable of being expressed more clearly and understood better'. In other words, the traditional formulations of dogma are open to varying interpretations in different contexts. This was the basis upon which the remainder of my affirmations rested. I maintained that there was no error proved in my writings, nor confession of any error by me. I accepted that there was confusion, but that this arose because 'doctrinal errors were *perceived* in my writing and therefore provoked negative reactions *from other parties*, affected relationships and led to unfortunate polarisation in the ecclesial community. I truly regret the harm *this* caused.' It is really all a question of perception. I also point out that no punishment was imposed in this reconciliation.

On the final day of the discussion, the Archbishop of Colombo was designated to carry out the canonical reconciliation. A text had been drafted for him to read to the media. But what he presented was different from what we had signed. It said that I 'regretted error'. I was taken aback. Despite a media embargo, the Vatican radio quoted Archbishop Fernando's comment that I 'regretted [my] error', and that went out all over the world as an accurate description of what I had accepted. It was totally unfair. When I told the nuncio that I was going public about this misrepresentation of my position, he accused Father Zago of drafting the text. Father Zago said: 'I drafted it and gave it to Archbishop Fernando. After that I don't know what happened.' So we started the affair with ecclesiastical 'hanky-panky' and we certainly ended with it! The real question is whether the CDF is ever really ready for reconciliation, and will it ever admit that it has made a mistake? I felt very betrayed by the misrepresentation. That is why I want to set the record straight.

First, I accepted that all dogmas are subject to interpretation. In other words, that God is one but the names of God and the paths to God are many; the truth is one, but the paths to truth are many; and that all theologies, as human expressions, are analogical, culture-bound and relative. Here I would point out that I did not accept that women cannot be ordained, and I did not accept original sin in the way it has been traditionally taught. That is very important for Asian theology. In Asia, where Christianity is a minority religion, we cannot accept that the whole of humanity is in original sin in the sense that they are alienated from God. We cannot accept that all our forebears are in hell. Regarding redemption, I have maintained my view that Jesus did not have to pay a price to God to save us, although this interpretation has so impregnated our prayers, hymns and attitudes. I believe in the story of the prodigal son in the Gospel, where the father, without preconditions, runs out to receive his erring offspring. Therefore, the mission of the Church is not so much to convert to Christianity as to convert all to humanity. There is now a little more space for a continuing debate about these issues and particularly about the role of other religions.

I am often asked how I make sense of it all. Personally, I think Cardinal Josef Ratzinger is trying to close the openings that occurred at Vatican II. Pope John Paul II seems not fully clear in his mind about this. He has the view that Jesus is somehow the only saviour. During the reconciliation process, Rome demanded that I accept this, but I refused. So we compromised and said Jesus was the 'universal saviour'. The question of what salvation is, from what, to what, by whom and how, remains a focal point for Asian theology. These questions are not being discussed so clearly in Europe or North America. The core of the problem for us is: if you say that the human Jesus is essential for salvation, then there is no future for the Church in Asia. However, if you talk about the message of Jesus, or Christ as the uncreated divine son of God, then Asians understand what you are talking about. But the human Jesus is seen as one among many saviours in Asian cultures.

Second, they wanted me to accept prior censorship of my books (what is called the *imprimatur*), and I accepted this 'in terms of Canon law'. However, this only applies if I translate the scriptures, or write a catechetical text for use in schools or a book that is sold in the Church porch. Later on, after I had written an article, they came back to me and demanded that I obtain the *imprimatur* because I was a member of a religious order. I told them I would accept that it if they imposed it universally on all members of religious orders. If it was imposed only on me it would be a punishment, and I am not subject to any punishment. They backed off.

Finally, I am often asked whether I think the CDF has a future role in the Church. I do, and I think that its role should be the promotion of theology, not the defence of orthodoxy. There needs to be a genuine rethinking for the twenty-first century, when the Church will be more of the South and the East than of the North and the West. It will be a Church of the poor not for the rich, of women and laity rather than clergy. That newly emerging Church will need a new body to assist in the orientation of theology. I would like a commission of inquiry to look at the activities of the CDF over the past fifty years, so that the truth about the suppression of creative theology can come out and we can ask pardon for the way theologians were treated. But, more importantly, this can become the basis for a creative body promoting theology. Membership of this creative body should be Catholic in the fullest sense and not just a ladder of promotion for ambitious clerics. There is nobody on the CDF from Asia, so membership should be broadened. Its theologians should be living and working with people – say six months in Rome and six months in our slums. In this way it would have people with real, pastoral experience.

We can no longer accept secret, anonymous denunciations. Those who accuse others to Rome must be subject to reasonable norms of inquiry. If they defame or falsely accuse someone, they should be subject to punishment. This is operative in civil society. A judge will not allow false witnesses in civil cases, but in the Church they hide behind a mask of righteousness and holiness. This is where the secular media becomes important. We should use it, and realise that the Holy Spirit speaks through it. The media are often far more respectful of truth, accuracy and authenticity than people in the Church. They are careful to see that what they say reflects what the person actually said. There is a whole younger generation moving into the media now, particularly women. My support for women's ordination particularly appealed to them.

The Apostolic Signatura needs to become more effective but it is stymied if the CDF has someone excommunicated *latae sententiae* – automatically. The CDF must be under the Signatura, at least concerning processes and procedure. It should not be possible to use a pope as accuser, judge and final source of appeal. The only result of that tactic is to paralyse the whole system. The CDF must be accountable and not hide behind a facade of being above Church law. The CDF tries to maintain that in matters of doctrine it is 'supreme'; this is a myth. There should also be a conscious networking of those people who are under investigation by the CDF. An association of those who have experienced investigation would be very useful; they could speak with a common voice, though they might not be necessarily in agreement on common theological positions.

It strikes me that there is widespread fear among Catholics when they deal with theology and institutions such as the CDF. As a result, almost all of the structures of the Church become inoperative. At all levels – diocesan, national and even the international level – everyone becomes stymied. There is a sort of 'holy fear', a kind of religious reign of terror, with threats of hell, excommunication and exclusion. These psychological weapons are used to frighten people, as the threat of torture was in the past by the Inquisition. That is why it is important to emphasise that where there is love, there is no fear. If we do not become a community of love and acceptance, people will just bypass the Church.

For me Jesus is the spiritual leader who gives profound meaning to life, and the identifiable community in which I have discovered him is the Catholic Church. But I do not want the Church to be taken over by people who think they have the monopoly of truth. This is the community to which I have belonged throughout my life. If you are a Catholic you are in communion with one-sixth of humanity all over the world. It transcends nationality and frontiers. The crisis over the book and excommunication confronted me with the need to struggle for human rights in the Church and to work for the reform of theology. These changes will eventually come from the base Catholic community, rather than from the top. The great joy for me in the whole process was the confirmation of my Catholicity and my solidarity with people, as well as the formal and informal support I received from several thousands of laity, religious, bishops and even cardinals.

At the heart of all this is the question of conscience. We cannot accept arbitrary authority, and there comes a point when we must say that eternal destiny is not determined by particular persons, or what is called 'orthodoxy', but by one's conscience and by our relationship to the divine. In India and Sri Lanka there is a tradition of spiritual resistance to dominant establishments. This comes originally from the Buddha and is exemplified by Gandhi and others. As a result, people in this culture support you if you are poor and manifest an understanding of the divine as universal, beneficent and compassionate. The tradition here is that a priest or monk will never die of hunger because it is part of our culture that someone who has opted for religion and the search for the transcendent will be looked after by the community.

In my case, ultimately, no matter what happened, I was never afraid of being hungry and on the street!

CHAPTER 5

Ministry in a Minefield:
Jeannine Gramick and Robert Nugent

For more than twenty-five years, Sister Jeannine Gramick and Father Robert Nugent have been household names among those working in the pastoral ministry of the Catholic Church in North America. Throughout that period they have laboured constantly in what Bishop John Synder of St Augustine, Florida, has called the 'minefield' of ministry to lesbian and gay Catholics, their parents and families. In 'this delicate and highly charged' atmosphere (Archbishop Raymond Hunthausen, Seattle), they have often faced the homophobia found among many in the Church and among otherwise intelligent people in broader society. While the structures of a democratic system are at least subject to the pressures of social and legal processes, and anti-discrimination laws can be used to protect and enhance the rights of homosexual people, some US bishops and the Vatican have proven resistant to such pressures. As a result Gramick and Nugent have been subjected to ongoing examinations and questioning about their ministry for most of their working lives.

Ironically, some lesbian and gay Catholics, as well as others inside and outside the Church, consider that Gramick and Nugent have been far too cautious in their approach to gay issues. They have been criticised for being too deferential to Church authority and too conservative in their approach to the issue. However, this has not saved them from the condemnation of the CDF. On 13 July 1999 the Congregation released a Notification barring them permanently from ministry to homosexual persons and their families, and banned both of them for an indefinite period from holding any office in their religious orders. The CDF claimed that since the beginning of their ministry 'they have continually called central elements of [Church] teaching into question', they have promoted 'ambiguous [moral] positions on homosexuality', and they have failed homosexual people by not giving them 'the authentic teaching of the Church'.

Yet, despite the CDF's focus on Gramick's and Nugent's ministry to the gay Catholic community, there is a sense in which this whole affair is not so much about homosexuality as it is about basic and long-accepted Catholic moral principles. The CDF seems determined to restrict some of the freedoms embedded for centuries in the Catholic approach to morality, and at times its assessors and theologians seem not to know or to understand the very tradition that they claim to uphold. Essentially there are two issues at the heart of the CDF critique of Gramick and Nugent: the first concerns the use and meaning of the language of moral discourse and the pastoral consequences of that language. The second is an attempt by the CDF to force both of them to reveal their individual consciences.

Taking the issue of language first, the Vatican has insisted that homosexual behaviour be described as 'intrinsically evil'. Gramick and Nugent presented this concept as part of the Church's teaching in their workshops. But when the Vatican asked for their personal convictions about the Church's teaching on the immorality of homosexual acts, Nugent questioned the pastoral consequences of using such language. To the Catholic moralist who is familiar with the technicalities of moral discourse, the phrase is not necessarily problematic. However, in the pastoral situation of a young woman or man struggling with the question of sexual identity it could seem particularly problematic, even repulsive. For that very reason Nugent chose to avoid using the phrase. He knew how easy it was for morally confused people not only to see their actions but also themselves as 'intrinsically evil'.

Nugent told the CDF he was willing to call homosexual behaviour 'objectively immoral', but the Vatican would have none of that. Their argument was that even for pastoral motives it is not acceptable to replace the phrase 'intrinsically evil' with something 'far less clear'. The CDF was determined to maintain what Dominican Father Bruce Williams, Gramick and Nugent's sometime theological adviser, has called the 'brutal clarity' of the phrase. The Vatican also insisted that a negative judgment must be passed even on homosexual orientation. As the US moralist Richard McCormick remarks: 'To say that someone's sexuality is "disordered" is a massive assault on the dignity of the human person.' The authorities in Rome made it clear that they feared the term 'objectively immoral' might be construed as 'subjectively moral'. Yet, in fact, the long-held and traditional Catholic moral position is that there are circumstances in which what is objectively immoral can be subjectively moral. As Boston College theologian Lisa Sowle Cahill says: 'The author of the CDF response [to Nugent and Gramick] himself contradicts Catholic moral teaching by denying that an objectively immoral act could be subjectively moral for the sincere but erroneous conscience.' (America, 14 August 1999, p. 9).

Moral principles are one thing, but principles have to be applied in practice and this is where the 'sincere but erroneous conscience' becomes a reality. In many situations the process of moral decision-making is not merely a simple matter of applying principles to practice. The actual business of moral discernment is complex and often ambiguous and confusing, even for the ethically aware. As Bernard Häring, probably the greatest Catholic moral theologian of the twentieth century, says: 'The decision regarding the correctness of an action surely does not depend solely on universal moral principles. It depends also on the correct and sound understanding of the unique and concrete in particular instances in which the principles must be applied. And often numberless factors enter into the situation, and these may be quite obscure in our present dark and fallen state' (The Law of Christ, vol. 1 (1963), p. 170). According to Häring, prudence is a central element in moral decision-making and conscience must be guided by it. Traditionally, Catholic moral theology has always recognised the complexity of making a conscientious decision, yet this very element seems to be completely missing from the CDF's analysis of the Gramick–Nugent approach to talking about the morality of homosexual acts.

The CDF now also seems to be demanding that those working in ministry disclose the full panoply of Church teaching on specific moral issues, regardless of the pastoral or political consequences. So the question arises as to whether this should apply, for instance, the next time a pope visits a country ruled by a Catholic dictator engaged in torture or murder. Since political murder and torture are public acts, is a pope bound publicly to confront the dictator and disclose the full teaching of the Church on the 'intrinsic evil' of killing and torturing opponents? Or should he, as Pope John Paul II did when he visited Chile's dictator Augusto Pinochet, in April 1987, merely maintain a disapproving but discreet silence? Will this 'maximalist criterion' as Lisa Sowle Cahill calls it, be applied to wealthy Catholics? Will they be constantly reminded of the Church's 'preferential option for the poor'? Or will the CDF's criterion applied only to sexual ethics?

Certainly, that seems the most likely scenario, although homosexual activity is not the only area singled out in John Paul II's encyclical Veritatis Splendor (1993), which says that there is a whole array of universal negative norms which identify actions that are similarly 'intrinsically evil'. It cites 'any kind of homocide, genocide, abortion, euthanasia and voluntary suicide; whatever violates the integrity of the human person ... whatever is offensive to human dignity, such as subhuman living conditions ... slavery, prostitution ... degrading conditions of work ... [and] contraceptive practices whereby the conjugal act is intentionally rendered infertile' (Veritatis Splendor, paragraph 30).

In this context it is worth reminding ourselves that ethical and moral norms are fundamentally human discoveries that arise from the very nature of human existence which Christians have come to accept. As the German moralist Josef Fuchs says: 'Concrete ethical norms are not divine revelation. They do not become divine revelation by virtue of traditional or official teaching. They are the discoveries of human beings, accepted by Christians' (Josef Fuchs, Ethics in a Secular Arena, (1984), p. 7). As such, like human beings themselves, they are surely subject to change and evolution.

The second fundamental issue in the case concerns the question of the revelation of individual conscience. The CDF demanded that Gramick and Nugent explain Church teaching on the morality of homosexual acts in their workshops (something that they were already doing very carefully), and that they strive to give internal assent to that teaching. It also demanded that they publicly manifest their own personal consciences on the issue. On the face of it, this seems an utterly unjustifiable invasion of what had traditionally been held by the Church to be completely inviolable. No one has a right to demand a manifestation of a person's essential integrity as they stand before God. By any estimation this is a matter of the internal forum which, in the Catholic understanding, refers to issues that effect the private spiritual and moral life of individuals, especially but not entirely linked to the sacrament of confession. The internal forum is traditionally characterised by a complete and inviolable confidentiality. This is clearly recognised by canon law. Canon 630, paragraph 5, says: '[Religious] superiors are forbidden to induce their subjects in any way whatever to make a manifestation of conscience to them.' If this applies to religious superiors, it certainly also applies to the CDF, which is not above canon law. To demand any form of revelation of individual conscience is an invasion of both personal dignity and integrity. It is a misuse of power.

One of those most intimately connected with the Gramick–Nugent case, Father Bruce Williams, who now teaches moral theology at the Angelicum University in Rome, maintains that implicit in this whole conflict is a very profound question about the credibility of the Church's profession of love and compassion towards gay people.

Williams says that 'the consistent endeavour' of the Gramick–Nugent ministry:

> ... was to convey the full range of Church teaching about homosexuality with special emphasis on the lesser-known, positive aspects of that teaching: the dignity of homosexual persons as bearers of the divine image, their baptismal right to an active presence in the Church, their special claim to pastoral care, the evil of violent and prejudicial behaviour directed against them, and so forth. There's a sad irony here. Rome complained that Jeannine and Bob were sowing confusion among the faithful. I doubt if anybody, as a result of listening to them, was at all unclear about where the Church stands on the parameters of what is sexually wholesome and acceptable. What

does sow confusion among the faithful is when the Church makes all these positive affirmations about the precious and inviolable dignity of homosexual persons, but then proceeds to oppose every concrete initiative to provide legal protection for their civil rights. Rome has even advised bishops that discrimination based on sexual orientation would not be unjust in screening for the military, or for certain professions such as teaching or athletic coaching, or in regard to the adoption of children. So, on the one hand, in general and rather theoretical terms, the Church professes to welcome and embrace gay people as brothers and sisters in Christ and as fellow human beings made in God's image. But on the other hand, in very specific and practical terms, Rome indicates that these people are dangerous to the family and to society because of their 'objectively disordered' sexual orientation inclining them to 'intrinsically evil' acts. That doublespeak is what really confuses the faithful. In the eyes of many, even outside the gay community, the Church's overall teaching about homosexuality appears duplicitous. And Rome's action against Jeannine and Bob will tend to strengthen that impression.

Another issue with which the CDF faults Gramick and Nugent is that while they state the Church's teaching regarding homosexuality, they also set out theological opinions which place that teaching within the context of the Catholic theological tradition. Two of the important moral theologians quoted by Gramick and Nugent are Richard McCormick and Charles Curran. Both of these emphasise that ethical decision-making always occurs in a specific context, and that all the circumstances operative in that context must be taken into account. These include intention, foreseeable consequences and a genuine proportion between the values one is trying to maintain and the evils (often called 'disvalues') that result from the act.

This becomes much more complex when applied to life situations involving relationships and the exercise of sexuality. In fact, a number of moralists opposed to McCormick and Curran argue that some human values are so fundamental that they can never be infringed, no matter what the circumstances or purpose. To a considerable extent this is also the view of the encyclical Veritatis Splendor.

Jeannine Gramick and Robert Nugent have worked in this pastoral 'minefield' for most of their ministerial lives. They have been tested and tried as few others in the Church, and right until the end they remained true to the vision of service that first inspired them. There is a strength and toughness about them both, as well as a sense of realism and a quiet humility. Both come from the Philadelphia area and both come from Catholic backgrounds, one Polish, the other Irish. They first met in the early 1970s and slowly began to cooperate in ministering to homosexual people. Jeannine Gramick begins their story:

I am a School Sister of Notre Dame. I come from Philadelphia, a traditional, conservative city that is almost 50 per cent Catholic. I went to Catholic grade school and Catholic high school. All my friends were Catholic. When I was growing up in the 1940s and 1950s we lived in a Catholic enclave. We did not mix with the 'publics', as we called the children who went to public school. So I grew up in a very provincial milieu, and had a very provincial attitude. I suppose that reflected something of the whole US Church at the time, although mid-west Catholicism was always more progressive than the Church on the east coast.

My family was very Polish, but my parents were Catholic in name only. They never went to Church, but they observed all the Polish rituals. I am an only child, and I don't quite know why I am the person I am. I attribute my closeness to the Church to some extent to the fact that I was taught by a sister in the first and second grades whom I admired very much. She was a very kind, holy and wonderful woman. It was probably through her example that I felt that I had a religious vocation. I attended mass every day. I was an excellent student. I was always first in the class academically and I was well liked by teachers. I could have been a complete 'Miss Goody Two-Shoes', but I was also popular among my peers, and in high school I was elected president of my class and of the student council.

From the age of seven I knew that I wanted to be a religious sister, but it was really immaterial to me which community I joined. For me it was a question of giving my life to God and to

God's people. The community I was going to join really depended upon which nun I was friendly with at the time. In my high school we had half a dozen or more different religious congregations of women teaching us, with about sixty or seventy nuns on the faculty. One year I was being taught French by a Mercy Sister; she was a great teacher, and I knew I was going to be a Mercy. Then the next year it would be an Immaculate Heart Sister. In my junior year I was taught history by a Notre Dame Sister; she moderated the debating club, which I joined. So in the end I became a Notre Dame Sister! The congregation was founded as a teaching order in 1833 in Bavaria, and the sisters came to the United States in 1847 to provide education for German immigrants.

The School Sisters of Notre Dame's main work is education. After my initial formation I taught for four years in preparatory and grade school, and then in 1969 my community leaders asked me to do graduate studies. I went to the University of Pennsylvania to get a doctorate in mathematics and education so that I could teach at the College of Notre Dame of Maryland, a liberal arts college for women which our community operates in Baltimore. In my third year at the university, I met a young gay man with whom I became very good friends. He asked me what the Church was doing for his gay brothers and sisters. He kept asking me this question, and it eventually became a call from God through him to do what I could to be a reconciler and a bridge-builder between lesbian and gay Catholics and the Church.

After university, in 1972, I came back to Baltimore and taught at the College of Notre Dame of Maryland. While there I found out about Dignity, a Catholic group founded in 1969 that still tries to help homosexual Catholics integrate their spirituality with their sexuality, and supports them in participating fully in all aspects of life in church and society. So I worked as a part-time chaplain for Dignity, and helped to start the chapters in Washington and Baltimore. In 1977 I was assigned by my community to work full-time with lesbian and gay people.

That year Father Bob Nugent and I founded New Ways Ministry, working for the reconciliation of lesbian and gay

Catholics with the Church. Its fundamental purpose is to serve as a bridge for alienated lesbian and gay Catholics to try to bring them back to the Church. It also tries to raise consciousness and awareness among Catholics in the larger Church about the rights of lesbian and gay people, and how those rights have been denied both civilly and within the Church. It aims to combat attitudes of discrimination, as well as violence and prejudice. It is important to note that this was not a ministry I took on and then later more or less obliged the congregation to own. I was actually assigned to it. After I had met the young gay man at the University of Pennsylvania, I used to talk over his challenge with my apostolate director, who subsequently became the provincial. It was she who assigned me full-time to this work. She was a woman of great vision and she believed that the Church had neglected this group of people, and she encouraged me to do what I could.

Initially I had not mentioned my ministry to my parents, but there was an article in one of the local Philadelphia newspapers. It was entitled 'Nun Meeting with Gays in Convent', and was accompanied by a picture of me. My father saw it and asked me why I was doing this. I said, 'Well, someone has to help this group of people.' His reaction was, 'Then let other nuns do it. You don't have to do it.' This was at the height of the anti-Vietnam war protests, and he suddenly said to me, 'You're not going to start burning draft records, are you?' I told him, 'Probably not. I believe in the peace movement, but I am not all that heavily involved in it. But what if I did?' He said, 'Well, you know, that's against our country.' He paused, and then he said, 'But if you do it, that's okay, because you're my daughter.' For many years that remark of my father mirrored for me the unconditional love of God. My mother's attitude was similar to my dad's. My father is now eighty-four, and he recently said to me, 'People change when they get older.' Sadly, what I'm finding is that he has a lot of deep-seated prejudice against lesbian and gay people, and people of colour. I did not see it before, but now he is letting his attitudes be more known. So we have had some discussions that have been very painful.

Father Robert Nugent comes from a similar background. He has a great
sense of humour and often laughs as he talks. His development both as
a seminarian and a priest has been less conventional than that of most
who entered his seminary in the late 1950s.

I grew up in a small town near Philadelphia, in an Irish–
American Catholic family. I have one sister. I was educated in a
Catholic grade school and secondary school, and graduated in
1955. Those were the days when everything was neat and tidy in
Catholicism in the United States.

I entered the Philadelphia archdiocesan seminary at Overbrook
in 1955. One hundred other young men entered in my group that
same year. I went to the seminary because I had met some very
good priests. I had been an altar server for ten or eleven years, and
I saw that the priesthood was a vocation where I could help people.
I had already seen the effect that priests had on people's lives. I was
not just attracted to the status which, of course, was important in
an Irish–American family. But I think I was attracted because one
of my needs is to influence people either individually or on a larger
scale, and I feel it was this which primarily motivated me. Also the
teaching aspect interested me; by nature I am a kind of educator
and researcher.

The Overbrook course in those days involved two years of
preparatory study, four years of college, and four years in the
seminary. We lived on campus and did everything there with the
same faculty. It was a very provincial and narrow education.
Fortunately, I was one of the few who were interested in worship,
and so throughout my seminary career I travelled to various parts
of the United States during the vacations attending liturgy
conferences. This was fortunate because it exposed me to the
Church beyond Philadelphia. Of course, in the conservative
Philadelphia archdiocese you were considered very odd if you were
interested in the renewal of worship, and you certainly did not
want the seminary authorities to know that you went to liturgical
conferences. I got to know some of the top people in the liturgical
movement, like Robert Hovda and Godfrey Diekmann, who had

great influence on the renewal of worship in the English-speaking world. Travelling to other dioceses, getting to know priests and students from other parts of the country, and visiting Benedictine and Trappist monasteries exposed me to a different world and to a wider understanding of the Church than that which was presented to me in the seminary. It helped me to break out of the narrow mould of a provincial Philadelphia priest whose whole life centred on a large east-coast city in which the Church was very powerful, and in which your priestly role was clearly and literally defined in black and white.

I was also of that transitional generation which was in the seminary at the same time that Vatican II was happening. My four years of theology exactly paralleled the Council; I was ordained in 1965, the year the Council ended. We students probably knew a lot more about what was happening in Rome than most of the seminary faculty, who were still using pre-conciliar textbooks and whose theology and attitudes were certainly backward-looking. Yet, oddly enough, we had the four books by Xavier Rynne read to us in the refectory. They had begun as articles in the *New Yorker Magazine* and they reported what actually happened at each of the sessions of the Council. It is surprising, looking back now, that a book like that was chosen to be read. Also the books and tapes of modern theologians, especially Hans Küng, were in great demand and were very carefully smuggled in and out of the seminary. I remember people coming to my door at night, knocking gently and saying, 'I understand you have a tape by Hans Küng.' I would say, 'Yes, but don't tell anybody where you got it.' We even had to carry on a long fight with the authorities to be able to sing 'A Mighty Fortress is Our God' in the chapel; in those days that was a big, controversial issue.

It really was a time of turmoil. One of my best friends was suspended from the priesthood because he came back to the seminary and said mass without vestments, using ordinary bread. It took place at night in the basement. Looking back it all seems quite humorous, but that actually became a big scandal in Philadelphia. My friend has since left the priesthood and married.

After ordination, in 1965, by the then Archbishop John Krol (he was appointed a cardinal in 1967), I went into my first suburban parish and was there for three years. From there I was sent to a south Philadelphia Italian parish, and then went to an inner-city Black parish. After that I was sent to teach high school. The pastors I worked with were not exactly the healthiest human beings, especially in terms of relationships with other people. They were quite autocratic. I began to wonder if this was what my life was going to amount to, and if I would follow the same pattern. I found rectory living very lonely and difficult, and I needed to live and work with a community. So I thought I would try to get some further education, even though in Philadelphia you did not ask for such things; only specially selected priests were normally chosen to go on and get degrees. Nevertheless, I asked for a leave of absence from parish work to get further education, but that was denied. So I took a personal leave; it was almost like leaving the priesthood for a period. I went to live with a community of De LaSalle Christian Brothers as a kind of unofficial chaplain to them and to their high school. During that period I got a degree in library science at Villanova University, where I had been given a scholarship. I also worked on skid row, met a supportive community of people there and was again the unofficial chaplain. I then asked the archdiocesan chancery if skid row could be my assignment, because I wanted to stay in Philadelphia. The answer was, 'No. We want you back in a parish.'

Around this time I met two priests who were studying for advanced degrees from the Society of the Divine Saviour (Salvatorians), a religious order founded in 1881 in Rome, which is devoted to education, running parishes and giving retreats. By this time I knew that if I wanted to stay in the priesthood, I was not going to last in Philadelphia. While I liked parish life and was reasonably good at it, I wanted something different, something bigger and more exciting. So I met with the Salvatorian vocation director, and they were interested in me. They invited me to come to live with them in Washington for a year, in a kind of mutual getting-to-know-you exercise. However, I warned the Salvatorian superiors that I would not get a good recommendation from the

Philadelphia archdiocese. Their reply was, 'If you did get a good recommendation, we might not be interested in you.' So I spent the year in Washington living in their community.

The next year was my formal novitiate year, and the order had to inform the archdiocese. So they wrote and said that I was interested in joining the community and asked if Cardinal Krol would give permission. The reply said that, 'Father Nugent has trouble with authority and obedience, but if you feel he would make a good religious, then we will give him leave.' After the novitiate I went to Baltimore to work at a Catholic women's college. There I was on the same campus where Sister Jeannine Gramick had taught.

My first meeting with Jeannine Gramick had occurred in the early 1970s. There had been an article in a newspaper about Jeannine meeting in the convent with a group of gay men. It was a kind of modern *Nun's Story*. She was pictured as the archetypical contemporary sister, studying and teaching at university, wearing lay clothes, bringing homosexuals into the convent. The article said something about her riding a motorcycle, but she denies that to this day. I am a great believer in supporting people and writing letters, and so I wrote to her and offered to help. I always say that if I had not written that letter, I could have gone right up the ecclesiastical ladder, and become a happy and successful monsignor in Philadelphia. Two days later she called back and said that I could help, because a lot of these people wanted to talk to a sympathetic priest: some wanted to go to confession, others just wanted to find out where they were regarding the Church.

I went to meet her group, but I must admit that I had to muster up all my courage. I had all of the usual fears and anxieties about homosexuality. In the seminary it was a taboo topic. Sometimes students there would simply 'disappear' because someone was found in their room at night, or something similar to that. There were the usual warnings about the dangers of 'particular friendships'. One of our seminary rectors used to give a regular talk about aftershave lotion. He got very upset with seminarians who used aftershave lotion because he felt that was probably a sign that they had difficulties with sexual identity or at least they were too effeminate. He was the 'jock' type. (He later became a bishop.) So in the seminary the whole subject of homosexuality was taboo and the closest we got to it was the rector's 'aftershave lotion' talk.

Thus I met these people who had gathered around Jeannine, most of whom were Roman Catholic or Episcopalian. In the early 1970s I began to celebrate the Eucharist for them, did a lot of counselling, and heard their stories. They had a great love for the Church; many of them were former religious and seminarians who could not stay because they were homosexual. Some of them had been expelled. They were deeply committed to the Church, but they felt the Church had rejected them. There was a kind of love-hate relationship. So Jeannine and I began to read and do courses so we could understand the psychological dynamics of homosexuality. At that time the Episcopal Church was doing a lot, and we went to some of their meetings and courses.

In 1975 I left Philadelphia for Washington and the Salvatorians, but one thing I did just before that was to testify on behalf of a gay rights bill. Every year this bill came up before the City Council of Philadelphia, but the Catholic, Baptist and fundamentalist churches objected to it, and that was always enough to kill it. There had never been any Catholic support for it. The gay rights movement in Philadelphia asked me to support it publicly. I thought about it, and agreed. I felt that at least on the basis of social justice and anti-discrimination, I could testify in favour of it. I could reasonably say that the morality of sexual behaviour was a separate issue. So I went before the City Council hearings and testified.

I sat there nervously at City Hall, waiting my turn to speak. The first speaker was a priest whom the archdiocese had sent down to testify against the bill. He got up and explained to the council why this bill was threatening to the family. Then a young Catholic man got up and testified to his sense of pain and alienation about being gay. Then it was my turn. The timing was perfect. But the first question they asked me was what was my official assignment from the Philadelphia archdiocese. Obviously, the chancery had got through to them and this was an attempt to discredit me. So I admitted that I was on leave of absence, but that I was still a Catholic priest. I quoted a lot of the documents of Vatican II about eliminating discrimination, and explained that this was a justice issue about civil bias against a specific group of people. I made it clear that I was not addressing the moral issue of homosexual relations. What I said got in the newspapers, and they played my 'compassionate and intelligent testimony' against the 'biased and prejudiced testimony' of the priest from the archdiocese.

Understandably, that did not go down very well at the chancery. So a letter was sent out to every priest and religious house in the archdiocese with the opening sentence: 'Father Nugent, whose name does not appear in the Official Directory ...' had testified before the City Council. It did not say what the issue was or what I had said, but it emphasised that if I continued speaking publicly I would be subject to severe ecclesiastical penalties. Basically it was to put pressure on me. But I got a lot of support from many people, including one of my seminary classmates who sent out a letter saying: 'We have heard from the archdiocese. Now we should hear from Father Nugent.' By that time I knew that I was probably not going to get anywhere in Philadelphia, so I decided to join the Salvatorians and went down to Washington in 1975. But it had been my first really public stand on behalf of gay rights.

In 1976 Jeannine came to Washington. We were both working at the Quixote Center, a broad-based peace and justice organisation, located in Brentwood, Maryland, and we began to run workshops for counsellors and priests on homosexuality, mainly in the Washington area. As we became known, we began to get more invitations to speak, so in 1977 we decided to put our energies and resources into a Catholic centre which focused on the gay issue. There were all kinds of centres working on other issues, but no Catholic group working on this. So New Ways Ministry was born. The federal government gave a small grant to Jeannine to do a study of lesbian women and this helped with the funding of the ministry.

But almost as soon as they began work together, they found themselves under ecclesiastical scrutiny. Even before New Ways Ministry was founded, a book that Gramick and Nugent wrote together quickly found its way to Rome, so Nugent took the initiative by travelling to Rome himself to talk to Vatican officials about it. He admits that he was not very successful.

In the early days of our cooperation, Jeannine, a Holy Cross priest and I published a short book entitled *Homosexual Catholics: A Primer for Discussion*, published by Dignity [1976]. It was a question-and-answer book. The first question concerned the teaching of the Church, which we laid out clearly; the second question concerned theological opinions, which we tried to lay out with equal clarity.

I went to Rome because there had been questions from the Vatican to our superiors about this book. The then superior-general of the Salvatorians, a Pole, had been advised by a friend of his, Archbishop [later Cardinal] Augustin Meyer, a German Benedictine who worked in the Vatican, that it would be good for me to come to Rome and meet with some of the officials, and in that way the whole thing could be quietly cleared up. My first appointment was with Meyer himself. He was a gaunt, ascetic-looking person. The interview lasted no longer than fifteen minutes. I tried to explain what our ministry was, but he suddenly got up and said, 'Well, you will have to answer to God for what you are doing', and then walked out of the room. I was stunned. I thought, here is the man who advised me to come to Rome, and he treated me so shabbily. Then I went to an appointment at the Congregation for Religious and Secular Institutes (CRSI), as it was called then. There I met a priest on the staff who came in with a very thick folder. Apparently it was all the information that had been sent to Rome about us. It included a copy of *Homosexual Catholics*. He pointed to the first question and said: 'That's fine. That is the teaching of the Church. But look at the second question.' The objection was that we had gone beyond the teaching of the Church and had given theological opinions. Their problem was that we should not be sharing theological 'opinion' with lay people; it could too easily lead them astray.

My third interview was with Archbishop Alberto Bovone, the

then secretary of the CDF. He was accompanied by an American priest on the staff, and he and Bovone came into the parlour to meet me. Bovone asked, 'Why had I come?' We spoke in English and he was annoyed at that. He complained that all of these people kept coming over to Rome expecting him to speak English. Why didn't they learn Italian? I tried to explain who we were and what we were doing, but he seemed more concerned that I would be speaking to other congregations in the Curia. He insisted that I tell them that the CDF had not called me over to Rome, and that I had come of my own accord. He seemed concerned that I would give the impression to other congregations that I had a pleasant meeting with him. Needless to say, it was not a very productive encounter. The American priest said, 'You know you are very popular among Dignity?' I said, 'Yes.' He said, 'Well, that is certainly not helpful to you.' All in all, my visit to Rome had not achieved much.

We were also soon in trouble with the archdiocese of Washington and the then archbishop, Cardinal William Wakefield Baum. As I mentioned, Jeannine had received a government grant from the National Institute of Mental Health to research the coming-out process of lesbian women. The diocesan newspaper claimed that our involvement in this study implied that we approved of homosexual behaviour. The chancery office notified Catholic groups and individuals in the Washington archdiocese that New Ways Ministry was not officially recognised in the archdiocese.

Jeannine Gramick takes up the story of ongoing hierarchical interference in New Ways Ministry:

The next intervention was in 1979, when New Ways Ministry was sponsoring a retreat for lesbian nuns, and Cardinal Baum was still Archbishop of Washington. It was just before he moved to a curial position in Rome. This retreat involved no more than eight or ten people. Baum must have complained to CRSI in Rome. CRSI felt that it was a scandal to talk about 'lesbian nuns'. Indeed, we found out that even among more progressive Catholics there was surprise that we associated the words 'lesbian' or 'gay' with nuns or priests.

They were working under the assumption that if you were homosexual, you were sexually active. In the 1970s even intelligent people had difficulty understanding the difference between orientation and behaviour. We were asked by our community leaders not to involve ourselves in the retreat. We had previously asked a sister to facilitate the retreat with New Ways Ministry as its sponsor. The retreat went ahead as planned.

Then, in 1980, Archbishop James Hickey succeeded Baum in Washington; he had come from the diocese of Cleveland. Bob and I requested a meeting with him to explain our ministry, but it took a whole year before we were able to get an appointment. We finally got the appointment because in 1981 New Ways Ministry was sponsoring a national symposium for religious and church leaders on homosexuality. We had invited the archbishop to give the opening address, or to give one of the talks. We heard nothing until we sent out the publicity on the symposium. Then his secretary called us to tell us to come to a meeting with the archbishop. At this meeting Hickey made it clear that he did not approve of our ministry. About two hundred Church leaders did come to the symposium. No one cancelled, despite a letter from Hickey to all the bishops and leaders of men's and women's congregations discouraging participation in the symposium. No doubt this was very frustrating for Archbishop Hickey. Unbeknown to us, from that point onwards, he began a campaign to get us out of this ministry.

What happened at this meeting with Hickey was significant because it sets the scene for all that occurred subsequently. It should be noted here that New Ways Ministry is ecclesiastically within Washington archdiocese, even though it is geographically just over the border in Maryland. Bob Nugent describes in detail what happened:

When the brochure went out for the symposium, we got a call from the chancery saying, 'The archbishop wants to meet with you.' So we went to his private residence and we thought it was going to be just the archbishop and us. When we got there we were ushered in, and the young priest-secretary even indicated in which chairs we were to sit. I had sat in the wrong one and he said, 'No, Father, you are to sit here', indicating another chair. Hickey walked in with his chancellor [a priest who in canon law acts as a legal notary and who may, as in this case, be given broad powers by the bishop to grant faculties to priests]. They were accompanied by a rather conservative moral theologian from Chicago, the Jesuit Father John Connery. I realised immediately that we were outgunned; we could have brought Richard McCormick or Charles Curran with us. But at that stage we were too naive.

Hickey had an agenda and Jeannine said that she wanted to add some points. He put her off because he wanted to talk about faculties for me. Faculties are the permissions granted by a local bishop to all priests in the diocese to celebrate mass publicly, hear confessions and celebrate the sacraments. My Washington faculties had expired when I went to Baltimore to work as a college chaplain from 1979 to 1981. When I came back I applied for them again. I said that one of the reasons for this application was that I had heard the confessions of homosexual priests. That did not go down well. I was denied faculties for Washington, although I still had them for Baltimore, and according to canon law if you have them in one diocese they are valid in all others unless specifically withdrawn. After some discussion it became clear that Hickey was concerned that we were giving workshops not just to priests but for lay people as well. If we were giving them to priests that would probably be all right because they 'understood'; but lay people would get 'confused'. I told Hickey that in my presentation of sexual morality I was doing the same thing that seminary professors were doing: giving the Church's teaching on homosexuality and then explaining what different moral theologians, such as Curran and McCormick, were saying. Hickey replied, 'If that is true, something should be done about that.' The other thing he was concerned with was that we were using a pastoral document put out by the Catholic Bishops of England and Wales, *The Pastoral Care of Homosexual People*. He did not approve of the document, even though it was had been written by another episcopal conference.

Clearly he thought that we were putting the official teaching of the Church on the same level as theological opinion, and from then on that charge has stuck with us. Hickey would also later accuse us of being 'ambiguous' on Church teaching on homosexual acts. He wanted us to tell people that these opinions were wrong and could not be followed. Connery sat through all this; he was obviously uncomfortable and I suspect that he felt that he was being used. The chancellor took notes. At the end I asked him if I could have faculties and he said, 'No, if we gave you faculties, all the homosexuals would come to you for confession.' If I had been quick enough I would have replied, 'But surely, Monsignor, that's exactly what you want, isn't it?'

After the meeting we were still naive enough to think that we had begun a dialogue. About two weeks later Hickey sent a letter to every bishop in the country telling them that he had met with us and that he was not satisfied that we were presenting the authentic teaching of the Church. That charge originated with him and has hung over us like a cloud for almost thirty years. He also wrote a letter to all the religious communities that supported the symposium, asking them to withdraw their sponsorship and participation, but none of them did. We went ahead with the symposium and about two hundred people attended. From then on our reputation was tainted. Some bishops would say to us, 'Didn't you have some trouble with Hickey?' He pursued us in any way he could. If we were giving workshops in a diocese and he found out about it, he would write to the local bishop and say that he had examined us and that he had difficulty with our 'lack of adherence' to Church teaching, and that we should not be allowed to speak in a Catholic location. Some of them barred us, but most of them just ignored his interference. And several of them with whom we met personally asked us why Hickey was so obsessed with us and the issue of homosexuality.

It is hard to understand, given that he is archbishop of the capital of the country, with an immense range of national and international issues facing society and government, why he would be so preoccupied with the issue of homosexuality and with us. I like to think it is his concern with the teaching of the Church. He once told some nuns that he had a table with two big piles of records in his office: one was material on Latin America and the other on New Ways Ministry. Despite considerable efforts by the US provincials of our two congregations, and our expression of a willingness to modify our methodology in light of his concerns, he simply refused to negotiate. Another of his advisors, Monsignor Lorenzo Albacete, told Jeannine's provincial that he would be willing to meet with us to work things out, but Hickey would not allow him to do this. He just wanted us out of this ministry and out of Washington.

A couple of years after this incident, there was another run-in with Archbishop Hickey. New Ways Ministry was planning another symposium, and this time they had a bishop who was willing to speak. He would have been happy if Hickey had simply remained neutral, but he did want some assurance that the archbishop would not send out a letter opposing it. Following their previous experience, Jeannine Gramick went to the chancery accompanied by two lay people from New Ways Ministry. She takes up the story:

I asked for and got an appointment. I took two people from the staff of New Ways Ministry with me. When we arrived at the chancery the secretary ushered me into the archbishop's office but would not let the others accompany me. When he arrived, the archbishop said that he was very disturbed that I had brought these people with me to the meeting, and that I should be grateful that he had given me a private interview. I responded, 'Well, the last time we met, Bob and I thought it was a private interview, but you brought your chancellor and a theologian. So if you can bring two people to a meeting, why can't I bring two people with me?' He was very surprised, and he drew himself up to his full height and said, 'Well, Sister, I'm the archbishop.' To which I said, 'What's good for the goose, is good for the gander!' After a pause, he said, 'Well, then let's begin with a prayer.' There was a long silence, so I began to pray, 'God, our Mother and Father ...' and followed with a spontaneous prayer. I heard later from friends in the chancery that he was furious because I had the audacity not only to begin the prayer but also to call God 'our Mother'. He said, 'No one can make me angry like that woman.'

I have thought a bit about Cardinal Hickey's motivation [he was made a cardinal in 1988]. I think that he sincerely believes that Bob and I are undermining the teaching of the Church on the question of homosexuality. He believes that his role as an archbishop is to maintain that teaching and make sure that it does not change. I think that explains why he delated us to Rome. We know that he has been writing letters and personally intervening with our community superiors and with both the CDF and CRSI since his arrival in Washington. He has continued to ask our congregations to get us out of Washington, out of gay ministry, and to 'retrain' us for other ministries.

Unable to obtain his objective directly through our community leaders, he then tried to achieve his objective through the Vatican. In 1982 Rome asked our community leaders to investigate us as a result of his complaints. Both groups of superiors produced a positive evaluation of the ministry. They said that we were not doing anything opposed to Church teaching, and that the ministry was good and should be strengthened. However, in 1984 our superiors-general received notification from CRSI that we were to separate ourselves from New Ways Ministry and if we continued this pastoral work, we were to make clear the intrinsic evil of homosexual acts. This directive was passed on to us, and we both resigned as co-directors. We were still engaged in lesbian and gay ministry, but not under the umbrella of New Ways Ministry. We continued to make clear the teaching of the Church about the immorality of homosexuality, but in 1985 CRSI again asked our religious communities to conduct another internal investigation. This resulted in another positive evaluation of our work.

Despite these endorsements from their communities, Archbishop Hickey continued his pressure. The pair eventually left Washington. Jeannine Gramick went to New York for a time and then moved to Baltimore.

Robert Nugent went to New Jersey for pastoral work in the archdiocese of Newark and then spent a year on sabbatical leave at Yale Divinity School. However, they continued with their workshops and writing, and the ministry continued to grow. By that stage they had attained a national profile and had spoken in more than half the dioceses of the United States. But, as Nugent describes it, the trouble with Rome continued:

In 1983 I published my book, *A Challenge to Love: Gay and Lesbian Catholics in the Church*, with an introduction by Bishop Walter Sullivan of Richmond, Virginia. I heard from one of his advisors that Hickey was furious when the book was published. In fact, he apparently read it while recuperating from some illness. In the meantime, Sullivan went to Rome for his *ad limina* visit [every five years diocesan bishops have to make a visit to Rome]. He walked into Ratzinger's office in the CDF to see my book sitting on the cardinal's desk. Ratzinger asked Sullivan, 'What is the meaning of this?' He then proceeded to order Sullivan to have his name removed from the cover, but he did not ask him to withdraw the introduction. Ratzinger said that Sullivan's name on the cover implied approval for the contents of the book. Walter Sullivan issued a press statement explaining his decision to take his name off the cover, but defended the publication of the book at the same time. The CDF asked my superiors to have me withdraw the book from any future printings. But there was no way I could tell the publisher to withdraw the book from sale and distribution.

In 1982 and 1985 there had been internal investigations of our ministry by our religious congregations, and our communities had given approval and support on both occasions. Every time there was a flare-up the CRSI ordered an internal investigation. The CRSI wanted our religious congregations to order us to withdraw from this ministry, but each time our superiors recommended that we be permitted to continue. In the meantime several bishops who had sponsored or attended our workshops wrote letters of endorsement saying that they had heard nothing against Church teaching.

Having failed to persuade the School Sisters of Notre Dame and the Salvatorians to order Gramick and Nugent out of their ministry, the CRSI – which by this stage had changed its name to the Congregation for Institutes of Consecrated Life and Societies of Apostolic Life (CICLSAL) – appointed their own commission to investigate them. In 1988 Gramick and Nugent heard that the 'Maida Commission' had been set up. The chairman was Bishop Adam J. Maida, then Bishop of Green Bay, Wisconsin. He was appointed Archbishop of Detroit in 1990. (In 1994 he was made a cardinal.) The members of the Commission were to be Monsignor James J. Mulligan, a moral theologian from the diocese of Allentown, Pennsylvania, and Sister Sharon Holland, an Immaculate Heart of Mary Sister and a canon lawyer teaching at the Catholic University in Washington, DC.

Maida is both a canon and civil lawyer, and Nugent says that 'he has often played a key behind-the-scenes-role in major ecclesiastical cases in the US, including the bankruptcy of dioceses. He is trusted by Rome and is a powerful figure in the US Church. He headed up a multimillion-dollar project for the John Paul II Center in Washington, DC. Maida prefers a rather low-key approach in the public forum.'

Neither Gramick nor Nugent, nor their congregations, had any say in the composition of the Commission. When one mid-western archbishop saw the list of appointees he was 'aghast'. So both congregations requested that they be able to nominate two other people to join the Commission as members. Jeannine Gramick describes what then happened:

The CICLSAL said that our communities could submit a list of names for the Commission, because by then Sharon Holland had resigned to join the staff of CICLSAL itself. She still works for them in Rome. The secretary of the CICLSAL, Archbishop [later Cardinal] Vincenzo Fagiolo, in a letter of 23 July 1988, told me that 'We [the Congregation] would be disposed to your superiors-general submitting a list of names who could possibly replace her [Sharon Holland]. The Congregation would then make a choice of the person.' In fact, the two superiors–general submitted two lists, one of canon lawyers and one of bishops, and asked that Rome choose one from each list. All of the bishops nominated were canon lawyers who had been involved in drawing up the US bishops' document, *Doctrinal Responsibilities*, which included a process for resolving difficulties between theologians and bishops. Drafted by the Canon Law Society of America and the Catholic Theological Society of America, the document was approved by the bishops. We had read it carefully and would have been very happy to use the investigation process that it outlines. The lists of names were submitted on 27 May 1989. We heard nothing further about the Commission until 1994. There had been rumours, but nothing official, so we presumed that the idea had been abandoned.

In the fall of 1993, Gramick and Nugent were scheduled to give a workshop in a Detroit parish. When Archbishop Maida barred them from the parish, they gave the workshop at a Catholic hospital. They went to see Maida the following day. Nugent describes the visit: 'He welcomed us warmly and was the perfect gentleman. He lit a fire and said, "Well, I guess it's time to get this Commission off the ground".' They were concerned because Maida had barred them from speaking at the Catholic parish. Nugent told Maida it seemed like he had pre-judged them even before the study had got under way. Maida admitted that he had some difficulties with their approach to gay ministry, but said that 'he wanted to get things going'. So on 24 January 1994 they were informed that the Commission had been reactivated. No reason was given as to why it had been allowed to lapse since 1988. Jeannine Gramick says:

It was then that we discovered that someone who was on neither of our religious orders' lists had been named to fill the vacant space on the Commission. When my superior-general asked Cardinal Eduardo Martinez Somalo, the new prefect of CICLSAL, about this, he replied that 'there was no commitment by the Congregation either to augment the membership of the Commission or to choose names only from those the authors or their superiors might submit'. She responded that she had a different understanding of my meeting [in 1988] with Archbishop Fagiolo about the number and composition of the original Commission. Bob and I did not want to cooperate with the Commission, but our community leaders urged us to do so. At the first hearing on 18 March 1994, we issued a statement saying we were attending the Commission under duress. We did not believe in the justice of the process, but out of respect for Church authority we attended. The Commission had two further hearings in May and July 1994. On 8 April 1994, the Commission sent a set of questions and a set of quotations from our new book, *Building Bridges: Lesbian and Gay Reality and the Catholic Church* (1992). We responded to these questions and sent them to the Commission on 24 June. We brought our written responses to the selected passages from our book to the third hearing and, upon discussion, felt that we adequately explained the passages that raised concerns.

Gramick and Nugent considered the first meeting of the Commission, which was concerned with procedure, as well as the second, to be a waste of time. They would not discuss substantive issues without the presence of their episcopal, canonical and theological consultants. The second meeting was spent correcting the minutes of the first meeting. Cardinal Maida insisted that the second meeting take place on 25 May and would not reschedule it, despite the unavailability of Gramick's and Nugent's consultants. The only substantive meeting of the Commission was held on 26 June 1994. Just before the first meeting, Gramick, Nugent and their religious superiors were told the name of the new member of the Commission: Dr Janet Smith. As already pointed out, she had not been on either list submitted to CICLSAL. Nugent describes the situation:

The next thing we heard was that Dr Janet Smith, an associate professor of philosophy at the University of Dallas, had been appointed to the Commission. She is not a theologian, but a classical scholar. She published a book defending the encyclical *Humanae Vitae* and criticising all dissenting theologians. She often speaks at the conferences of right-wing Catholic fundamentalist groups. Clearly the Vatican chose her because they knew that she would evaluate us negatively. We complained because we already knew where she stood. Several years earlier, when she was asked by the Bishop of Fort Wayne–South Bend to evaluate our writings, she recommended that we not be allowed to speak on Catholic premises. The biggest problem of all was that she is not a theologian.

The other member, Monsignor James Mulligan, had no experience at all in ministry with homosexuals. The US bishops' document *Doctrinal Responsibilities* says clearly that any commission should represent the 'broad theological spectrum' on any issue, and should have people with pastoral experience in the area under discussion. We complained that it was a kangaroo court from the very beginning. Jeannine's superior-general, Sister Patricia Flynn, protested but to no avail. We wrote to CICLSAL to ask if we could use *Doctrinal Responsibilities* as the basis for discussion. The reply was: 'No. That is for theologians. You're not theologians. This is a pastoral ministry case.' Maida said that we would use a modified version of the process, but that never really happened.

Incidentally, in terms of costs, Jeannine at one point asked Maida who was going to assume the financial burdens. He said: 'Well, when I work for Rome, I always pay my own expenses. It is kind of a contribution to the Holy See. Now, if you want to you can write to the Congregation to see if they would be willing to underwrite the expenses.' Jeannine considered writing to Rome to ask for financial reimbursement, but in the end our communities volunteered to assume all of the expenses involved in our defence. They paid for us to go to and from Detroit three times, and also paid for four experts to come from all over the country for the final meeting of the Commission.

At the first meeting Maida told us about the formal documents of the Commission which set out its terms of reference and scope. One of these was a letter to Maida from the then papal nuncio in Washington, Archbishop [later Cardinal] Pio Larghi. We asked for a copy of this letter. Maida offered to give us the parts that referred to the Commission. A few weeks later we got three sentences, beginning with an ellipsis and ending with an ellipsis. We were canonically advised that we needed the whole letter. According to Maida it formed part of the official mandate of the Commission, though later it simply disappeared from the list of official documents. It was obvious to us that Maida was protecting the nuncio in refusing to give us the entire document. I can only wonder if it was at this point that it was said or implied in polite ecclesiastical language that 'these people have to be stopped'.

Our theologians were Father Bruce Williams, then pastor of a New York parish, and Professor James Hanigan, chair of the theology department at Duquesne University in Pittsburgh, who wrote a fine book on the morality of homosexuality. Our episcopal advisor was Bishop John Snyder from St Augustine in Florida, and our canonist was Monsignor Leonard Scott, the head of the marriage tribunal of the diocese of Camden, New Jersey, a brilliant canon lawyer and the first African–American president of the Canon Law Society. Our consultants accompanied us to the third hearing. Our provincials, Sister Christine Mulcahy, SSND, and Father Paul Portland, SDS, attended all the hearings with us and gave us deep moral and verbal support. In addition, my provincial-elect, Father Dennis Thiessen, SDS, also attended the third hearing.

The substantive hearing on 26 July 1994 was held at the Sacred Heart Seminary in Detroit. Mulligan had had a stroke and could not participate. So we were working with Maida and Smith. When we arrived, we went into this room which was all set up with name cards, the whole bit. A professional group was taping the proceedings behind the Commission's table. There was a table up-front for Maida and Smith. There was another table facing it for Jeannine and myself. About thirty feet [ten metres] back another table was set up for our consultants. As we stood around having coffee before the hearing, Monsignor Scott said to me, 'This arrangement is not going to work.' I agreed. Clearly, the idea was to isolate the consultants. So Scott told Maida that he needed to be sitting at the same table with his clients. Maida said, 'This is the arrangement we always have, but I guess it's okay to move the tables.' So then there was a lot of shuffling and last minute rearrangements. We all ended up at the same table facing Maida, Smith and Maida's clerical secretary.

One of the key issues became the contents of the letter from Larghi to

Maida. Despite considerable pressure from Scott, Maida refused to reveal its contents. It may have suggested an outcome for the process that would be 'acceptable' to Rome. It was obviously so embarrassing that it was later dropped as part of the official list of documents forming the mandate of the Commission. Jeannine Gramick describes what happened in the morning session:

The whole morning was taken up with Monsignor Leonard Scott's canonical issues. He went through every procedure. He demanded access to all the materials in possession of the Commission, including all letters, and warned that there was evidence that the Commission was being pressured toward a specific conclusion. As an example, Scott produced a copy of a letter dated 10 October 1989 from Cardinal Hickey to Cardinal Jérôme Hamer, then prefect of the CICLSAL. The second paragraph of the letter began, 'I respectfully urge that pressure be brought to bear on Sister Jeannine's superiors to ensure that she cease this work in view of her ambiguity with regard to the wrongness of homosexual activity.' Scott noted that Hickey was not asking for an objective study of our ministry, but 'pressure' to close it down. He also produced a second letter from Hickey to Maida himself, dated the same day, perhaps written, Scott suggested, with the same thought in mind. This letter was the type to which we had a right, Scott claimed, in order to defend ourselves. The letter was ambiguous, or at worst deceptive, because it alleged that I had been directed to 'refrain from participating in such [gay/lesbian] workshops'. That, Scott noted emphatically, was false. To withhold this letter, as the Commission had done, compromised our right to defence. Scott's appeal had no effect. Maida refused to release any letters that the Commission had received from bishops, priests, religious and lay Catholics on the grounds that some had been written 'in confidence'. Father Paul Portland, Bob's provincial, responded that he returns letters of complaint if the author is not willing to stand behind what he or she writes. Under questioning from Scott, Maida conceded that the Commission had joint competency from both CICLSAL and the CDF. Scott suggested that this was a form of 'double jeopardy'. Maida responded that the concept of 'double jeopardy' does not exist in canon law.

The question of the letters sent spontaneously by individuals to the Commission became a real bone of contention. The fact of the Commission's investigation of our ministry had been made public, but the substantive details had not. Because people knew about the Commission, more than 250 groups or individuals had written to Maida supporting us. At the outset in 1988, we had been assured that we would have access to all information that the Commission had. But, despite further pressure from our canonist, Monsignor Scott, the Commission would not show us the letters. Maida told us that only about ten were negative. However, the written report of the Commission stated that it had a number of letters, some positive and some negative. While that information is strictly true, it hides the full truth that only a tiny proportion was negative. We believe that a few negative letters unduly influenced the Commission. One solicited negative critique from Monsignor Leonard P. Blair [who has subsequently been named a bishop] was made part of the official record, while positive critiques, and even supportive letters from nineteen bishops, were not made part of the official acts of the Commission.

During the afternoon Gramick and Nugent did most of the talking. Their reports are complementary. First, here is Nugent's version of what happened:

After lunch Janet Smith started the questioning. Our written answers sent to the Commission in June were incorporated in questions about certain passages in the book, *Building Bridges*. The discussion went on for the entire afternoon. Generally it was friendly, although it became testy once in a while. For instance, we were sparring about the meaning of the phrase 'intrinsic disorder', its pastoral implications and potential harm to people who don't understand technical Church language. Bishop Snyder said that he worked with disabled people and he would never use a word like 'disorder'. He said: 'What Jeannine and Bob have been doing is breaking through what wasn't there. I would see it still evolving, but I wouldn't want to talk to the parents that I'll see this weekend and talk about their children as "disordered".' Hanigan expressed his admiration and stated that he could not imagine 'there would be any result but a letter to thank them [Nugent and Gramick] for their ministry'.

Gramick's emphasis is slightly different:

The rest of the day was spent dealing with the theological and moral issues arising from our book *Building Bridges*. Despite all our misgivings, we went away feeling that the discussion with the Commission had been a very useful experience. While there were differences of opinion, we had a chance to explain the passages from *Building Bridges* which were under scrutiny. If there was any confusion in those passages, we felt we had explained that confusion, and had clarified our position. We said that what we were trying to do in *Building Bridges* was to articulate the actual views of the lesbian and gay Catholics with whom we had worked over more than twenty years, rather than explaining our own views. The Commission's admonition was that we needed to make it clearer as to whether we were speaking in their voice or our own, and we committed ourselves to do that in the future. Other issues discussed were whether we promoted Church teaching or tried to change it, and whether we should use the Vatican's preferred word 'disordered' to describe a homosexual orientation.

The whole Gramick–Nugent team came away from the day feeling that it had been a success. They felt that the Commission had responded positively to them. That is why the Commission's written account, when it appeared on 4 October 1994, was a real bombshell. They were not even given access to the whole account. As Gramick points out, 'Maida made a Jesuitical distinction between the "recommendations" and "findings". He said that we could have access to the Commission's findings and respond to them, but we would not receive the recommendations. These would go straight to Rome. As it turned out, the findings were very negative and skewed against us.' Nugent felt that: 'They could have written the findings without us being at the meeting. This was not a fair, objective hearing. The findings raised new material and new quotations from our books that had not been discussed in the hearings. I don't know who wrote the findings. Things we had answered in the meeting itself were simply ignored.' Gramick now outlines in detail what was in the findings:

Certainly, the report recognised positive aspects of our ministry. It said:

> Many homosexual persons have had alienating experiences at the hands of Church people, are estranged from the Church, and need someone to reach out to them with love, compassion and understanding. This task of reaching out to others is sometimes made more difficult because the Church's teaching has traditionally been expressed in language whose meaning is not easily grasped by those not familiar with the history of moral theology. This language can sometimes sound insensitive and even offensive if not properly understood. The Commission believes that Sister Gramick and Father Nugent are to be commended for recognizing these important needs and for having the courage and zeal to attempt to address them. Their love and compassion for those who need someone to reach out to is clear and commendable.

But the Commission's criticism outweighed its praise.

One of the issues highlighted by the report, which was subsequently seized upon by the CDF, and which was ultimately to become the key issue for Rome, was the question of our personal, internal conviction about the Church's teaching. The findings stated:

> While Sister Gramick and Father Nugent take care to state clearly the Church's teaching about homosexuality, they themselves are not manifest advocates of the Church's

position. They merely *present* (the Commission's emphasis) the Church's teaching, but give no evidence of personal advocacy of it. Neither was prepared to give personal assent to the Church's teaching on homogenital behaviour. Both were ambiguous in their responses regarding legislation that would allow for single-sex marriages or adoption by homosexual individuals.

We were given an opportunity to respond to the findings, and we pointed out some of its inadequacies. In the passage quoted above it says: 'Neither was prepared to give personal assent to the Church's teaching on homogenital behaviour.' However, the findings fail to note that at the actual hearing, before we could give an answer to this question, Archbishop Maida interjected, 'Maybe that's not a fair question', and immediately moved off the subject. If it was not fair to raise the question in the hearing, and we were not asked to pursue it on that occasion, then it is hardly fair for the findings to raise the question again and then to complain that it was left unresolved. In many ways the findings focus almost entirely on the adequacy of our teaching on homogenital acts. We are accused of not being 'manifest advocates of the Church's teaching'. Yet we consistently told the Commission that in our workshops we insist on the full range of the Church's teaching which includes: 1. the immorality of homogenital behaviour; 2. the moral neutrality of a homosexual orientation; 3. the need for pastoral care; 4. the immorality of prejudice and discrimination against homosexual persons; and 5. support for their human and civil rights.

But the findings seem almost exclusively focused on the single issue of the Church's teaching on homogenital behaviour. As we honestly told the Commission in the July meeting, we do not overemphasise the Church's well-known teaching. Rather, we place it in a wider moral context. To require that ministers to gay and lesbian persons concentrate on an emphatic proclamation of the objective immorality of homogenital acts makes the pastoral task of reconciliation more difficult. When Jesus was confronted with a pastoral situation involving a woman about to be stoned for adultery, he did not take the occasion to deliver a sermon on the evils of extramarital sex. Those who minister to the divorced and remarried are not expected to constantly harp on the immorality of divorce and remarriage. Hospital chaplains are not expected to constantly proclaim the immorality of neglecting and endangering one's health by smoking or not getting any exercise. Those in prison ministry are not expected to constantly proclaim the immorality of criminal acts. Military chaplains are not expected to constantly proclaim the immorality of war. The expectations of those in lesbian and gay ministry should be similar.

The findings are also concerned about our use of the words 'natural' and 'disordered'. While they have quite specific meanings within the context of Catholic moral theology, they convey quite different meanings to people today. We reminded the Commission that the word 'natural' is not equivalent to 'morally permissible'. Yet the findings say that our use of the word in the psychological sense 'appears' to imply that we think that homogenital acts should be morally permissible. For the modern American, the word 'disorder' implies psychological illness. We reminded the Commission that the National Conference of Catholic Bishops expressly rejected the use of this word to describe a homosexual orientation in the text of their document *Human Sexuality* precisely because it would be confusing, pastorally insensitive and add further pain. It is unfair of the Commission to fault us for maintaining a position held by the US bishops.

We heard nothing for about a year. Then, in December 1995, we were told through Maida that the Vatican had three more questions to ask us. Apparently, from Rome's perspective, what we had said to the Maida Commission was not sufficient to convict us, so there had to be further questioning. The questions were:

1. Is a homosexual orientation in any sense a defect?
2. Are there any moral limitations on homosexual activity that do not apply to heterosexual activity? What are these limitations?
3. If there are such moral limitations, what is their basis?

We were advised to answer the questions briefly and to the point, which we did. Essentially, it was all a repeat of the question concerning what we present about Church teaching on homosexual activity and orientation in our workshops. I thought that we had made it quite clear in both the hearings and in our written responses to the Commission's questions that while we do present the Church's teaching on these two aspects, we don't dwell exclusively on them because there is much more to the Church's teaching. We think it is imperative to spend the bulk of the time talking about what people don't know about the Church's teaching, namely the need for pastoral care, the dignity and human and civil rights of lesbian and gay people that are encoded in Church teaching, as well as the Church's teaching about the immorality of discrimination, prejudice and violence against homosexual people. While not neglecting homosexual activity and orientation, we have focused on these other issues.

What we did not know at that time was that our case had already been transferred in 1995 entirely to the CDF, because it involved doctrinal issues. Our superiors-general were informed of this at a meeting with Cardinal Josef Ratzinger and Archbishop Tarcisio Bertone, at the CDF on 19 December 1997. We discovered that a *contestatio* (this is an assessment of our written work drawn up by a CDF consultor) had been prepared by the CDF in October 1997, and this was forwarded to us in late December through our superiors-general. We were told we were to answer it independently and personally within two canonical months. We also discovered that our case was being processed by the CDF under the procedure of 'Examination in cases of urgency' (Arts 23–27 of the CDF's *Regulations for Doctrinal Examination*). The *contestatio* was entitled 'Erroneous and Dangerous Propositions in the Publications *Building Bridges* and *Voices of Hope* by Sister Jeannine Gramick, SSND, and Father Robert Nugent, SDS'. The CDF had re-examined the book *Building Bridges*, and they also looked at our 1995 book *Voices of Hope: A Collection of Positive Catholic Writings on Gay and Lesbian Issues*. The *contestatio* said that our writings 'favour and indeed advance dissent from the Church's teaching while consistently lacking a clear, accurate and sympathetic presentation of that teaching'. It was claimed that our approach was 'unacceptable from every standpoint'. It said that our work involved 'a studied ambiguity' and that we did a 'disservice to the Church, to those engaged in the pastoral care of homosexual persons and to those seeking guidance from the Church'.

From this point onwards the two stories diverge because the interaction between the CDF and Gramick differed from that with Nugent. However, despite the difference in process, in July 1999 both were banned permanently from ministry to homosexual persons. Gramick tells of her encounter with the CDF:

We both responded separately, and in detail, to the *contestatio* in early February 1998. On 27 June 1998, I was informed that my response to the *contestatio* was unsatisfactory because I did not reveal my personal assent to the Church's teaching on homosexuality, and because I frequently sought to justify points in my writings. I was asked to make a public declaration agreeing with the Church's teaching on homosexuality, to accept responsibility for errors in the two books and to ask for pardon. I made a directed retreat to ponder my response. My community leaders and I knew that the consequences could be serious. We even worried that I might be excommunicated if I did not satisfy the CDF. My provincial, Sister Jane Burke, proposed that we both make a pilgrimage to Munich to pray at the tomb of our foundress, Blessed Theresa Gerhardinger, at the site of our original motherhouse.

On 25 July 1998, my provincial and I were waiting to board our Lufthansa flight to Munich at DaVinci Airport in Rome when we saw an elderly, white-haired man we thought we recognised. As we took our seats, I noticed that he was sitting five rows behind us, next to the window, with two vacant seats beside him. I sat down next to him and asked, 'Do you speak English?' 'A little,' he smiled back. I ascertained that he was a priest, that his deceased aunt had been a School Sister of Notre Dame, and that her name was Ratzinger! When the cardinal learned my identity, he whimsically said, 'I have known you for twenty years.' I told him how I had become involved in this ministry. He asked what we did in the workshops and if bishops invite us to conduct them. I responded, 'Yes, some do and some don't. We are also invited by religious communities, colleges and universities.' I asked if he had ever met any gay people and he responded, 'Yes, in Berlin. They were demonstrating against the pope.' We discussed the Vatican's suggested changes to the document *Always Our Children* [the US bishops' pastoral message]. I told him that the US bishops' had accepted the revisions and had printed a new edition. He looked surprised and said, 'Oh, I do not yet have a copy.' 'Well, I would have brought you one if I had known we would meet,' I quipped. We then conversed pleasantly about broader topics: US schools, religious vocations, his first book, and his pending visit to his only living relative, a brother who, now retired, had been rector of the cathedral at Regensburg. Several times in the twenty-minute conversation he said, 'This [meeting] is providence.' As we were landing he said, 'Pray for me and I will pray for you.' My provincial also had an opportunity to speak with Cardinal Ratzinger on the plane. She said: 'Jeannine is a good sister. She may not tell you all you want to hear, but she is speaking from her heart. We are worried that Jeannine might be excommunicated.' To ease her fear of excommunication, Cardinal Ratzinger said, 'It is not at that level of doctrine.'

Both my provincial and I agreed that Cardinal Ratzinger was gracious and personable. My provincial felt that we had experienced a miracle. I believe that the real miracle for me was the opportunity to put a human face to the Vatican bureaucracy. I sensed in Cardinal Ratzinger an intelligent, gentle and prayerful man, filled with the love of God, who has devoted a lifetime of service to the Church, even in the face of enormous unpopularity among the people of the Vatican II Church. I have continually tried to believe that our Church leaders act from a sincere conviction of responsibility to God and God's people. However, the miracle I received was an intense experience of feeling the goodness of those with whom we disagree or who hinder our accomplishment of the perceived will of God. These kinds of miracles teach us how to live as followers of Christ with our intellectual antagonists.

So on 29 July 1998 I responded personally to the CDF. I told them:

> In freedom, I choose not to publicly reveal my personal beliefs regarding any doctrinal positions on homogenital behaviour and homosexual orientation. The approach I have taken in my pastoral ministry requires this reticence. In my desire to spread the Gospel of Christ to lesbian and gay people who have felt alienated from the Church, I have tried to be a 'bridge builder' or mediator whose personal views on contentious issues remain as far as possible in the background.

In my response I also accepted responsibility for the contents of the books. I stated that I thought I had corrected the propositions by:

1. pointing out how the opinions I report were in conflict with Church teaching;
2. showing how the meaning of words or statements can be reconciled with Church teaching; and
3. acknowledging omissions, correcting ambiguities, and resolving to be clear in the future. I apologised to anyone I may have misled, confused or offended by the contents of the books *Building Bridges* and *Voices of Hope*.

To some extent this was the end of the affair for me until the following summer. On 10 July 1999, Sister Rosemary Howarth, our superior-general in Rome, informed me that the CDF had decided that we were to be permanently banned from 'any pastoral work involving homosexual persons'. We were also declared ineligible for leadership positions in our religious congregations for an indeterminate period of time. In a further clarification given to the superiors-general by Cardinal Ratzinger, it was explained that the banning meant that we were not to engage in retreats, workshops, liturgical celebrations, or any other pastoral initiatives for lesbian and gay Catholics or their parents. Canon lawyers have assured me that punitive measures are to be interpreted in the narrowest possible way. Therefore, I have not been 'silenced' as has been reported in the media. I have been forbidden only to engage in pastoral ministry with gay Catholics or their parents. I may speak or write about homosexuality in academic or educational forums.

After the banning, I cancelled my ministerial commitments for the summer so that I could take the time needed to discern where God was calling me in the future. In a public statement on 24 July 1999, I expressed great concern that lesbian and gay Catholics and their families would be angered by this action. To them I said: 'Use your anger creatively. Don't leave the Church. It is your spiritual home. The people of God are welcoming you into our parishes. They are coming to see that the whole community is diminished when we exclude lesbian and gay persons from the table of Eucharist and dialogue. Believe what our US bishops said in their pastoral message, *Always Our Children*: "In you God's love is revealed".' I also expressed profound gratitude to the Congregation of the School Sisters of Notre Dame, and to the Baltimore Province in particular. Their advocacy of this ministry for more than two decades, especially when it was new in the Church, has been a witness to their commitment to Jesus' way to comfort and liberate the oppressed and marginalised of this world. I saw that I was faced with a decision of whether or not to accept the outcome of a process that I believed was fundamentally unfair. I still felt called by God to lesbian and gay ministry. I also felt called to serve the people of God as a loyal member of the School Sisters of Notre Dame in the Catholic Church. Thus, the censure from the Vatican presented a dilemma for me.

In my discernment I reflected on the significance of a call or vocation, the meaning of obedience to God's will to which all Christians are called, the process leading to the CDF decision, the implications of following the CDF order for lesbian and gay Catholics, for me and my religious community, and for the whole Church, and the call of the School Sisters of Notre Dame's community documents to eliminate unjust structures of oppression. I expressed my conclusion in a statement of 23 September 1999: 'As a woman religious I give special attention to the directives of our Church leadership as a source of knowing God's call for me. Obedience to God, however, is not reducible to blind acceptance of Church injunctions.' I said that: 'While I see no benefits for lesbian and gay Catholics and their parents if I passively accept the CDF decision, I believe it is more beneficial to minister on their behalf with the blessing of Church leadership than without it. Therefore, I believe it is important to work within Church structures to have the CDF decision reconsidered and, hopefully, ultimately reversed.' I asked my Notre Dame sisters, other women and men religious, lesbian and gay Catholics and their families, our US bishops, and all the people of God to help me find creative, collaborative ways to lift the burden of this directive from my shoulders. Creative solutions will ultimately be advantageous to lesbian and gay Catholics and to the whole Church. I view my decision not as passive acceptance of an order, but as an active seeking to rectify an unjust directive.

My view still remains that the CDF has never been able to demonstrate any specific instance where we did not adequately present the Church's teaching. So the focus of the investigation gradually shifted to hone in on our personal beliefs. When the Maida Commission was set up, the mandate was to examine us on our public presentation of the Church's teaching on homosexuality. Because the Vatican could not find adequate reasons to condemn us on that issue, they invaded our private views. As we saw, our private opinions were questioned in the Maida Commission, but Maida himself acknowledged that 'maybe it's not a fair question'. Recall that later in the Commission's written findings we were faulted because we did not express personal assent to the Church's teaching. Gradually, this became the pivotal issue. I have no problem saying that the Vatican teaches that homosexual activity is intrinsically evil, and that a homosexual orientation is objectively disordered. This is the Vatican's position. The US bishops take a more pastoral approach. They try to avoid the words 'objectively disordered' or 'intrinsically disordered', although they would still make negative judgments about homosexual activity. They have put these words in footnotes in their documents because they know the pastoral harm these words cause. As I said, I have no trouble articulating the Vatican's position, and in our workshops I have done that.

The problem is that the Vatican has demanded to know if I actually believe that. My view is that as a baptised Catholic, and as a public minister in the Church, I have an obligation to present what the Church teaches and to explain why the Church teaches it. However, I do not have an obligation to give my personal viewpoint. Church authorities have a right to ask me if I assent to the essential beliefs of the Catholic Church, to what it means to be Catholic. But what the Church teaches about homosexuality is not one of the core beliefs of being Christian or Catholic. My status as a vowed religious and a public minister in the Church should not deprive me of the right which every believer has to maintain the privacy of her or his internal conscience in matters which are not central to our faith. To intrude, uninvited, into the sanctuary of another's conscience is both disrespectful and wrong. Even priests in parishes need not make a public Profession of Faith in non-essential teachings, so why should I as a pastoral minister?

As one letter writer to the *Tablet* in London pointed out, if all the priests in parishes who minister to heterosexual Catholics had to make a Profession of Faith in *Humanae Vitae*, we would immediately be very short of priests. In the final analysis, I believe the case has been a political one: a very powerful cardinal used, by his own admission, 'pressure' on Church authorities to remove us from lesbian and gay ministry.

Perhaps because he is a priest, the Vatican seemingly tried to 'squeeze more' out of Nugent than out of Gramick. In February 1998 both of them responded to the CDF's contestatio. On 4 July Nugent was informed that his response was not satisfactory because he did not express in sufficiently unequivocal terms his adherence to the Church's teaching on homosexuality, and because he sought to justify points in his writings. Both of them were told that they had to produce within one month a declaration of personal assent to the Church's teaching. Nugent submitted a one-page draft on 6 August 1998.

Also, the apostolic letter Ad Tuendam Fidem *(30 June 1998) came out right in the middle of the period when their cases were being considered in Rome. The letter distinguishes three levels of revealed doctrine. The first articulates all that is contained in the word of God and divine revelation. The second covers doctrine on faith or morals 'definitively' proposed by the papal magisterium. The third refers to other teachings of the pope or bishops when they do not intend to be 'definitive'.*

Prior to the introduction of the 'second level', all non-infallible or non-defined teaching was exactly that: teaching that should be respected and offered submission of mind and will, but still open to debate, discussion and development within the Church community. But what Ad Tuendam Fidem *has done is to introduce formally another category of 'definitive' but non-defined teaching. In his commentary on the apostolic letter Ratzinger says that this second-level teaching is, in fact, infallible. However, it has to be said that this assertion has a note of theological 'novelty' about it in the sense that it is not strictly traditional. Ratzinger says that this 'second-level definitive teaching' includes 'all those teachings in the dogmatic or moral area which are necessary for faithfully keeping and expounding the deposit of faith, even if they have not been proposed by the magisterium as formally revealed'. As examples he gives the Church's teaching on euthanasia, the canonisation of saints, the legitimacy of a papal election, and even the invalidity of Anglican orders. Nugent takes up the story from the time of submission of his personal declaration:*

In the personal declaration I said that I offered *obsequium religiosum* or submission of mind and will to the teaching of the Church because it was non-definitive and it could still be probed and discussed. As I said in the declaration: 'I have never deliberately denied or placed in doubt any Catholic teaching which requires the assent of theological faith. I have never publicly rejected or opposed any proposition that is to be held definitively. I have never been charged with public dissent from magisterial teaching.' But in the meantime *Ad Tuendam Fidem* had come out, and the minute I saw it

I thought, we are going to be the first victims of *Ad Tuendam Fidem*, because it has introduced this middle-level definitive but infallible teaching of the universal, ordinary magisterium. So when I did not give them the words they wanted they wrote up a document with the precise language and words they wanted me to say.

From June 1998 until January 1999, I was doing pastoral work in several dioceses in England. Two weeks before Christmas, on 15 December 1998, the superior-general called me. He said that the CDF had found my statement contained some positive things, but that my declaration was still not clear enough in indicating my interior assent to Church teaching. A Profession of Faith had been especially drawn up by the CDF for me. Jeannine meanwhile had heard nothing. In July she had her 'providential' encounter with Ratzinger on the plane to Munich. She felt that after their conversation the CDF would handle her case differently. I said: 'I don't think so. I think they know they can't squeeze you for anything more, but they are going to put more pressure on me.'

The Profession was faxed to me and I immediately realised that there was no way I could sign it, yet the pressure was on to do so within two weeks. I asked for more time. I needed to talk with people like Charles Curran, Richard McCormick, Joseph Selling and the canon lawyer, Ladislas Örsy, at Georgetown University. Others were not so helpful. My first thought was to ask the CDF if I could substitute certain words, but then Charlie Curran said, 'Bob, why not just write what you think you can sign and send it in.' He was right, and that is what I did. The first part of the Profession of Faith had to do with the creation of man and woman, marriage and the call to chastity according to one's state in life. I had no difficulty with any of this. The second part was more problematic. It said: 'I also firmly accept and hold that homosexual acts are always objectively evil. On the solid foundation of a constant biblical testimony, which presents homosexual acts as acts of grave depravity, tradition has always declared that homosexual acts are intrinsically disordered.' The issue, as always, was the use of words. So I substituted 'objectively evil' with 'morally wrong', 'grave depravity' with 'serious abuse', and 'intrinsically disordered' with 'objectively disordered'. I felt I could interpret those terms in ways that I could live with if I were called upon to explain them.

Some people felt I had given the CDF too much. Even a few traditional theologians told me they couldn't sign the statement as a Profession of Faith, but they would give religious submission of mind and will to it as authentic teaching. This teaching about homosexual acts was now clearly being placed in the category of second-level 'definitive but non-defined' though virtually infallible teaching. So I also added a paragraph near the end alluding to the 'difficulties in determining whether a particular teaching has in fact been taught infallibly by a non-defining act of the ordinary and universal magisterium'.

The third section of the Profession dealt with homosexual inclination. It said that though this was 'not in itself a sin, it constitutes a tendency toward behavior that is intrinsically evil, and therefore must be considered objectively disordered'. This required only *obsequium religiosum*, was not definitive, certainly not infallible and was, therefore, capable of further development. So I sent in my alternative version of the Profession of Faith on 25 January 1999, the Feast of the Conversion of St Paul. We heard no more until 8 July 1999. On that day we were both summoned to Rome, and on 10 July my superior-general informed me of the CDF decision that I could no longer work in ministry with gay people. This means that I can still preach and minister the sacraments, but not to groups of homosexuals or their parents. I am also allowed to write and publish provided the traditional canon law requiring permission from my religious superiors is observed. My superior-general also handed me one sheet of paper which contained *Some Observations on a Response to a Profession of Faith by Father Robert Nugent, SDS*. It said that the term 'intrinsically evil' should not be replaced, even for pastoral motives, with terminology which is far less clear and, because I noted the difficulties in determining when something is taught infallibly by the universal, ordinary magisterium, it accused me of questioning 'the definitive status of doctrines regarding homosexuality'.

As in the case of Tissa Balasuriya, there was clearly an attempt by Church officials to get to the media before Gramick and Nugent. A copy of the notification had been mailed to the US bishops and to the press on 9 July 1999, embargoed to 14 July. Gramick and Nugent did not get a copy of this notification until 14 July. However, a copy was on the Internet on 13 July. Nugent feels that some of the senior US bishops and cardinals had a copy of the notification weeks before. Among them were probably cardinals Hickey and Maida. He continues:

Some bishops, like Hickey, had already given it to the editors of their diocesan newspapers. When the Washington archdiocese's *Catholic Standard* came out with the story on the Notification, it said, 'Father Nugent could not be contacted for comment'. The fact was that Father Nugent was on the plane coming back from Rome that very day without the Notification that the editor already had. So hierarchy had all their ducks in line, ready to go. Hickey and Maida had media statements prepared. Hickey had a chronological list in his paper of the whole affair from beginning to end. It was incredible. That week the whole Washington *Catholic Standard* was filled with the story. I called the editor a week later and told him that the reason I was not available for comment was because I was on a plane coming back from Rome without having seen the Notification. He had the grace to admit that he had the Notification before I did, and to his credit he ran a second story quoting a lot of my public statement.

When we got back all hell broke loose. When I arrived at JFK airport there was a page for me: 'Meet your party at the baggage claim.' I said to Jeannine and Father Bruce Williams, who met us at the airport, 'I don't have any party.' It was actually a reporter from the *New York Times*. They had already picked up the story from the website of the US Bishops' Conference. I decided for a few days not to talk to the press until I had some time to sort the whole thing out in my own mind. Then I started initially with an interview on NPR [National Public Radio]. I said that I accepted the decision, after having outlined the whole case and emphasising the injustice of the decision. As I said in my public statement, after five major studies 'the most serious charge raised about my pastoral ministry during the entire twenty-five years has been a perception by some of ambiguity'. Actually, in terms of the media, the only rude treatment I received was from a thuggish presenter on the BBC Sunday morning religious program. In an antagonistic tone, he said, 'Well, surely, Father, you don't believe in this Church teaching in your heart of hearts?' I said, 'That's a question I would not answer for the CDF, and I certainly will not answer it for you.' I came close to simply walking out on the long-distance phone interview.

At this time Jeannine did not speak to the media; she wanted more time to think about it. So the first wave of interviews involved me, and I got a good chance to lay out the whole story. After about two months Jeannine issued her statement saying that she would live with the decision and work to reverse it.

But this was still not the end of the affair. On 17 November 1999 Bishop Joseph A. Fiorenza, the president of the United States Bishops' Conference and the Bishop of Galveston–Houston, Texas, issued a statement on the affair as a result of the reaction of Catholics in the US to the CDF's action against Gramick and Nugent. Among other things, Fiorenza addressed the question of the violation of conscience involved in the CDF's action. He said: 'It is not an invasion of conscience for the Church to ask those who minister in her name about their adherence to Church teaching. Thus no invasion is involved in asking those serving in ministry to homosexual persons whether they adhere to the Church's teaching on the intrinsic immorality of homosexual acts. Their personal beliefs have pastoral, and therefore public, significance.'

Aside from the fact that this statement does not distinguish between the different levels of adherence to different levels of teaching, and that it treats belief in the 'intrinsic immorality of homosexual acts' as though this were the equivalent of belief in the Trinity or the humanity of Christ, imagine the consequences if all bishops and priests had to manifest their internal conscientious commitment to the teaching contained in, for instance, the encyclical on birth control, Humanae Vitae. *Here Nugent responds to Fiorenza:*

What Fiorenza is saying is that you cannot maintain a personal and private interior dissent in conscience and be a public minister in the Church. So we would have to say goodbye to a very high percentage of both the clergy and bishops. If we put this test to every priest and bishop on the issue of contraception and we asked them, 'Do you personally and interiorly really believe in and adhere to the papal teaching that every act of contraception is intrinsically evil?', the result would be a serious crisis in the Church. Actually I think that the CDF acknowledges in the 1990 *Instruction of the Ecclesial Vocation of the Theologian* that a theologian can have personal struggles with certain teachings about which he or she is not convinced. It says: 'If the theologian has serious difficulties for reasons that appear to him or her to be well founded in accepting a non-irreformable magisterial teaching, the theologian has a duty to make that known in an evangelical spirit with a desire to resolve difficulties. The objection to a certain wording of Church teaching can serve as a stimulus to the magisterium to propose the teaching in a greater depth and a clearer presentation.' This is saying that just because a theologian has difficulties with a teaching, it does not mean that they cannot do pastoral ministry, or teach on that issue. So I think you can separate one's interior struggles from one's public teaching and pastoral ministry. But now both the CDF and Fiorenza are saying, 'No. Unless you adhere internally in conscience to that teaching and make that adherence public, you cannot even do pastoral ministry.'

I also argued that a very traditional principle of law is that silence gives consent. So it is just as logical to assume that if one is silent about some Church teaching, then one can be seen to be assenting to it as long as one does not speak against it. So where do Fiorenza and the CDF stand on freedom of conscience? They seem to be arguing that the only valid and correctly formed conscience is one that comes to the same conclusion or conforms perfectly to Church teaching. Any other conclusion is erroneous.

The US bishops in their 1990 document on human sexuality have a wonderful section on how Catholics make moral decisions as to what is right or wrong or what vocation to follow. It says that even after using all the available help, including Church teaching, the decision is made by the person who takes responsibility for that decision before God. It is in the innermost sanctuary that we are alone with God and it is there that God speaks to us. We simply cannot abdicate that decision-making process or give it over to anyone else, including the Church hierarchy.

What is the effect of all this? What has it done to Gramick and Nugent personally? And what about the future? Here is Gramick's view.

As I look back over the whole affair, I feel that Church authorities follow rigid and totalitarian procedures. While I knew that in theory before, I now know it experientially. I guess it has made me more convinced than ever that we need governmental changes in our Church. In 1989, when we saw the totalitarian structures in Eastern Europe crumbling, we facetiously said that the Church is really the last bastion of totalitarianism, and I think it is true. We need to work harder to have processes in our Church that are more mutual, collaborative, open and respectful of due process. We already have organisations such as the Association for the Rights of Catholics in the Church, but we need to have more support and stronger voices for the reformation of Church procedures.

We often hear people say, 'the Church is not a democracy'. Well, I say, 'Why isn't it now? It used to be in the early Church.' I do not claim that a democratic form of government is ideal, but it would give us a greater opportunity to act justly towards people within our own community. I must admit that at times I got very distressed and dejected during this long process. There were moments when I felt that my energy had been sapped, and yet I think that I have been able to keep going because the investigation has been an opportunity for more education. It has even been a chance to touch some of the people in the Vatican. They have had to read our books and our answers to questions. So I somehow hope that it will give people in the Vatican pause to think.

I guess that one frustrating part of it is that most of the correspondence has been secret, not been open to the public or to the media. The fact that the investigation was being conducted was publicly known, but the particulars of the investigation were kept secret. Had they been made public from the beginning, I think there would have been more opportunity for education. One advantage of the Vatican decision is that we can make the details public and there is a chance for further education. Certainly, I have had my periods of feeling despondent, but in the long run I hope, indeed believe, that it all had some good effect.

As to the future of the CDF and the Roman Curia: I am not a professional ecclesiologist, just a lay person looking in from the outside. It is clear to me that any bishop, including the Bishop of Rome, needs administrative helpers. But the administrators of the Bishop of Rome should be just that: administrators. The problem is that they assume authority and hierarchical power that they should not have. I have to admit that in the US the future of Church reform looks bleak. For reform to happen you need two things: reform-minded people who are in authority, like the bishops, and a willingness to work for reform at the grass-roots. On both counts, I see grave deficiencies.

We have a body of bishops in the US, most of whom have been appointed by John Paul II, who are subservient 'yes-men'. By and large, most Catholics are not concerned about Rome. They simply want a good liturgy in their parishes, good religious education and good schools for their children. There is a reform movement, but it is very small. It is not like the reform movement in Austria or Germany, for instance, where millions of people have at least shown support for change in the Church. Our bishops certainly could not be compared to the bishops of Germany for resisting or questioning the Vatican.

I keep going because I believe in justice, because I think it is important to support people who believe in the same things as I do, and above all because of my faith in God. In all of this I have learned more and more to depend on God. Things do not happen the way you expect or would like them to happen. I have had my convictions reaffirmed that in the long run things will come right. One of my favourite quotations from St Paul's Letter to the

Romans is: 'For those who love God all things work together unto good' (Romans 8:28). Somehow, I still believe that.

As terrible as the ordeal has been for me, for my religious community, and for lesbian and gay people, many of whom have found this the last straw and have left the Church altogether, we have to believe in the resurrection. For some reason this is all part of the mystery of suffering and redemption. I believe that somehow it will be a catalyst for good. My faith is still very strong.

The last word goes to Bob Nugent. He reflects on the whole question of the invasion of private conscience, an issue that is at the heart of this whole affair:

I think that this is the first time that a pastoral minister has been asked by the CDF to reveal publicly his or her own position, or even personal struggles in being convinced of the truth of a definitive, second-level teaching. (Here let us abstract from the fact that there are real problems with this business of 'second-level' teaching, its validity, its relationship to infallibility, and its origins.) I think this is the first time that anyone has been asked to reveal his or her conscience in order to be able to continue a particular ministry. I am willing to say that I accept the teaching of the Church about homosexual acts, but only in language that I can explain and live with, and explain with some degree of intellectual integrity and understand in light of the approach of some contemporary moral theologians. But I simply could not do this when the teaching is couched in such language as 'intrinsically evil' and 'objectively disordered', when these terms are under intense debate among respectable theologians. Jeannine, on the other hand, maintains absolute discretion regarding her own interior conscience. However, I keep my struggles to myself. I don't project them onto others in workshops. I have never publicly dissented from Church teaching, and that has been acknowledged.

As Boston College moralist, Lisa Sowle Cahill, said in *America* [14 August, 1999]: 'Now people are being silenced not for contradicting any doctrine, and not even for contradicting any non-infallible teaching, but for staying within the Church teaching while not equally emphasizing or including other points.' I am even willing to assent to the position that homosexual behaviour is objectively immoral while being aware of the problems related to it being definitive. I can understand and nuance what 'immoral' means in the larger picture, and I feel I would be able to explain it to someone else, though they might not agree with some of my basic assumptions about human sexuality. But that is a lot different from using the terminology of 'intrinsically evil'. There is no way I could explain that language in a pastoral way that someone struggling with sexual identity could understand or would not be heard as hurtful, alienating or passing judgments on a personal decision in conscience. Janet Smith told us in the Maida Commission that once she explains to married couples the Church's teaching against contraception, they understand it and accept it. She wanted us to do the same: to explain in a certain philosophical or anthropological way what the Church really means by 'intrinsically evil'. She maintained that once homosexuals heard about and understood the 'intrinsic evil' of homosexual acts, they could reject it and live out the Church's moral teaching. I felt like saying, 'You obviously have had no real pastoral experience with homosexual people.'

As someone said, 'Authority can only coerce your will; it cannot coerce your intellect.' They can stop you from speaking or writing or doing pastoral ministry. They can ask you to maintain silence about your difficulties. But they can't get inside your head and make your intellect believe and accept something that you are unable to do for very good reasons. Over all these years I have been extremely careful, and the thing that upsets me the most is that no matter how careful I have been walking this fine line, I have still been condemned. I certainly ask challenging and probing questions. I try to get people to think and analyse their experiences, but I have never rejected the Church's teaching on this question. I can't even be accused of open or public dissent. The irony is that I come across in many workshops looking like a conservative.

People who come to the workshops criticise or reject Church teaching much more strongly than I would ever think of doing.

Truthfully, I can say that throughout my entire ministry in this area I have resolutely refused to give my personal opinion or reveal whatever struggles I might have with second- or third-level teachings. It was only when I was coerced to do this that I used different language and alluded to struggles, that I was accused of calling that teaching into question and punished severely for this.

One of the reasons I believe that the goal of the whole process was to stop our ministry is the fact that although I tried to cooperate with the CDF in signing the Profession of Faith while Jeannine did not, in the end the punishment for both of us was identical. I honestly believe now that even had I signed the original Profession of Faith, it would have made no difference whatsoever. They would have said, 'Yes, we now know that you accept Church teaching, but since your ministry has already caused so much harm, we are going to shut it down.'

As I see it, there are really two issues: 1. the language of Church teaching; and 2. the truth of that teaching. I have already explained my difficulties using particular language in the pastoral area when it can be misunderstood or even used to justify physical or psychological violence. I simply could not, in good conscience, align myself publicly with such language that has such a potential for real harm after devoting a great part of my life promoting respect for the dignity of homosexual people. As for the truth of the teaching, I have an obligation to give the teaching the respect due it as authentic teaching and try to internalise it. But since I have never rejected it, I find no persuading or justifiable reason to be coerced to make a public manifestation of my heart of hearts on the issue of the intrinsic evil of homosexual acts. I do have to promote that teaching, but always in a balanced and pastorally sensitive way. I also have to continue to struggle with whatever personal difficulties I might have either about the wording or the reasons supporting it.

The current ongoing theological debate about the existence, nature and description of 'intrinsically evil' acts is too recent to have any impact on magisterial teaching, but has to be considered in this discussion. So what really disturbed me was that even though I tried to walk a little further with the Church authorities and make concessions to them, it made no difference.

The goal of the exercise was not to find out whether the ministry was helpful, or whether it did any good for people, or even whether it seriously violated doctrinal or pastoral principles. The sole aim was to close the ministry down. And that ultimately goes back to Cardinal James Hickey.

Just before the manuscript of the book was delivered to the Australian publisher in late May 2000, Jeannine Gramick and Robert Nugent, were summoned to Rome again by their religious superiors. They were told that both the CDF and CICLSAL considered that they had not shown the 'proper attitude' to the Notification of the CDF of 14 July 1999. They were also informed that they were now prohibited from writing or speaking in the public forum about the 1999 Notification itself, about the ecclesiastical processes that led to it, as well as the issue of homosexuality. Effectively, what the CDF and CICLSAL was doing was attempting to muzzle them completely, and denying them any voice whatsoever. They were to be stripped of any right to defend themselves.

Jeannine Gramick was unwilling to accept this. Despite the risk of expulsion from her order, she was determined to be true to her conscience. In a public statement she declared: 'For eleven years the Vatican investigated my pastoral ministry to lesbian and gay persons, after my religious order, the School Sisters of Notre Dame, conducted two studies resulting in positive evaluations of my work. I gave no particulars publicly about these investigations because church authorities requested that I remain silent during the investigation process in the interests of confidentiality. The publication of the Notification from the Congregation of the Doctrine of the Faith on July 14, 1999 presented the details of the investigation from the perspective of the hierarchy. Since July 1999 I have offered my own viewpoint by revealing additional facts, which show that the process violated principles of fair judicial procedure outlined in the Catholic church's 1971 document, 'Justice in the World'. Gradually I have found my own voice and have told my story to various Catholic and ecumenical audiences...I have gravely considered the requests of my community leaders...I feel pained that the Vatican and my community leaders now ask me to silence myself. After finding my voice to tell my story, I choose not to collaborate in my own oppression by restricting a basic human right. To me this is a matter of conscience' (Statement from Sister Jeannine Gramick, 23 May 2000).

For perfectly understandable and equally conscientious reasons, Robert Nugent took a different tack. Responding to the imposed 'silence' he simply stated: 'As a result of a recent clarification of the Notification by the CDF and CICLSAL...I am now prohibited from speaking or writing in the public forum about the Notification itself, about the ecclesiastical processes that led to it or about the issue of homosexuality'. In other words Nugent decided that his best witness would be silence. He felt that if he were expelled from his religious order and the priesthood for disobedience, the work he had already done in ministry would be endangered. While their responses differ, Gramick and Nugent both give abundant witness to the integrity which has always characterised their ministry.

It is important to note that Nugent's piece in this book is based on a discussion I had with him in early November 1999, in which he participated in perfectly good faith fully six months before he was informed by his superiors about the prohibition of speaking in public or writing about the CDF's 14 July 1999 Notification, and the ecclesiastical processes that led to it. His silencing created a dilemma for me as editor. Because Gramick and Nugent's ministries had been so interconnected, I had combined their interviews into parallel accounts. Their pieces were complementary. To withdraw Nugent's contribution would be a failure to tell the whole story. As well as that, this whole book is posited on a commitment to tell the truth about the CDF and its activities and behaviour. Since I am not bound by CDF strictures about silence, I decided to run with the piece as it stood. To do anything else would have been to fail to be consistent. The decision to run with the whole piece is mine. I have not consulted him about this since 'silence' was imposed on him on 23 May 2000.

However, this story is on-going. By speaking out Gramick was placed in an invidious position in relationship to the School Sisters of Notre Dame. It could have resulted in a process that led to her being expelled from her order. For twelve months after May 2000 she continued to speak out. Then on 28 June 2001 she announced that she had transferred religious orders from the School Sisters to the Sisters of Loretto, a US congregation founded in Kentucky in 1812. At that period Kentucky was on the frontier of the

United States, and the Sisters of Loretto are well known for their pioneering spirit.

With the transition she is no longer subject to the jurisdiction of the School Sisters of Notre Dame. Therefore the formal command issued by the School Sisters' superior general in May 2000 not to speak or write about homosexuality or the Vatican investigation is no longer binding on her. However, the command of the Vatican's CDF of July 1999 not to engage in pastoral work with lesbian or gay persons still stands.

Despite the draconian nature of the Vatican's action, there is a possible silver lining. Church lawyers maintain that disciplinary actions and punishments die with the pope who imposes them, and to be effective again they would have to be formally re-imposed by the new pope. So the silencing will automatically cease when John Paul II dies, and it remains to be seen what the next pope will do.

The story continues.

CHAPTER 6

Woman at the Altar:
Lavinia Byrne

The first time I interviewed her for television, I discovered that Lavinia Byrne spoke in almost perfect sentences. Unlike most interviewees, she required very little editing. It reflects the discipline and clarity of her mind. Her speech is also enlivened by a thoughtful impatience and by an energy that is eager to discover and articulate how we might make sense of the Church and its significance for us.

The fact that she is a dream interviewee is no doubt closely connected to her media experience: she is the UK's best-known Catholic broadcaster, having regularly presented the BBC's 'Thought for the Day' since 1988, and she has been a frequent presenter of the 'Daily Service' on Radio 4 since 1994. The author of eighteen books on spirituality and theology, she was university preacher at Oxford in 1993 and select preacher for Cambridge University in 1996. Until January 2000 she was a member of the Institute of the Blessed Virgin Mary (IBVM), a religious order founded by the Englishwoman Mary Ward in the early years of the seventeenth century, a very difficult period of persecution for Catholics in England.

Talking to Lavinia Byrne you have a sense of a woman who delights in her femininity and who, at the same time, enjoys the satisfaction of equal companionship and collegiality with men. There is nothing of the Dresden-china image of womanhood about her. She clearly loves Catholicism and wants to communicate this to others. Her work excites the thinking faithful who are so often intellectually compromised and torn by current Church praxis in worship, preaching, music, and in the rules and regulations that so often prevent Catholics from being generous and pluralist – in a word 'Catholic'!

Lavinia Byrne's troubles with the CDF began in 1998 after the publication of her book Woman at the Altar. *When she left the Institute of the Blessed Virgin Mary in January 2000 she said: 'What I'm concerned about is not so much the debate about the ordination of women, because if it is God's will it is going to happen anyway. My concern is the way the people in the Congregation for the Doctrine of the Faith deal with dissenters.'*

It is the CDF's failure to communicate directly with the person accused and to listen to them that outrages Lavinia Byrne's sense of justice most. She says:

> *This means that a legitimate chain of trust within the community is broken, and the rightful and necessary administration of the Church becomes a faceless bureaucracy condemning individuals without hearing their story or point of view. Religious women do some of the most bold and adventurous work in the Church, working worldwide with the poor ... as well as in universities, hospitals and schools. It is too easy to make them a sitting target by questioning their integrity and undermining their commitment to the Gospel.*

Lavinia Byrne begins by describing her background.

I was born a Catholic in 1947. My parents wanted to have a Catholic child, and that part of my identity was presented as central when I was little. I still have my first communion medal, certificate and photograph. For my fifteenth birthday my mother even gave me my first communion dress. It's ravishing! It's like a little bride's dress with a veil made of lace, and it has a hanging pocket and a silk underskirt that come right down to the ground.

I still treasure it, because that kind of quality of Catholic inheritance seems really important to me.

My birthplace was Edgbaston in Birmingham, and that is quite significant because the Oratory Church there was founded by the great English theologian and writer, Cardinal John Henry Newman [1801–90] and he actually lived in the parish. The priest who baptised me, Father Denis Sheil, was the last novice whom Newman had admitted into the Oratory community. He was a very good friend of the family, and that was significant because there was a small, very middle-class ghetto of Catholics in Birmingham who met up with each other all the time, and my family was right in the middle of that. My mother's father was a doctor. He attended to the Oratory Fathers and the local bishop, as well as to J. R. R. Tolkien who wrote wonderful stories like *The Lord of the Rings* and *The Hobbit*. So my parents occupied a very comfortable place in this secure Edgbaston Catholic world. My mother used to take me to the Oratory to light a candle every time we were out shopping.

My first communion preparation was extraordinary. We even had a day's retreat when we were aged about six, and I remember we built altars in the garden during that retreat. It made me think very hard about the mass, and it placed communion right at the heart of my personal Catholic spirituality. So when I realised a bit later that I could not be a priest, I was quite distressed and used to say mass a lot in my bedroom. At one time I was ill and was given some paper to play with and a pair of scissors, and I spent my time making hosts, cutting them out of the paper. My mother was thrilled when she discovered this; she thought I was making confetti for a wedding. In fact, I was preparing to celebrate mass in my bed!

I went with my brothers and sister to the local convent school until I was eleven; again, my grandfather had been doctor to the nuns. Then we moved house and went to live in Somerset in the southwest of England, where again we were very much part of the parish. In 1958 I was sent to boarding school at St Mary's Convent, Shaftesbury. It was here that I first met the sisters of the Institute of the Blessed Virgin Mary (IBVM). I was very impressed by them:

they were such intelligent, witty, enthusiastic women. They were very young and huge fun to be with. We had mass every day and the girls were expected to attend at least three times a week, as well as Sunday. Quite soon I began learning Latin for answering mass, and by the age of thirteen I was one of a group who sat up at the front of the Church on the left and answered the priest in Latin. We felt we were helping the priest celebrate the mass. At that time communion was the centre of my spirituality. If you had asked me then what prayer was I would have said prayer is lighting candles in Church on the way to go shopping, and attending mass and benediction. Our spirituality was very eucharistic.

I wanted to be like the nuns who taught me at school. People still talk far too blandly and easily about the call of God, as though it comes from outer space, and is directed to a part of oneself that is very personal and private. I don't think that God works like that at all. God works through the everyday and through what attracts us. That was why the way of life represented by the sisters really attracted me. I saw it as an opportunity to have the preaching of the Gospel at the centre of my life, and as a chance to be a strong, independent and intelligent woman in the service of the Church. Also, part of the attraction to the IBVM was the woman who founded our community: Mary Ward [1585–1645]. She was the product of a time in British history – the time of the penal laws – when it was impossible to be a Catholic and live in peace in this country. So travel became integral to her spiritual journey. She went to an English community in St Omer, in northeast France, to become a nun, but then realised that the enclosed religious life was not for her.

She came back to England and began something that was absolutely new in the service of the Church. She and her cousins got together and began a way of life that was modelled on that of the Jesuit Fathers. Her desire was to have the same constitutions and freedom that the Jesuits had. She wanted government by a woman general-superior, which is really important because it says that God can speak directly to a woman; a woman can take the place of Christ, be Christ, for other people. She wanted no enclosure [the separation of contemplative nuns from the civil community], and that was very daring in the period after the Council of Trent [its sessions were held between 1545 and 1563]. Trent had decreed that religious women had to live not only in a nuns' enclosure, but also in fortified and walled towns and cities. It is an irony that within forty years of her death, her sisters had deliberately bought a house outside the walls of the city of York, in Blossom Street, where the community still lives. They specifically chose to be outside the fortified city in order to be free enough to practise as Catholics. So already the precepts of the Council of Trent did not match the actual position of Catholics in England. It did not take into account the fact that in York there is no way sisters could live as Catholics inside a fortified Protestant city. The third thing was that she did not want religious dress of any sort. In fact, the sisters wore what widows in polite society would have worn. There is a reference in one of her letters where she writes to a friend in Germany: 'Please bring my red silk taffeta petticoat.' So I can't believe she was not one for looking smart and dressing appropriately. We are also told that sometimes when she was working in London she would swap clothes with her maid in order to go out looking like a servant in order to gain access to houses where Catholics lived.

When I joined the community in 1964 there were sixteen of us in the noviceship. We were there for the first three years of training for the religious life. My companions were huge fun and we had a great time together. We actually formed each other. They were devout, fervent and very gifted women, and after novitiate most of us were sent off to teacher-training college, or to university. I went to London University and read French and Spanish, and my great interest in language and communication dates from that time. In 1971 I went to Cambridge for a year to do a post-graduate certificate in education. It was at a time when linguistics were all the rage and people were beginning to study communications, and I took to it like a duck to water.

Almost as soon as I joined the community things began changing radically in the Church. It was the time of Vatican II. The mass went into English and the participation of the laity began to be perceived as something that would transform the Church. Sisters began to develop aspirations in line with the education they had received. For if you educate somebody as highly as we had been, then clearly their aspirations change. Ours certainly did. In the early 1970s I had began to study theology which, as a women who was a member of a teaching order, I had to do by correspondence. The idea of going off and doing a further three years' theology at university over and above all that I had already done was out of the question. I really revelled in theology.

For the first fifteen years of my religious life I was perfectly happy teaching in a number of girls' schools which were owned by the community. I began by teaching French and Spanish, which I dropped quite soon because I also began teaching religious studies. That became my real interest. I taught girls aged fourteen to eighteen. I felt that I was exercising a very diaconal ministry in the service of the girls with whom I was working. Most of the schools were boarding schools and we did everything with the girls; we were with them morning, noon and night. I believe that we were bringing the Word of God to them. We were proclaiming the Word both by what we said and what we did; we were actually serving them in the same way as Jesus washed his disciples' feet. It was lovely watching them grow and blossom and discover their intelligence and learn to think.

As part of our ongoing formation as sisters, we had to do a 'tertianship' – a final third year of study and experience. That came for me about fifteen years into my life as a teacher. It was a transforming year: I was taken right out of school and was given a variety of experiences where, for example, I worked in an all-night refuge, in a hospice, and with the Afro-Caribbean community in Bayswater, a very mixed-race part of London. In each of these places I found that what mattered in communicating the Gospel to people was very basic and simple. Often it was just the example of a life lived in the service of others.

As a result of the tertianship I realised that I could not go back to being a schoolteacher. During the tertian year, I met up with a couple of Jesuit friends who were editors of *The Way* and *The Way Supplement*, periodicals devoted to spirituality with an international authorship and readership. It also soon became clear that there would be an opening for me in the Institute of Spirituality at the Jesuit-run Heythrop College in London University. I went there in 1985 and worked there for six years. I also shared increasingly in responsibility for editing *The Way* and *The Way Supplement*. I travelled quite extensively and gave lectures in Australia, the United States and Canada. What strongly attracted me to the ministry of the Institute of Spirituality was working with adults, after having been so long with adolescents. The other facet of the ministry that appealed to me was that it was ecumenical. We trained people to be spiritual directors in the tradition of St Ignatius Loyola, the founder of the Jesuit order. This meant that we were working with a group of adults from across all the churches who shared a common interest in Ignatian and Jesuit spirituality. I began to realise that some of them, particularly some of the women, had vocations to the priesthood. As my work at Heythrop became better known, I found that I was asked to lead retreats for people, and one of the peer groups I began to work with was Anglican women deacons. I did many retreats for them, and I made many firm and lasting friends among them.

When I moved to my next job in 1991 – with the Council of Churches for Great Britain and Ireland – I found myself fully in ecumenical work. I had a job with a ridiculously long title: Associate Secretary for the Community of Women and Men in the Church. It was a World Council of Churches project trying to bring the contribution of women in public life and in the Church into the light of the public domain. That work became thrilling because it was all about promoting the interests of women, reading masses of both secular and religious literature about women, disseminating information about women and making sure women's contribution was valued in all the meetings I attended. I also discovered I was mixing with people from the Congregational Church, that had first began ordaining women in Great Britain in 1917. The Methodist Church, too, has been ordaining women for nearly thirty years. This changed the way I thought about women's roles. I also began working with married ministers and priests. Being married clearly makes a difference to their ministry. Some of the restrictions that I had taken for granted as a Catholic seemed meaningless.

A pivotal time for Lavinia Byrne was the period of the debate about the ordination of women in the Church of England. The first Anglican woman priest, Florence Li, had been ordained by the Bishop of Hong Kong in 1944. Discussion of the issue within the Anglican communion continued until two more women were ordained in Hong Kong. In 1971, eleven women were ordained priests validly but irregularly by three retired bishops in Philadelphia. Four more were ordained in Washington in 1975. In 1976 the US Episcopal Church passed legislation for women to be legally ordained. Canada also allowed the ordination of women in 1976, and New Zealand in 1977. By 1989 the Episcopal Church had ordained a woman bishop. After a long and difficult debate, the Australian Anglican Church ordained its first women in 1992. At the same time the Church of England slowly worked its way through the arguments about the ordination of women.

So when the debate about the ordination of women took place in the Anglican Church, I was one of twenty people with a ticket to the gallery in virtue of the ecumenical work I had done with the Church over the proceeding years. It was a very powerful experience to watch the debate take place in the Church of England, to see the votes come in, and to realise that the ordination of women had been carried. I then went to both the houses of Commons and of Lords to hear the women's ordination debate in those places. The air I breathed was full of the narrative of people who were either preparing for ordination or who supported the ordination of women.

When I first began working with the Jesuits at Heythrop, I was caught up in a wonderful world of equality, because my colleagues were keen to nurture the gifts I had and to encourage me to read more widely. I was actually the reviews editor of *The Way* for several years. I had equal access with the Jesuit priests to all the decision-making that we did. That was a time of real change for me, because I would hear stories of certain of my IBVM sisters who were also moving out into other ministerial work in the Church, but they learned very quickly that in the average parish set-up the sisters were always in an ancillary role.

In 1988 I published a book called *Women Before God*. I cannot tell you what an impressive set of letters I received from women from both the Catholic and the other churches telling me that I had written a book that made a lot of sense to them. What fascinated them was the fact that I held up the idea that women can represent Christ, that women can be 'Christ-bearers'. This does not mean that they are to be passive, meek and mild. I argued that women bring particular skills into the public domain and that nowadays we see this everywhere. Women have the ability to listen, to use both hemispheres of their brain at the same time, and as a result they are good at multitasking. All of that comes naturally to women. In the book I quoted something that Pope John Paul I said when he was still Cardinal of Venice. He claimed that a wife will always want her husband to eat well, that she will want to be a 'queen of the sparkling floors' and to bring up the children as 'little flowers', while still maintaining the ability to read Shakespeare and Tolstoy. This really annoyed me. Sure, the cardinal was admitting that women can multitask, they can do all of those things, that they can do housework and be cultured at the same time. The problem for me was he was so sentimental about it, and that trivialised women's achievements. Women are not just 'queens of the sparkling floors', because that assumes that man, 'king of the universe', is going to come in and walk all over them!

Then I thought, perhaps this is more part of the macho Mediterranean culture than it is of Anglo-Saxon culture. But something inside me rebelled when I read this. As a British person, I was brought up to believe that democracy is not a gift but a natural human right. I also grew up surrounded by highly intelligent women who ran completely autonomous organisations, the girls' convent boarding schools into which some rather elderly priest was brought to celebrate mass. Now, school chaplaincy has changed a great deal since that time, and very different sorts of priests now function as chaplains in schools. But at the time, the sisters were so evidently in control and exercised leadership roles without turning a hair. To move out into the public life of the Church and to find that women were expected to be in subservient roles seemed such an anachronism. The very gifts of leadership that come to women naturally through organising their homes, families and budgets make them ideal persons to lead in Church communities.

When I left Heythrop in 1989 and began working with the Council of Churches, I gained extraordinary access to the major libraries of the British Christian communities. I had just begun work on a book called *The Hidden Tradition*, which was an anthology of women's spirituality. Through my access to these libraries I discovered material that I had not realised existed, which is why I came to entitle the book the *hidden* tradition. For instance, in the nineteenth century, Catherine Booth, the wife and co-founder of the Salvation Army with William Booth, wrote: 'Who should dare to put my light with my lamp which God has lit under a bushel; who should presume to cast women out of the Church's operations?' She wrote that 150 years ago! I was also impressed by things that Quaker women had written about God's direct access to them, and also by some of the great Anglican laywomen at the beginning of this century, particularly Maude Royden, a social worker, preacher at the Temple Church in London and editor of the women's suffrage magazine, *The Common Cause*. Another was Dorothy L. Sayers, a vicar's daughter who was extraordinarily intelligent and learned: she translated the whole of Dante and wrote detective stories. She said: 'Perhaps it is no wonder that women were first at the cradle and last at the cross. They had never met a man like this man.' The sense that women were known and recognised by God, and that women had been active in the Church's service for so long, brought something into the light for me. And then I re-read some of Mary Ward's writings, particularly a series of conferences she gave in 1616, where she said: 'And it will be seen in time to come that women will do much.' It struck me that maybe this is the time that she envisaged, a time when women can and must do much.

Once I finished *The Hidden Tradition*, I began gathering books, and over the next five years I amassed a collection of 3000 of them by and about women. From these books I produced two further anthologies. The first was *The Hidden Journey*, about women missionaries and their work in the service of the Gospel. Again I came upon many extraordinary women such as Mary Slessor, a Scottish Presbyterian, who in 1875 went to Calabar in southeast Nigeria, and eventually persuaded the people there to stop the slaying of twins, human sacrifice and various forms of cruelty. She died in 1915 and is revered by the people of Nigeria to this day. They said of her, 'Her skin was white, but her heart was black'.

Other missionary women worked in China, India and places in the Far East where child prostitution was practised, and they condemned it roundly. These were women of great integrity and courage in the service of God, and they were also women who enjoyed real autonomy in their ministry. The final book in my trilogy was called *The Hidden Voice* and was about the emergence of women as educators, and in public life. I was particularly impressed by the great number of daughters of parsonages and manses who went out to campaign for the women's suffrage movement. They adapted the sorts of things that we use in Church – medals, ribbons, lights, colours and statues – in order to pursue universal suffrage for women.

The debate about the ordination of women in the Church of England took place in 1992. But the debate was not just about the Church of England; it was about all women in the UK. The general public was very aware of the debate and there was considerable media coverage. So there were glasses raised in wine bars and pubs all over London when the vote for women's ordination was passed. People throughout the country were genuinely thrilled for the Anglican women. The *Sun*, the popular newspaper, had an extraordinary headline the day after the vote was passed: 'Vicars in knickers!'. Obviously, this is popular journalism, but the fact that the decision was noted even in the most popular of newspapers says something about how the issue spoke to public consciousness.

Having been at the debate and heard the arguments both for and against, I was not surprised when my publishers contacted me and asked me to write a book about the ordination of women in the Roman Catholic Church. There was a clear perception that the arguments would now be picked up by Catholic women and that campaigning would begin in Catholicism. As I was doing a job that required me to think about the position of women, I was very happy to take on the proposed book. It was a logical step after all that I had written about women previously. The book was called *Woman at the Altar*. I had it read by a number of people before I submitted it for publication. This was not because I believe in censorship in the sense that a book has to be cleared by some foreign and possibly hostile authority, but because good sense dictates that if you write something, you should subject it to the judgment of other people in order for it to be as good as possible.

I have often been asked about the key arguments for the ordination of women. For me the question of representation is at the heart of the matter: can women represent Christ? If they can, then they must be able to represent Christ at the altar, just as they can in so many other places in public. If you take the logic of the argument that says that only a man can represent Jesus in the action of the mass, then you would only be able to have Jewish men ordained as priests, because there is a sort of absolutist, biological determinism embedded in that argument. It just does not hold water that only people who are constructed physically according to one of the normative expressions of human life can represent Christ. It trivialises the rest of human experience. Here it is also worth mentioning another negative aspect of the Catholic argument. This aspect trails the activity of Eve as temptress in the second creation narrative at the beginning of the Book of Genesis, right up to the present day, and plants this notion like a deadly seed inside the heads of women, so that they are made to feel that somehow they corrupt and tempt men. That is pernicious. That is not about honouring and respecting human life in all of its manifestations.

The arguments against the ordination of women really break down into two categories: one is historical and claims that women have never been ordained before; the other is a kind of constellation of things that are fundamentally emotional, but they usually get called 'theological'. The historical argument does not hold water. The BBC recently produced a documentary called, oddly enough, 'The Hidden Tradition', which presented clear archaeological evidence that women in the early Church were ordained and led the community in eucharistic worship. The argument against this is that these women were actually members of heretical communities. But it is so easy to stamp the label 'heretical' onto something you want to reject. In that way you drive it underground and make it hidden, which is precisely why the documentary was called the *hidden* tradition. I want to know who hid the experience of women in the early Church. In our time, as women have emerged into every other sphere of public life – the law, medicine, the academy, industry, the armed forces – it becomes a mockery for the Church to deny women access to the public domain and maintain that our work is private.

Then you get the series of arguments that are basically emotional, but which are put in a kind of theological language that can be quite intimidating. They do seem to suggest that women are made *for* men instead of *with* men. They presuppose that women were created for a servant role. They are often very beautifully phrased: they constantly talk about the 'dignity and mystique of women'. But if you say that dignity can only be expressed in the home and in the private sphere, you are restricting God's work through women. There is a wonderful line from the poet Thomas Blackburn which I put at the beginning of *Woman at the Altar*: 'God, through his daughters here, is taking aim.' When I worked with Anglican women deacons they would often say, 'I feel God is calling me to the priesthood'. I would reply: 'Nonsense. Don't use the phrase "I feel" because it suggests the same as "I feel like a can of Diet Coke, or a Mars Bar ice cream". What you are talking about is much more significant. You are telling me that you believe that God is calling you to priesthood, and that has been manifested to you as a call that your Church recognises.'

Returning to the story of *Woman at the Altar* just when it was being printed in May 1994, Pope John Paul II issued the Apostolic Letter, *Ordinatio Sacerdotalis*, reserving ordination to men only. It was the death knell of discussion of this issue in the Catholic Church because, in effect, the pope was saying that there is no case to be made and that all discussion must now cease. Since the book was being printed, I tentatively contacted the editorial director of my publishers and asked that the pope's document be included at the back of the book. At great inconvenience, the publishers included the papal text. So what the pope says ends up as the final word in the book. When the book was published in 1994, it went out as a total text. After publication nothing was said to me other than compliments about my attempt to hold the middle ground, and to write in a journalistic way describing the events of the previous three years. This was very much a book of the moment. It did not claim to be anything particularly theologically intense. It was simply a faithful record of what had happened, and what I had experienced as an onlooker.

Then, out of the blue, on 21 June 1995, the Chilean Archbishop Francisco Javier Errazuriz Ossa, at that time secretary of the Congregation for Institutes of Consecrated Life and Societies of Apostolic Life in Rome [the section of the Roman bureaucracy that supervises religious orders], wrote to the general superior of the Institute of the Blessed Virgin Mary. The letter said:

> Recently Sister Lavinia Bryne, IBVM, has published a book entitled *Woman at the Altar.* This book advocates the ordination of women as priests in the Catholic Church, a position which is counter to the teaching of *Ordinatio Sacerdotalis*, the Apostolic Letter issued by our Holy Father, Pope John Paul II, on 22 May 1994. Though the volume contains the text of the Apostolic Letter as an appendix, and though there is an explanatory note on page 9 which explains the book was written before publication of the Apostolic Letter, the author proposes her

thesis with no recognition of our Holy Father's pontifical magisterium and she expresses no acceptance of that magisterium. Further, she states 'I also write quite deliberately as a Roman Catholic woman and a religious sister.'

The letter went on to ask whether the general-superior had permitted the book to be published. I was able to write back and remind the superior-general that I had a letter from her predecessor supporting my writing apostolate, and encouraging me to liaise with the English provincial-superior on this matter. So she wrote back to Archbishop Ossa explaining this, and no more was heard about it.

Then, suddenly, in 1998, Archbishop Tarcisio Bertone, secretary of the Congregation for the Doctrine of the Faith in Rome, wrote to the general-superior of the IBVM saying that the Holy See was concerned that the book was still being distributed. It had been published in the UK by Mowbrays, a secular publishing company associated with Cassells. There was no way that I could have had the book withdrawn from sale. A contract bound both writer and publisher. The people at Mowbrays had published the book in good faith, and they have a right to earn their living. I had written the book in equally good faith at a time when the debate was free and open. So, as far as I was concerned, the case was closed.

But in the US the book was published by Liturgical Press of St John's Abbey, Collegeville, Minnesota. Apparently, they had done a reprint just before the local Catholic Bishop of St Cloud, Bishop John F. Kinney, at the request of the CDF, asked them to withdraw the book from circulation. Liturgical Press acquiesced and the book was withdrawn. This was all done behind my back, and the first I heard of it was when a second letter from Archbishop Bertone of the CDF was sent to the general-superior. He said: 'This Congregation wishes to inform you that Liturgical Press of St John's Abbey has recently agreed to discontinue the sale of this book. This action undertaken by St John's Abbey resolves the problem of the continued distribution of *Woman at the Altar.*' Certainly it resolved the problem of US distribution to the CDF's satisfaction, but it was far from the end of the problem for me.

Before getting to that, however, another question occurred to me: I sometimes wondered what Liturgical Press did with the remaindered copies. I have been told that they burned them. Do we still burn books in the late 1990s? Did they put them in the incinerator, so that the monks' toes could be warmed by *Woman at the Altar*, and their bathwater heated? Or did they pulp it? Or are the books sitting vegetating in some monastic attic somewhere? I was told 1400 copies were withdrawn from distribution. Meanwhile, the publishers in this country continue to distribute it freely, and they have found another North American publisher, so it is still available in the US and Canada. It is also available on the Internet.

But back to Bertone's letter. He also told the general-superior of the IBVM: 'This Dicastry asks you to inform Sister Lavinia Byrne that it will be necessary for her to correct the errors disseminated by her book by making some form of public declaration of assent to the specific teaching of the magisterial documents *Humanae Vitae* and *Ordinatio Sacerdotalis*. Such a public statement is all the more necessary given Sister Lavinia Byrne's public activities on behalf of the Church, and, as mentioned in your letter, on behalf of the Holy See.' This last clause referred to some work I had been doing for the Pontifical Council for Interreligious Dialogue. So apparently one part of the Vatican [the CDF] does not talk to another part [the Council for Interreligious Dialogue]. Bertone continued: 'Therefore this Congregation asks you to provide it with the text of Sister Lavinia Byrne's public statement of assent to the teaching of the Church at which time this unfortunate case will be considered closed.'

The thing that I found personally distressing in all of this was that these people did not write directly to me. I did not deal face to face with somebody who knew me, who experienced me as a person, with my vitality and energy. Everything I do, I do in the service of the Gospel in this country. If the CDF knew me, I genuinely believe that they would not have written to the general superior as they did. Also, they would not have demanded that I make a public statement in support of two very specific bits of Catholic teaching: namely, the encyclical *Humanae Vitae*, condemning birth control, and *Ordinatio Sacerdotalis*, excluding the ordination of women. People have been puzzled by the demand that I publicly accept the teaching on contraception in *Humanae Vitae*. How this arose was that in *Woman at the Altar* I said that there had been two scientific facts this century which had transformed the way in which we experience human reality. One was the landing on the moon, whereby we saw the Earth for the first time from space. That relativised things and we realised fully for the first time that we live on a tiny, frail, fragile, blue-green marble hanging in space. The other was the invention of the contraceptive pill. You may be against it, but as a straightforward piece of journalistic information, I believe that the invention of the pill has completely changed women's self-perception. They have gained access to the control of their own fertility. That changes everything. So I was not surprised that *Humanae Vitae* was singled out.

The things that hurt me most in this war of nerves and attrition between the CDF and myself was first, that they did not know me; second, that they did not know my work; and third, that they thought it a good idea to ask me to sign up to two discrete bits of Catholic teaching, taking no account of my assent to the rest of the Church's teaching. You trivialise people's religious experience by demanding to know, 'Do you believe this or that particular teaching?' I would have thought an attempt would be made to discern from the overall quality of my committed life in the service of the Gospel, whether I was what Mary Ward called 'a loyal daughter of holy mother Church'. But no attempt was made to discern if this was true or not; it was simply, 'Do you accept this and that particular bit of teaching?'.

As Cardinal Basil Hume commented later, if I accepted this demand it would have been the thin end of the wedge. If people in public life like me were forced to sign up to discrete pieces of doctrine, it would be the beginning of a whole wave of demands that all types of people publicly support certain bits of teaching, as though these were the most important things the Church had to say. If they had asked me to sign the creed, or the great Vatican II document *Gaudium et Spes* on the Church in the modern world, I might have thought differently because that produces an image of the Church which is entirely positive and fruitful. I have consistently said that I would be happy to profess my faith in what anyone entering the Church as a convert had to say; namely, to recite the Nicene creed and the declaration that I believe whatever the Catholic Church believes and teaches.

Then there was the question of a *public* statement: if I were to make any kind of public assent to two particular documents, it would make the Church in Britain a laughing stock. There was no way I was prepared to do that, because it would confirm the public perception that the only things that the Catholic Church was interested in were sex and keeping women in their place. I was not prepared to make a fool of the Church like that. So I held out.

The reaction of my family was interesting. My father is dead, and my mother, who is half-French, had inherited a certain amount of anti-clericalism from my *grandmère*. Before all the troubles with the CDF, I was taken out of my mother's will with my consent, because it seemed to me that my brothers and sister needed the money more than I did. Eventually, I thought I ought to tell my mother about this CDF investigation. She was nearly ninety at the time, and very frail. With my elder brother, I talked her through what was happening. I told her that if things got really ugly I might actually be dismissed by the Vatican from the IBVM congregation. She was lying on the sofa with a blanket over her legs. She immediately swung her legs over the edge, stood up very shakily, and said, 'I am going to go and see the solicitor now.' He lived across the street in her village. Her intention was to put me straight back into the will, and in fact there is a codicil now which says that if the Church dismisses me, I should inherit my share of the estate. I was very moved by this immediate, concrete gesture of support which was so generous and practical.

Since I don't expect that the CDF reads every Catholic book that is published, the question of who reported me to Rome arises. When I worked at the National Council of Churches I became aware of a group known as the Association of Catholic Women. They are, for the most part, very middle-class, well-educated and leisured women, with time on their hands to write letters to Rome. Two of them invited me to the London Royal Air Force Club. I arrived on my bicycle, tied it to the outside railings, brushed myself down and went in. It was quite a witty experience, because I felt quite at home in the club. I don't know if I was supposed to be overawed by it. The three of us had a perfectly pleasant lunch together, during which I 'entertained' them by talking freely about my work and my background; I am fairly well connected in the Catholic Church in the UK. It was all very charming. Then they withdrew to the Ladies' Room, where they clearly decided that I was not going to be allowed to get away with this. When they returned, they demanded to know if I supported 'Church teaching' on questions like contraception, abortion and a whole range of other things. I did not feel the slightest bit accountable to them. I am accountable to God and my conscience. So I gave them a run for their money. But from then on I knew that I was actively targeted by them. It would not surprise me to know that certain of their members might have delated me to Rome but, I must say, I can't be sure of that.

Initially my religious community found it quite hard to support me. When the letter from the CDF first arrived, they were frightened; it was written in very adversarial and confronting language. The general feeling was that if something came from the CDF that said I was to make a public statement, it had to be obeyed. The general-superior of the IBVM, Sister Annunciata Pak, was put in an extraordinarily difficult position, so I went to see her. I could see she was anguished over this whole affair and, on one level, just hoped it would go away. I was anguished myself, because from the description I have given of my background it is obvious that my Catholic identity is at the core of my very being. When the whole thing became public I was drenched with letters and emails from all around the world, and many of them said: 'It must be difficult for you. Why don't you leave the Church? Why not pull out?' But I persisted in saying there is no way that I am going to leave the Roman Catholic Church, first because I have done nothing wrong and second because it is my spiritual home. It is where I belong. You can't ask somebody to give that up lightly. So there was conflict within the order because my superiors had a huge amount of strain put on them, to the extent that one of the letters sent by the CDF was never shown to me because it was deemed 'too disturbing'. Personally, I think that infantilises people. Of course everything should be shown to the person involved because you can't make out a case for yourself if you do not know all that is being said about you. I guess that the letter threatened me in some way with dismissal from the IBVM.

I really resent the fact that my superiors were put in that situation because it did not bring out the best in them. It has been an extremely painful time for them, as well as for me. Because the community found the whole thing so hard to accept, I was very unsupported, even with canonical advice. I simply had to activate my own networks. I did not get in touch with anyone specifically able to help me in terms of canon law. It shows the lack of resources that women's religious communities have in comparison to their male counterparts. But I was supported by many, including England's senior bishop, the late Cardinal Basil Hume, OSB, the Archbishop of Westminster.

I finally decided that if the CDF was asking me to make a public statement, the whole case should be in the public domain. So when John Cornwell, a journalist from the *Sunday Times*, contacted me and asked if we could have a chat, I was very happy to talk to him. Subsequently, an article was published in the *Sunday Times*. I also talked about the affair on a program I do regularly on BBC Radio 4, called 'Thought for the Day'. I talked about my feelings of fear and pain at having been so threatened. Curiously, by going public I got it out of my system; it was less of a private wound that I was carrying around which was turned in on me. I had actually got very depressed and unwell.

I think that the CDF people who write these letters should know that they cause intense pain. These are not just a couple of ideas banging around in somebodys' head, but are about one's root identity as a Roman Catholic. It was only after I had gone public that I realised how much secrecy wounds people. It was the kind of secrecy that even excluded Cardinal Hume from knowing what was going on. He only found out about it because I talked to somebody at the Bishops' Conference Secretariat about going public, and it was he who told the cardinal. I was told that Cardinal Hume was really angry and asked to see the English provincial of the IBVM. I went to that meeting, where he was extremely supportive of me. He said: 'This is not about obedience. It is about justice.' He was clear that I had written the book in good faith and this CDF judgment was, as it were, being made retroactive. That seemed to him to be acutely unjust.

As a result of the meeting with Cardinal Hume, he wrote to Bertone on 15 February 1998:

> Your Excellency,
> On Monday, 14 September I met with Sister Lavinia Byrne, IBVM, and her Provincial, Sister Cecilia Goodman. The purpose of our meeting was to discuss the aftermath of the publication of Sister Lavinia's book, *Woman at the Altar*. I explained to the two sisters that I had no mandate to interfere in the affairs of their religious institute. I also said that whereas I had to make certain that the teaching of the Church was known and accepted by the Catholics of England and Wales, at the same time I had to ensure that no harm would come to the Church. I, too, had to be concerned that every individual be treated with justice and charity.
>
> Having considered the present matter carefully, having spoken with Sister Lavinia and her Superior, taking also into account the sensitivities of people in our country, at a delicate moment in the Church in this country and abroad, I have concluded that I must advise, and strongly, that no further action be taken by the Congregation [for the Doctrine of the Faith] in the matter of Sister Lavinia's book.
>
> You will recall how Sister Lavinia had explained that her book, *Woman at the Altar*, was completed and with the publisher when the Holy Father issued his document entitled *Ordinatio Sacerdotalis*. It was Sister Lavinia who insisted that *Ordinatio Sacerdotalis* should be printed at the end of her book, even though this caused the publishers considerable inconvenience.
>
> I have read Sister Lavinia's press release of 1 August 1998 and

this confirmed my view that no further action should be taken. Sister Lavinia wrote: '*Woman at the Altar* was a book of that moment. There is no way in which I or any other theologian could write it nowadays. I have not spoken in public or lectured about the question of priestly ordination since I was asked not to by my legitimate superiors of the Institute of the Blessed Virgin Mary in July 1997. I should add that I believe and profess all that the Holy Catholic Church teaches and proclaims to be believed by God.' This statement was given publicity in the press.

Sister Lavinia is a much respected person in this country, and not only in the Catholic Church. She has done much good, and will continue to do so. I am sure the Congregation will act wisely and with prudence and now leave the matter to rest. Any other policy will be harmful for the Church in this country. Please accept my advice.

Yours respectfully, Basil Hume, OSB, Archbishop of Westminster.

I found that letter so supportive because the cardinal heard the logic of the chronology. I wrote that book before thinking about women's ordination was condemned.

I am not personally acquainted with any of the people in Rome who have been so adversarial in this case. They don't know me, I don't know them. I have a sense that the universe they occupy is very removed from the one I occupy. I have travelled extensively: I have seen the Church in the US, Canada, the Philippines, the Caribbean, Peru, India and Australia, and I have seen Catholic ministry and action on a scale that is heroic. And yet there are people who sit in darkened Roman offices, whose first concern seems to be with something very different from the concerns of most of the Catholics I have met.

There is an expression that is being used a lot lately: recently, I heard someone describe herself as 'post-Catholic'. That deeply saddens me. I want the Church of the future to be alive, and for it to offer spiritual resources to people and for it to empower them through the life of faith. How do you best secure that kind of energetic, empowered Church? What kind of bureaucracy should go with it? I wonder if we do not need a kind of 'post-Vatican' Church, one in which the way the Church is administered actually moves it into the twenty-first century. We need a much lighter mechanism for organising the Church, something much fleeter of foot, much more transparent, much more accountable. We need a Church structure which is missionary, zealous and apostolic. This would require a complete overhaul of what I see as the 'Whitehall' of the Church. In British politics, Whitehall administers what parliament decides, and it seems to me that the administration of the Church is out of kilter with the decision-making structures of the Church. True, there is a sense in which Whitehall at least is responsible to parliament. But this is not true of the Vatican, especially when we have a sick and weakened pope. It is tragic that the Church does not have law courts that are available to Catholics. Similarly it is sad that there is no system whereby representatives of the churches cannot come together to work with each other and not, as it appears in the CDF's attitude to me, against each other.

The Roman Catholic Church in England and Wales exists in a very secular world. That is part of Catholicism's attraction. The leading light in the Church was Cardinal Hume. He said things simply and accessibly. He would make statements such as, 'Prayer is as natural as breathing'. Anybody can hear that. He made prayer and the spiritual life very accessible to people. People experienced him as a prayerful man who wanted people to be close to God. That was his pulling power. Since his death in June 1999 we have no one like that, and we miss him a great deal. Catholics are a minority in the UK. We don't have power or influence, except that which we create ourselves.

Belief in this country is hugely in decline. Whole generations of people have left our schools knowing nothing about religion. The Catholic schools have done a good job, but there is a bit of a feeling around that once you are confirmed, you drop out for a few years. Maybe you come back to the Church, maybe you don't. Ministry among students in colleges and universities is of a very high quality, but having said that there are people who don't persevere, who lose the plot. There is also a worrying drop-out among women in their forties. They have brought up their children, they have done their best and suddenly the Church seems to have very little to offer them, so they quit. Priests are very happy to use women's talents and generosity, but they find it much harder to offer anything nourishing to them largely because of the discipline of celibacy which creates such an unfamiliarity with women. Certainly, some priests work collaboratively, and there are some things being done in the seminaries to improve things.

Since my major ministry is media and the public face of the Church, I have become very conscious that there is a genuine problem in a post-modern world with the idea of preaching a gospel which claims to be an overarching narrative in a world where all our other narratives are fragmented. I am so grateful that I am a religious communicator and I try to model my language on that of Cardinal Hume. I remind people in the broadcasting I do that God is accessible, that God is present and that you don't have to know special theological words in order to communicate with God.

One of the ironies of this entire affair with the CDF is that I have written nineteen books and have made Catholic teaching, thinking and spirituality available to people in a form that is easy to understand and assimilate. I have written eight lives of the saints. I also wrote a book of reflections that was used by the BBC during Lent in 1997, which sold 6000 copies in seven weeks. The book I have worked on for Advent 1999 and the millennium, *The Dome of Heaven*, is selling really well. I know that it has been read by many members of parliament and that there is a copy in Number 10 Downing Street. This means that the work of evangelisation which I believe in profoundly and which I support by broadcasting and writing is effective in showing something of the life of the Church and the richness of the Gospel. The slot that I do regularly on Radio 4, 'Thought for the Day', is listened to by six million people. It is part of the 'Today' program, and its audience is a very influential one. Most leading politicians, lawyers, doctors, people in professional life and the business community listen. One time a gas man came to my home, and as he walked down to the cellar he said: 'You're that Sister Thing-a-me? I knew that I'd bump into you one day, because I always hear you on the radio!'

Therefore, it is very destructive for the CDF to be trying to silence a Catholic voice which is heard both in the Catholic community and beyond in the secular world. I always speak on the assumption that the people I am speaking to want to know something about God, but that they are not necessarily churchgoers, or even people who believe. But they do want to have a reflective insight, based on the news of the day, that opens a window in their mind, so that it becomes their thought for the day, not my opinion for the day. I think that the very brevity of the 'thought for the day' is very well adapted to modern life. If we were more disciplined in our discourse in the Church, if we did not waste words but used them accurately and as precision tools, the Gospel would immediately become more attractive to people. But pious utterances and futile theology which is not geared to what people are actually dealing with and their desire for a transcendent God, is just so many words wasted.

On 12 January 2000 Lavinia Byrne released a statement saying that she had resigned from the Institute of the Blessed Virgin Mary. She said: 'I remain a loyal and committed member of the Roman Catholic Church and an enthusiastic supporter of my religious community.' What happened was that, although nothing had been heard from the CDF since Cardinal Hume's letter to Bertone, Byrne felt that the Congregation had failed to withdraw their charges and apologise, that they had never dealt with her directly, and that her integrity had been questioned. She says in her statement: 'The deal seemed to be that I had to keep silent on these matters [contraception and ordination of women]. The sense that I could not get on with the rest of my life became overwhelming. It came to head on a recent visit to New York where well over three million Catholics were reported to have attended mass on Christmas Day. These people give a lot of money to the Church, and I asked myself how many of them were practising birth control. Yet it was me that the Congregation for the Doctrine of the Faith was pounding away at.'

Byrne's statement correctly pointed out that women religious did some of the most 'bold and adventurous' work in the Church, but that she felt that the 'faceless bureaucracy' of the CDF belittled them 'by questioning their integrity and undermining their commitment to the Gospel'.

At the core of her concern is the appalling way in which the CDF and other Vatican dicasteries deal with people: they simply refuse to interact with them directly, instead treating them as though they were objects. I agree with Byrne. Once the CDF process begins there is this constant sense that you are a child and that you will only be dealt with by the Church authorities through your 'parents'. It is as though you are not capable of answering for yourself and that what you say needs to be mediated by a 'responsible adult'. And for members of religious orders this responsble adult is the superior of the order. What is astonishing is that religious orders have generally colluded completely in impersonal CDF procedures by acting as conduits for accusations and condemnations. The Institute of the Blessed Virgin Mary has not been alone in this. Ultimately none of the orders has ever really taken a stand against the CDF, which they could do if they acted collegially and simply refused to participate in what Lavinia Byne has correctly called an 'infantilising' process.

In concluding this chapter, I will give the last word to two letter-writers to the Tablet *(29 January 2000). Two women wrote in to say, 'We were angered and upset to read that Dr Lavinia Byrne has felt obliged to leave her order, the IBVM. Her ideas have helped many Catholics and non-Catholics alike, and in particular given hope, firm good sense, and a sense of solidarity to many Catholic women who feel that our clergy-dominated Church is sadly out of touch with their needs and spiritual experiences.' Another, male, letter-writer quoted the words of a then young theologian writing just after Vatican II on the question of the primacy of conscience in the book* Commentary on the Documents of Vatican II *(edited by Herbert Vorgrimler (vol. 5,p. 134): 'Over the pope as the expression of the binding claim of ecclesiastical authority, there still stands one's own conscience, which must be obeyed before all else, if necessary even against the requirement of ecclesiastical authority. This emphasis on the individual, whose conscience confronts him with a supreme and ultimate tribunal, and one which is beyond the claim of external social groups, even of the official Church, also establishes a principle in opposition to increasing totalitarianism.'*

The young theologian who wrote this was none other than Father Josef Ratzinger.

CHAPTER 7

Protocol Number 399/57/I:
Hans Küng

Hans Küng is now in his early seventies. Physically, he looks to be in his early fifties. This is the result of hard work and a very disciplined lifestyle. While he retired from Tübingen University in the winter semester of 1995–96, his work days are still up to eighteen or nineteen hours long when he is writing, and for years he has travelled constantly throughout the world giving lectures and seminars. A typical day in November 1999 saw him just returning home to Tübingen from Augsburg, before leaving in two days for Jordan, then going on to South Africa the following week.

For the past forty years Küng has been the world's most famous and accessible theologian, one of the very few religious thinkers whose works can be found in airport bookshops. At least twenty-seven of his books have been translated into English, and have sold hundreds of thousands of copies in many other languages. One reason for his popularity is his clarity of exposition. Leonard Swidler, a long-time friend who has often translated him into English, says, 'The flowing style of Küng's books (and the ease with which they can be understood) is due not least to the "oral testing" of the text by reading it aloud.' He does this by writing every page twice by hand, then he dictates it, listening at the same time to the flow of the sentence. He then goes over it again and finally hands it to an assistant for editing. It is this care with the text that gives Küng's books the 'feel' of direct speech.

Swidler says that Küng's other great characteristic is truthfulness. While some theologians fudge their conclusions and call contradictory or mutually exclusive Church statements a 'form of development', Küng tells his readers the truth: they can't both be true, so we have to admit that one of them was a mistake. It is precisely this directness and honesty which has made him a thorn in the side of the CDF. An example from recent Church history illustrates this: in the 1832 encyclical Mirari Vos, Pope Gregory XVI (1831–1846), threatened with revolts in the Papal States, called freedom of conscience and religion a 'derangement' and a 'pestilential error'. This teaching was re-enforced in similar language by his successor, Pius IX (1846–1878), in the Syllabus of Errors (1864). However, exactly 100 years later, Vatican II, in the Declaration on Religious Liberty, says religious freedom is founded 'in the very dignity of the human person as this dignity is known through the revealed word of God and by reason itself'. This statement could not possibly be construed as a 'development' of Gregory XVI's view; it is a contradiction. Küng is honest enough to point this out, but it is this which infuriates Church authority.

When you first hear him give a lecture you feel that there is something of the German academic about him. But when you meet him and get to know him, you discover an open, rather humble man who delights in the art of conversation. When you talk to Küng, he engages with you, listens, asks opinions, learns. As his close friend Walter Jens says, 'He loves dialogue, talk between equals, friendly conversation and cheerful, light parlando ... He finds monologues among friends wearisome; he would much rather learn something new than constantly be lecturing himself ... The culture of conversation shapes the scenery on the Waldhasen heights.' Küng lives in a three-storey, modern house, among a number of other elegant houses, on Waldhaser Strasse on the side of one of Tübingen's hills. There is a real sense in which Tübingen is the Cambridge of Germany. It is a lovely town with a kind of sixteenth-century feel to it, set in rolling hills on the banks of the Neckar River. It is physically dominated by the old ducal castle (it now houses the university institutes and museum), but it is the university, founded in 1477, which is the life-blood of the town. The great Philip Melanchthon lectured here from 1512 to 1518 before going to Wittenberg and joining Luther and the Reformation. With the Catholic Erasmus, Melanchthon was one of the most ecumenical men of *the sixteenth century. When Duke Ulrich of Württemberg adopted the Reformed faith in 1534, the university became a centre of Lutheran orthodoxy. For centuries the university has been a leader in the study of theology, and in 1817 a Roman Catholic faculty was added. Johann Adam Möhler (1796–1838), the great Catholic pioneer of ecclesiology, was professor of church history here from 1828. The university has an almost 200-year tradition of ecumenism. Hans Küng fits in well.*

Dialogue is a characteristic not only of the personality, but also of the theology of Küng. He always does theology in cultural context, respecting and engaging with other views and taking them into account as he develops his own. History also is central to his way of thinking. For him theology is a dynamic science, always 'developing' in the genuine sense in which John Henry Newman used the word. For the Spirit of God is never static, never confined by cultural constructs, historical contexts or dogmatic settings.

It is precisely the dynamic nature of Küng's theology – and personality – which leads to conflicts with those whose minds are static and whose opinions and lives are fixed. Küng's approach is the antithesis of the CDF's understanding of theology.

Ecumenism, in the broadest sense of the word, is at the heart of Küng's theology. In the 1960s he was an initiator of the dialogue between Catholics and Protestants with his major study of Karl Barth's theory of justification. Barth (1886–1968) is widely recognised as one of the greatest Protestant theologians of the twentieth century. Justification is the doctrine that deals with how a person is made right with God and saved, and it was one of the great dividing lines between Catholics and Protestants during the Reformation of the sixteenth century. While Protestants emphasised the sheer gratuity of God's grace and the necessity of faith for salvation (the famous cry was sola fides – faith alone), Catholics stressed the need for good works and the sacramental ministry of the Church. What Küng did was to reach across this largely artificial divide and show the compatibility between Barth's views and those of the Catholic tradition. His position was completely justified forty years later, when the Lutheran World Federation and the Pontifical Council for Promoting Christian Unity reached a final agreement on justification in the Augsburg Declaration of 1999.

In the early 1970s, Küng focused his theological energies on the structure of the Church, particularly papal infallibility, because it was these ecclesial doctrines that were the real obstacle to union between the Christian churches. In this context he often speaks of the cultural 'paradigm shifts' that Catholicism has omitted. Küng believes that for the past 500 years Catholicism has tried to maintain the medieval cultural paradigm in which the Church is all-powerful. But just as we cannot leave out parts of our human development, so the Church has had to confront the cultural shifts embedded in the sixteenth-century Reformation and the eighteenth-century Enlightenment.

From the mid-1970s, Küng's focus shifted to the possibility of Christian belief in the contemporary Western world, and to the obstacles to faith thrown up by philosophy over the last couple of hundred years. The key books of this period are his On Being a Christian *(1974),* Does God Exist? *(1978) and* Eternal Life? *(1982).*

Since the mid-1980s, Küng has been engaged in a profound dialogue with the great world religions. In this he has much in common with Tissa Balasuriya. As a result, his focus has shifted to the central question of the future of the world, and to the role that religion and ethics have to play in this. In 1991 he founded the Global Ethic Foundation, which is run out of the ground floor of his house on Waldhaser Strasse.

The CDF, by its actions in 1979, may have seized Hans Küng's so-called 'licence' to teach Catholic doctrine, but he remains a Catholic in the profoundest sense, and a priest held in the very highest standing. His affection, concern and interest in Catholicism have never waned. He remains one of the Church's most persuasive and widely read theologians, and one who still gives hope, inspiration and a sense of purpose to that vast group of contemporary, committed and intelligent Catholics, who have remained loyal to the Holy Spirit's call for a more open vision of the Church, despite all the condemnations, and all the attempts over the past thirty years to 'restore' a medieval vision of the Church. At the deepest level, Hans Küng is a man imbued with a profound and prophetic sense of hope.

I have always been proud that I was born into a German-speaking and traditional Catholic family in the rather conservative little town of Sursee, near Lucerne, in central Switzerland. The year was

1928. I would never have become a priest without the Catholic youth movement. We had a splendid assistant pastor in our parish, who was very good at working with young people, and he influenced me deeply. When I decided to become a priest I wanted to be like him, and I never expected to become a university professor. I attended a very liberal gymnasium [grammar school] in Lucerne, where I had a great deal of freedom. Even then there was co-education.

After school I entered the seminary for the Swiss diocese of Basel, and was almost immediately sent to Collegium Germanicum, the pontifical German college in Rome. I was a resident there from 1948 to 1955, and I did my entire priestly studies in philosophy and theology at the Gregorian University. During the whole time I was a student in Rome I was only allowed to go home once. However, it was in Rome that I realised that I had a chance to get a very good, classical Catholic education. At the Gregorian we were taught everything in Latin. One of my lecturers there was the Dutch Jesuit, Father Sebastian Tromp, who was to become famous as one of the leading conservative theologians at Vatican Council II. He became the secretary of the theological commission of the Council, and a theological advisor to Cardinal Alfredo Ottaviani, the then cardinal secretary of the Supreme Sacred Congregation of the Holy Office. At the Council Tromp and I were to be on opposite sides of the fence, but in the early days of my troubles with the Holy Office he supported me.

At the Germanicum we had to wear scarlet cassocks with a broad, black sash everywhere we went; in those days resident students at all of the national colleges had to wear a different coloured cassock. The story is that the Germans had to wear the scarlet cassock everywhere so that they could be recognised, because in past centuries they had a bad reputation for drinking and wild parties. Having lived for seven years in that kind of clerical outfit, I have completely lost my desire ever to become a cardinal! The irony is that my Roman training would have actually prepared me very well for a successful career in the Roman Curia. The spiritual director at the Germanicum was Father Wilhelm Klein, a Jesuit, and he had a great influence on me. He helped me to find my own way, so in those seven years I changed considerably, in the sense that the education we received and the cultural experience that we had in Rome gave us a chance to broaden our horizons. I was ordained priest in 1954.

I left Rome in 1955, spent some time in North Africa, which aroused my early interest in world religions, and then went to Paris, which even then was still viewed with a lot of suspicion in the Vatican. It was seen as a centre of the *nouvelle théologie*, condemned in Pius XII's encyclical *Humani Generis* [1950].This was the theological movement that formed an important part of the foundation of Vatican II, and it tried to integrate ministerial experience with theology, and to draw on the broad and rich tradition of biblical and historical resources in the Church. I did my doctorate in the Institut Catholique at the Sorbonne, graduating in 1957. That same year my dissertation was published as a book entitled *Justification: The Doctrine of Karl Barth and a Catholic Reflection*. In my dissertation I argued that there was a fundamental compatibility between Barth's views and Catholic views on justification. Nowadays, the debate about whether we are saved by faith or works seems unimportant, but it does touch on the important issue of how we respond as persons to God.

The approach I took in the book has been borne out by the ecumenical agreement reached between the Lutheran World Federation and the Catholic Church on 31 October 1999, which deals with the doctrine of justification. It took forty years to reach this accord, and it is widely recognised that my work was the first fundamental breakthrough on the issue. Apparently I was at the top of the list of those to be invited to the main celebration in Augsburg, but because of the mean and narrow-minded attitudes of some in Rome, my name was crossed out. I was not invited, but I felt that at least my work on justification had not been forgotten.

In those years of training, I learned a great deal from the wonderful generation of theologians who went before me, men such as Yves Congar, Henri de Lubac and Karl Rahner. After a brief time in pastoral work, in 1961 I was suddenly thrust into the limelight with my second book, *The Council and Reunion* (in the US it was entitled *The Council, Reform and Reunion*), especially because the editors of *Time* magazine put my photograph on their cover between Pope John XXIII and Martin Luther! I was rather shocked, for in those days being associated with Luther could be dangerous for a Catholic. The book set out a comprehensive and alternative agenda for the forthcoming Council that differed from the one articulated by the Roman Curia. Because there was enormous interest both inside and outside the Catholic Church in what the Council might achieve, many influential people read it, including probably John XXIII. This led to invitations to speak all over the world, especially in the US, where I was warmly welcomed in some dioceses but forbidden to speak in others.

In the meantime, back in 1960, after several more well-established theologians – including my fellow countryman, Hans Urs von Balthasar – had turned it down, at the age of thirty-three, I had been offered and took the chair of fundamental theology in the Catholic faculty at Tübingen University, even though I did not have my *habilitation* [the German post-doctoral lecturing qualification]. Josef Ratzinger came to the Tübingen Catholic faculty after Vatican II, and we were colleagues there between 1966 and 1969. In fact, we shared the honour of being called the 'teenage theologians' of Vatican Council II.

Actually, the Council gave me a new horizon on everything. As I look back on Vatican II, the great underlying thing that happened was the attempt to integrate two paradigm changes into the life of the Church that Catholicism had deliberately by-passed. The first was the paradigm of the Reformation with vernacular language in worship, participation of the laity in the liturgy, ministry and government of the Church, and the central importance of scripture and biblical studies. These were the important things that the Reformation had called for, and which the Catholic Church had rejected at the time. The second was Catholicism's acceptance of the paradigm of modernity and the Enlightenment. Thus the Council faced the questions of freedom of conscience and religion, which were pushed especially by the American bishops who had always lived with pluralism. But this shift also involved a new attitude towards the Jews and the other world religions. The Vatican II affirmation that even atheists can be saved if they follow their consciences went further even than the World Council of Churches had done to that point [if it had done so the World Council would have had problems with its fundamentalist members]. Unfortunately, while much of the work of Vatican II was done with a clear view towards the future, it was often only achieved by major compromise with the minority conservatives at the Council.

Because there were so many compromises, after the Council it was rather easy for the Roman Curia and the reactionaries to return eventually to formulas that allowed them to reinterpret Vatican II 'backwards'. The Church found itself gradually returning to the medieval paradigm that Vatican II had set out to leave behind.

The medieval paradigm only came in with the reforms of Pope Gregory VII [1073–85]. Here we have the assertion of the absolute primacy of the pope, the subordination of the laity to the clergy, and the law of celibacy. This is not essentially Catholic at all; rather it is a reflection of medieval culture and social structure. The Council of Trent in the sixteenth century confirmed the medieval paradigm against the Reformation, and the nineteenth-century papacy vehemently excluded modernity when it rejected the French Revolution, modern science and philosophy, and the new, more democratic concepts of the state and society. After Vatican II, the Roman Curia did everything it could to drag the Church back to this medieval, Counter-Reformation, anti-modern paradigm.

My troubles with the Holy Office go all the way back to 1957. My protocol number in the CDF's files is 399/57/i. The 'i' refers to the *Index of Prohibited Books*, and the '57' to the year 1957. So the file was opened in the days of my dissertation. I have to credit my teachers in Rome and Paris with the fact that the Holy Office did not act against me at that time. I later heard from one of the officials of the Holy Office, Father Franz X. Hürth, SJ, a well-known moralist who was behind most of Pius XII's moral encyclicals and statements on medical ethics and obstetrics, that the four Jesuits, including Tromp, who had taught me at the Gregorian University and who were consultors to the CDF, protected me. The *Council and Reunion* had no trouble because the German edition had a preface by Cardinal Franz König of Vienna, and the French translation one by Cardinal Achille Liénart of Lille.

But my next book, *Structures of the Church* [1962, English translation 1964], got into trouble with the Holy Office over the issues of ministry, the primacy and infallibility of the pope, and my evaluation of the Council of Constance [1414–18]. I argued that Constance's emphasis on the authority of general councils over the pope was a useful counterbalance to the emphasis on papal power at the First Vatican Council [1870]. As a result, I was invited during Vatican II to a rather solemn session with Cardinal Augustin Bea [who, despite his Italian-sounding surname was a German, born in Swabia], my own Bishop of Basel, and Bishop Karl Josef Leiprecht of Rottenburg-Stuttgart, in whose diocese Tübingen University was situated. I had also accompanied him to the Council as a *peritus* [expert]. There were also two professors from the Gregorian University present. Because Cardinal Bea had been a confessor in the German College when I was a student there, I knew I had nothing to fear. Their cross-questioning was rather gentle, and then they asked me to write up my answers in Latin. At the end of the meeting Cardinal Bea said, 'We shall see.' As a result, the whole thing was dropped.

At the end of the third session of the Council (14 September to 21 November 1964), I wrote a highly critical article on what had happened, and especially on the imposition by Pope Paul VI of the now infamous *nota explicativa praevia*, an explicative note imposed in advance and according to which the relationship between episcopal collegiality and papal primacy in the *Constitution on the Church* was to be understood. After its publication I was called in personally by Cardinal Alfredo Ottaviani, secretary of the Holy Office. He said: 'How can you speak in this way about the pope? You were educated here; you are one of us. You should not say this type of thing.' He talked for a long time and I knew I had to win him over. Eventually I asked, 'Am I allowed to say something?' 'Ah, yes, of course,' he replied. I said, 'Eminenza, I am still very young!' Then Ottaviani's half-blind eyes and face lit up, and he said, 'Yes, yes! You are still a young man! How true that is! I was young once upon a time. And I got up to a few things too when I was young!'

After that we had a good conversation. Nevertheless, as I was leaving he said, 'You should not go down now to the Piazza di San Pietro and hold a press conference!' The Curia is very afraid of any kind of public statement.

Küng has spoken of the challenge that Vatican II faced to go beyond the medieval paradigm of the Church as an hierarchical institution focused on power and authority. But the Constitution on the Church *(its Latin title was* Lumen Gentium*) reflects one of the monumental compromises of the Council. The source of this compromise was the determination of Pope Paul VI to keep the small minority of reactionary bishops and members of the Roman Curia on side with the Council. He wanted to avoid division at all costs. The Church is described in chapter three of* Lumen Gentium *as essentially a hierarchical structure. But the first two chapters are based much more on the New Testament, and they envisage the Church as a sacramental community. Many theologians have argued that the two views are complementary, and that the hierarchy can exercise a genuine leadership in a community Church. This might possibly be the case if popes, bishops and priests actually acted in a Christ-like way. But the fact is they do not.*

What we have learnt over the three and a half decades since the Council is that the two models are not only not complementary, but are in fact mutually corrosive and tear away at each other in a destructive manner. The Church cannot be fundamentally both a community structure and a hierarchy. Part of the deep hostility and suspicion among Catholics at present arises because people are often unconsciously working out of one specific model, and are antagonistic to others working out of the other model. These contradictions and compromises were to effect Küng considerably.

A chronology with all of the documentation for the period up to 1979 can be found in Leonard Swidler (ed.), Küng in Conflict *(1981). Küng takes up the story:*

Things became more serious in 1967 with my book *The Church.* I started *The Church* during the Council as a systematic approach to ecclesiology, and I wanted it to be comprehensive. I saw that the vision of the Church that I and many others had interiorised, which was based on the New Testament, was simply not being realised. The inclusion of the third chapter on the hierarchy in Vatican II's *Constitution on the Church* was the clue that it was going to be business as usual as soon as the Council finished.

Just before Christmas 1967 I was in Switzerland, where I received a letter from Ottaviani. The Holy Office seems to have a tradition of sending out condemnations just before Christmas. Perhaps they think there will be less publicity then. *The Church* was already out in German, and the letter instructed me to stop publication of the book in other languages. So I immediately phoned the publishers in London, New York and Paris, and encouraged them to get the translations out as quickly as possible! The English editions were published early in 1968. French and Spanish editions also appeared that same year. The Italian and Portuguese editions came out in 1969.

This was the period of the changeover from the Holy Office to the CDF. In a way the inquiry about *The Church* seemed to fade away, perhaps because the CDF was too busy dealing with the fallout from *Humanae Vitae*, the encyclical on contraception which came out in 1968. However, clearly my file was still active because early in 1970 the new prefect of the CDF, the Serbo-Croat Cardinal Franjo Seper, wrote to me mentioning a *Modus Procedendi in Examine Doctrinali* [this refers to a CDF document that came out in 1971 and set out the procedure for doctrinal examinations of books]. The CDF had moved at their usual snail's pace: Paul VI had requested the *Modus Procedendi* six years previously!

It was *Humanae Vitae*, of course, which precipitated my book *Infallible? An Inquiry*, which was published in mid-1970. I had always tried to insist on a biblical foundation for all ecclesiology, and in *Infallible?* I questioned the whole idea of infallibility when 'the errors of the Church's teaching office have been numerous and grave'. Vaticans I and II have created a situation in which there is no limit to the arbitrary and autocratic action of a pope. 'He is, of course, bound by revelation and the beliefs of the Church ... But he himself decides, with the means that seem appropriate to him, what the meaning of this revelation is and what the true beliefs of the Church are ... If he wishes to, he can act as he chooses, even without the Church' (*Infallible?*, p. 86).

What I called for in the book was a reappraisal in which we would recognise that the Church was 'indefectible'. By 'indefectible' I mean that the Church can make mistakes and be in error at particular times and in specific circumstances, but that what is guaranteed is that the Holy Spirit would remain with the Christian community and never let it abandon the core teaching of Christ, what I called the Church's 'perpetuity in the truth'. I would argue that this represents a more ancient tradition than the teaching on infallibility.

On 12 July 1971, I was informed that the CDF were proceeding against *Infallible?*. The CDF case against *The Church* was eventually conflated with the one against *Infallible?* and the whole thing dragged on with letters back and forth until 15 February 1975, when Cardinal Seper eventually informed me that the case against the two books was 'closed'. However, this was not a peace settlement; it was just a lull in the war.

Throughout this whole period I was enough of a Roman among the Romans to know that you cannot win by debating the substantial theological issues with the CDF. They are always right, and there is no other possibility. It is just like dealing with the Kremlin: what they ultimately want is for you to say exactly what they say. So I always tried to keep the argument with them confined to the level of process. I had always said that I was willing to go to Rome for discussions, but laid down certain conditions. I demanded to see my file, I debated questions of procedure and language, criticised the injustice of their processes, requested the right to know who my defence lawyer was, and asked for some type of appeal process. Occasionally, you won a point with them, but they were always adamant that I would not be allowed to see my file, was not permitted to know who would defend me, and was given no right of appeal. Perhaps one of the reasons why they would not let me see my CDF file was that Luigi Ciappi, OP, in those days the official papal theologian, and later a cardinal, had written some fairly sarcastic and bitter things about me in his critique for the CDF of *The Church*. In the meantime, the German bishops had became involved in the case. After the sudden death of Cardinal Julius Döpfner of Munich and the appointment in 1977 of Josef Ratzinger as his successor, I had less protection from the hierarchy. My vulnerability was increased by the appointment of Cardinal Josef Höffner to Cologne, who came from a strong, tough, traditionalist Roman background. The election in 1978 of Karol Wojtyla as Pope John Paul II sealed my fate.

Right from the beginning of the Wojtyla papacy, it was clear that theologians perceived as 'dissenters' and 'critics', such as Küng, and the Dutch Dominican, Edward Schillebeeckx, were going to be forced to adhere to the Vatican line. Around the same time, in 1979, a book appeared in German focusing on Pius IX and the First Vatican Council. The author was the Swiss August Bernhard Hasler (1937– 80) and the English edition was entitled How the Pope Became Infallible *(1981). The book argued that the validity of the decrees of Vatican I concerning papal infallibility and primacy could be called into question, because the sizeable minority of bishops who opposed the decrees were placed under considerable duress both by Pius IX and by widespread calls in the ultramontane (pro-papal) Catholic press for the most extreme possible definition of infallibility. Hasler's book also argued that those who supported infallibility were driven by an authoritarian ideology that was deeply contrary to the teaching of Jesus. Küng discusses his relationship to the book, which raised a storm in Germany.*

In 1979 I wrote an introduction to *How the Pope Became Infallible*. This was an English summary of a much longer two-volume work that [Hasler] had published two years previously, and which had raised considerable controversy in Germany. It was highly critical of Pius IX, the pope at the time of Vatican Council I, and it questioned whether the Council was really free enough from papal pressure and outside forces to have passed the doctrines of papal primacy and infallibility.

About the same time I had also published a book, *Truthfulness:*

The Future of the Church, in which I asked Pope John Paul II to appoint an ecumenical commission to examine the whole question of infallibility. It was these two brief works that were used by the CDF to demand that the local bishop withdraw my *missio canonica* [the licence to teach Catholic theology]. I had always felt that the CDF and the German bishops were extremely legalistic, and that both would observe their own procedural rules. I quickly learned that they did not, largely because they were not able to. Like an army general staff, they had obviously planned their campaign to get rid of me from Tübingen, and they withdrew the *missio canonica* in a way that completely surprised me. The period from 18 December 1979 (again just before Christmas) to mid-April 1980, was the most cruel and painful of my life. This is what happened.

On 14 December 1979, the day before the CDF Declaration that I could no longer 'be considered a Catholic theologian, or function as such in a teaching role' was issued, a secret meeting was held in Brussels between the Dominican Archbishop Jérôme Hamer, then secretary of the CDF, the papal nuncio to Germany, Archbishop Mestri, Cardinal Höffner, and Bishop Georg Moser of Rottenburg-Stuttgart, who, according to the 1933 concordat between Nazi Germany and the Vatican, was the competent authority to grant the *missio canonica*. Clearly a strategy to deal with the issue was agreed upon at the Brussels meeting.

A press conference was called by Höffner for 11:30 am on 18 December, although a copy of the text of the CDF Declaration was not delivered to my house until about 10 am that same morning. I was away in Austria at the time, and the first I heard about it all was when a friend telephoned me. Höffner gave copies of the CDF Declaration, as well as another statement from the German Bishops' Conference, to the journalists at the press conference. Bishop Moser declared his intention of informing the minister for science and art of the state of Baden-Württemberg that my teaching commission had been withdrawn. I had talked to Moser some months before and asked him to let me know if he was under pressure at any time, so that we could work out what to do. I am convinced that if he had resisted the CDF's demands, things could have worked out differently. But he did not.

I said that the CDF does not keep to its own rules. These required that if the CDF was concerned with my introduction to Hasler's *How the Pope Became Infallible*, and my book *Truthfulness: The Future of the Church*, they actually had to begin a new process against me. Also, there is a passing mention in the Declaration of my views on Christology. This was a completely new claim; there had been no previous discussion of my Christology. Again, this was just slipped in without any respect for canonical formalities. So instead of the process being mandated by its own rules, the CDF moved directly to a condemnation which seriously impinged upon my employment. Höffner's statement to the media attacked my Christology in great detail, as though that were the key issue. He publicly maintained that I had constantly refused for ten years to go to Rome to discuss the CDF's concerns with my theology, when in fact I had two long meetings with Seper and Hamer in 1973 and 1975. And that was despite all my reservations with the refusal of the CDF to agree to basic conditions of justice for the dialogue between us.

The Declaration led to protests both in Germany and across the world, especially the English-speaking countries. I suspect that the CDF and the German bishops totally underestimated the reaction that they eventually faced. The irony is that the whole thing gave me freedom. I only met Cardinal Ratzinger once subsequent to this Roman intervention and his appointment as prefect of the CDF. He said to me, 'You look good.' 'Yes,' I said, 'I feel good, but this was obviously not the intention of your Congregation.' 'I do not know the intentions of my predecessor!' he replied. However, many people were confused and thought I had been dismissed from the priesthood. Actually, the chancery office of the Rottenburg–Stuttgart diocese issued a helpful explanation of what the CDF Declaration meant. In part, it said:

> Professor Küng ... remains after as before within the community of the Catholic Church. [He] is neither hindered in the exercise of the priestly office, nor has [he] been removed from its functionings. He remains a priest with all the rights and obligations that are connected with this office.

The effective result of the Declaration was that I was no longer a member of the Catholic theological faculty of the university, but I remained as professor of ecumenical theology. In the end the Church authorities only compromised because the university was returning for the next semester and they were afraid of student upheavals. So I was able to keep my chair. The Ecumenical Institute was moved out of the Catholic faculty and, although they disputed this right up to the last minute, I was still able to present students as doctoral candidates and for habilitation.

Looking back, I realise that I was liberated from a four-year cycle of boring lectures on dogmatics and the tedium of examinations. I was now free to focus on world religions and global ethics. I even had a significant increase in the number of students attending my lectures. Before 1979 I had about 150 students. From 1980 onwards the numbers gradually increased up to almost two thousand!

In retrospect, I can see a pattern in my life that I did not plan. In the 1950s I concentrated on justification, in the 1960s on the Church, the council, infallibility, ecumenism and reunion, and in the 1970s on a new basis for theology in *On Being a Christian* [1974], *Does God Exist?* [1978], and *Eternal Life?* [1982]. After the withdrawal of the *missio canonica*, I was now free to move from Christianity, Christian existence and the Church, to the world at large: to world religions, world literature and finally to the notion of a global ethic. It seems to me that this is an example of divine providence. *Hominum confusione, Dei providentia* – God's plan emerges from our human confusion. I felt an invisible hand in my life guiding me, even when things seemed to be negative, such as the Roman intervention in 1979. Looking back, things seem to have worked out perfectly.

As we move into the new millennium I think we are in a 'dark' period in Catholicism. We face a whole range of issues from the Roman refusal to acknowledge women and women's ministries, to the rejection of the validity of the eucharist of the other churches. But what I see as the central challenge for Catholicism is a radical reform of the structure of the Catholic Church. The vast majority at Vatican II felt that we had left the medieval structure of the Church behind, but embedded in the conciliar documents there was an ambivalence:

on the one hand collegiality, on the other, the same old affirmation of jurisdictional primacy with things such as the *nota praevia*. While we remain caught in this ambivalence, the Roman Curia is stronger than ever before. All this is compounded by an exodus of women from the Church, while the young feel alienated and find no place in the community, as I certainly did when I was young, and there is an acute shortage of effective priests. Cardinal Joseph Bernardin of Chicago mentioned to me the last time I saw him before he died [in 1999] that we also have a de facto congregational system; that is, every congregation follows the parish priest or, if they do not like him, they go to another parish. Most of this division is along progressive–conservative lines. This creates an impossible situation.

I am convinced that many of the cardinals who once found Pope John Paul II a great leader will actually be very relieved to elect a new one. I hope that they will admit that the barque of St Peter has become stranded on a reactionary sandbar. We have to return to the centre and recover the direction set by John XXIII, who remains the greatest pope of this century for me. We need another council – Vatican III. We have to recover the New Testament ecclesiological emphases, and reform the papacy in the light of a biblical vision of the Church.

Despite all the failures of the papacy and all the disillusionment we have experienced over the last quarter century, I remain convinced that a pastoral primacy in the spirit of the Gospel and in the image of the very fallible popes of the past – St Peter or St Gregory the Great or John XXIII – still has a future. I do not believe that the maintenance of a medieval dictatorship has any future. In German-speaking countries the credibility of Pope John Paul II is now at rock-bottom. In the US a recent major survey shows that support for this pope has completely dissipated (see *National Catholic Reporter*, 29 October 1999, p 12).

All this demonstrates that the influence of the pope is increasingly limited: he can constantly travel the world and lecture Catholics through sermons and encyclicals, but he has not been able to change their views on one single controversial issue, neither on birth control, nor abortion, nor euthanasia, nor even on ecumenism. So now the Roman Curia tries to exercise control through manipulation: for example, the appointment of reactionary bishops, demanding special licences to teach theology, the marginalisation of those (including bishops) of whom the Curia disapproves, and above all through the use of the Inquisition.

In the end none of it has worked, nor will it work. In fact, I think that if there was another Council, many of the conservative bishops would change, just as they did at Vatican II. The reality is that the vast majority of them are not convinced of the Roman agenda. Whenever you talk to bishops who are not absolutely stubborn or stupid, you will now find a great deal of agreement that things will have to change radically in the Church.

People often ask me: why do you stay a Catholic, why do you keep going, what is it that sustains you? I have always felt that I am as much a Catholic as any bishop or pope. This is not because I am a saint or morally or spiritually better than them, but because I know that throughout my life I have remained in the great Catholic tradition of two thousand years. I know that I am defending that great tradition, not a medieval paradigm which did not emerge until the eleventh century. Ultimately, I feel rooted in the Gospel itself. If anyone can show that my position is opposed to the Gospel, then I would say immediately, 'I am ready to correct myself.' But I am not ready to correct myself when I have scripture behind me and only the CDF against me.

Ultimately, of course, it is the doctrine of justification that is basic for me. But it is not a question of looking back to and debating the formulas of the sixteenth century. In today's world it is the individual self and his or her achievements that are emphasised. But what I learned in my early days doing the thesis on Barth remains basic: that ultimately, when you stand before God, it is not a matter of who you are or what you have achieved or how you feel you have failed. The real question is: have you kept an unshakable confidence in God, who will be for us all a gracious, forgiving and merciful judge?

The challenge for me is to say again and again, especially in my last hours: 'I am a poor sinner. Lord have mercy on me.' My unshakable confidence is that God will.

CHAPTER 8

Antipodean Heretic:
Paul Collins

It may seem a strange place to start my own story, but I want to begin with an event that has shaped my attitude as an older adult perhaps more than anything else. It was one of those defining experiences that come once or twice in lifetime and that fashion your attitudes and values for years to come. It happened in a wonderful natural place that is now destroyed.

I was ordained in July 1967 in my home city of Melbourne, and in January 1970 I was sent by my religious order to work in a parish in Hobart, Tasmania. Australia's only island state is somewhat isolated, lying due south of the east coast of the mainland. It also lies in the path of the Roaring Forties, the powerful winds that cut across the southern Indian Ocean from west to east. The winds and the weather patterns of 40 degrees south latitude, as well as isolation, have given Tasmania a unique and extraordinary natural environment. In Hobart I did all the usual parish work – celebrating masses, baptisms, weddings, visiting schools, and even acting as chaplain to the local Polish migrant community for a year or so.

But the most important thing that happened to me in Tasmania was that in 1971 I walked for two days to Lake Pedder, a then untouched wilderness area in the central-western part of the state. It was a uniquely beautiful place, a cathedral of nature, that was suggestive of a transcendent and transforming presence. For me that day at Pedder was both the locus and stimulus for an experience that put me in touch with a presence far beyond myself, something that I had never experienced before, even in the context of the Church. I hesitate to use the word 'God' here, for sadly that word inevitably comes loaded with personal connotations that I did not experience. But I know that at Lake Pedder I did face out into a transcendent and mysterious presence that touched me deeply. The sense of it has remained with me ever since.

Lake Pedder is now destroyed. It was so beautiful that it was incomprehensible that its destruction could ever have even been contemplated, let alone carried out. Yet, despite a massive public campaign to save the lake and its unique species, it was destroyed in 1972 behind a huge dam, for an un-needed hydro-electric scheme by a myopic state government, which was dominated by a Hydro-Electricity Commission that even today is still driven by an inane and unquestioned technologism. It was an immoral and sinful action and a triumph of the barbarians. We sometimes forget that stupidity, wilfulness and appalling small-mindedness can often lead to profoundly evil actions. It was the beginning of my sense that the natural world was a sacrament or icon of the divine presence, but that despite this it was very vulnerable. It was also the source of my deep outrage at what was happening to it.

While my revulsion at the time was real, there is a sense in which for a number of years I left the experience of Lake Pedder behind. For a decade or so more practical ecclesiastical affairs dominated my life. But somehow what happened to me that day sat there at the back of my mind, ready to return to consciousness when the moment was right.

At the beginning of 1973 I moved back to Sydney, where I taught Church history and helped run the ministry formation program in a seminary for mature men training for the priesthood. I also worked in a parish and did some part-time hospital chaplaincy. The mid-1970s were a very happy period for me and I was very much caught up in traditional ministry. I enjoyed it thoroughly. In 1976 I was appointed pastor in a very large inner-urban parish in the Sydney suburb of Randwick. But a number of things caught up with me in the late

1970s, not least of which was a disagreement with my provincial over the administration of the parish. It all eventually led to my resigning as parish pastor in 1977 and leaving Australia for post-graduate study at the Divinity School of Harvard University in Cambridge, Massachusetts. My years in the US were to be something of a turning point. They certainly gave me a chance to reflect on my home country from a very different perspective.

I had been born in 1940 in Richmond, then a tough, working-class suburb, in inner Melbourne. My parents ran a corner shop that sold all the basic foods, as well as cigarettes, candy and confectionery. The shop was open seven days a week for long hours. My parents subsequently bought a number of run-down shops, spending several years working them up, and then selling them for a small profit. By 1948 we were back in another shop in Richmond and at about the age of ten I began serving at the altar, first at St Ignatius Church, Richmond, the local parish which was run by the Jesuits. The parish church, on top of Richmond's highest hill and still visible from many parts of Melbourne's inner suburbs, was a fine nineteenth-century French-style gothic building. I recall especially the choir and the singing, and how well the old Holy Week and Easter liturgy was celebrated. Soon after this I also began serving mass at St Patrick's Cathedral in East Melbourne, perhaps the finest neo-gothic church anywhere in the English-speaking world. My father and uncle had also been altar boys there from about 1915, so my sense of connection with the cathedral was strong.

I mention this because I believe it had a cumulative effect. I belong to that generation and group of Catholics who do not despise the Church of the Counter-Reformation past. Instead, I respect it for all of the qualities and values that were embedded there, above all for the experience of divine transcendence that was a part of its milieu. Its influence was more cumulative and pervasive than direct and tangible, as on that day at Pedder, and it was always contextualised by the human reality and amusing frailty of the priests and brothers with whom I came in contact. I am certainly aware that this was not the experience of all Catholics of my time, but I do look back with appreciation for the foundation of faith that was laid in my life then. I think that nothing replaces the pristine and youthful experiences of spiritualty and faith, especially when they are conveyed through the medium of fine music and good liturgy.

My chronology makes me a classic product of Vatican II. The theology I learned was open to development and change, and the Church I inhabited as a young man embraced renewal and looked outward towards the world not as hostile, evil territory, but as a place permeated by the grace of God, as well as by the effects of sin. At the core of the theology I learned was the emphasis of the great Austrian theologian, Karl Rahner, on the complete permeation of the whole world by God's grace.

This still intimately underpins my belief that the natural world is itself a symbolic sacrament of transcendent presence. That is not to pretend that there is no evil or selfishness or destruction in the world, but it is to embrace the truth of the words of Jesus that, 'God so loved the world that he gave his only son' (John 3:16). The Greek word for 'world' here is 'cosmos' and it explicitly refers to the natural world. St Paul picks up a similar theological theme: for him the world is the product of God's creative love in Christ. If it is, it must mirror the splendour of God's creativity. Certainly, this what I experienced that day at Lake Pedder.

Some of us who grew up in the Church of the 1960s have never lost this vision of a Church open to the world. There is also a sense in which we have moved on and we are now in the post-post-Vatican II era. But the greatest failure of progressive Catholics in the period after Vatican II was our lack of insistence on enshrining in structural form the theological vision that we had internalised. There is no doubt that this has been blocked every step of the way by those whose power and influence will be lessened, such as the bureaucrats of the Roman Curia, as well as by those Catholics who want to live in the past. But the failure is primarily ours. Those of us who were the leaders of change in the late 1960s and the 1970s were lacking political savvy and did not take the need to change Church structures seriously enough. We thought that people would embrace the vision if we talked enough about it, that the structures of the Counter-Reformation Church would be changed by discussion, and that everyone would quickly shift from a hierarchical model of the Church to a communal one. What was lacking was a sense of realpolitik: we failed to take the issue of power seriously and did not *realise that our renewed vision of the Church would only be realised when it took shape within the context of new, participative, more democratic structures.*

Conservatives have always instinctively understood power and the way that institutions work. However, assuming goodwill, we post-Vatican II Catholics felt the need to get everybody to agree and we waited far too long in the effort to bring even the slowest on board. Instead of seizing the initiative, we became crippled by seeking a consensus that could never be achieved. It has been this failure of nerve and a lack of recognition that real change is achieved by people with a vision acting quickly and decisively that has contributed considerably to the impasse in which Catholicism now finds itself. This does not mean the process has to be necessarily undemocratic, but it does mean that you cannot wait until everyone agrees. We have also become crippled by the compromises inherent in the Vatican II documents themselves.

In 1986, during the visit of Pope John Paul II to Australia, Penguin published my first book, Mixed Blessings. *It was an attempt to see the contemporary Church in light of all that had happened since Vatican II. This led to my being invited to be a radio commentator on the papal visit by the Australian Broadcasting Corporation (ABC), and eventually to a full-time job in radio and TV as a religious broadcaster with the ABC. Eventually I was appointed specialist editor–religion for ABC radio. I remained with the ABC until 1996 when, after finding myself more and more a manager, I resigned to become a freelance writer and broadcaster. I was fortunate that the Missionaries of the Sacred Heart, my religious order, were very tolerant in all of this. Superiors here in Australia have allowed me to make my own way and have been truly supportive.*

In 1995 HarperCollins published my book God's Earth: Religion as if Matter Really Mattered. *I have to say that increasingly it is ecology and its relationship to spirituality and theology that I really care about. While living in the US I had seen the deleterious effects of a massive population and rampant industrialisation on a wonderful and bountiful natural environment. It was also in the US that I first encountered the writings of Thomas Berry on ecology. Berry is one of the most provocative and integrative Catholic thinkers on the whole issue of our relationship with the natural world. He is really the Teilhard de Chardin of our time. Later, during my years with the ABC, I visited him on two occasions in his Riverdale Center for Religious Research in New York City and interviewed him for radio. He has subsequently returned to where he was born, near Greensboro in North Carolina. Berry is a startling and original environmental thinker who has influenced many people both inside and especially outside the churches.*

It was also at this time that I began to realise that the pressure of human population was a key element in most environmental degradation scenarios. Yet the fact is that it is not only the Catholic Church, but all of the Christian traditions that have shied away from the question of overpopulation. This flows from Christian anthropocentrism, from our deep fear of pantheism and our aversion to tackling ethical issues not related to humankind.

But in the 1980s I also began to realise that environmentalism is not just theory; the Lake Pedder experience was a constant reminder that the vandals were still riding high. While I was sorting out my theories, Australian old-growth forests were being destroyed for woodchips, the seas fished out, uranium mining was continuing, and the only major river system in Australia, the driest continent on Earth, was steadily being destroyed by irrigation and use as a sewer. At the same time an Australian multinational corporation was destroying the Fly River in western Papua New Guinea. For me it is these destruction scenarios that are the real ethical issues facing humankind and the churches. There is a sense in which the failure to change the Catholic Church institutionally is merely a subset of the broader problems that face us as a culture.

But it is specifically to the issue of the Church that I will turn now and recount the story of my encounter with the CDF and my response.

Even though it is very late in the day, I remain optimistic that we still have a chance to change things for the better in the Church. It was this conviction that led to the writing of my book *Papal Power: A Proposal for Change in Catholicism's Third Millennium*, published in February 1997 in Australia and in the UK. To this point there has been no American edition. It was my fourth book, and fundamentally it attempted to argue, from an examination of papal history and by putting forward more participative models of Church governance, that Catholics today can move beyond the highly centralised and hierarchical notions that dominate the contemporary Church.

Papal Power used Church history and the dynamic nature of the Catholic tradition as a way of suggesting how these new models might be used in governing the Church. For instance, drawing on the conciliar tradition of Catholicism, the book called for a series of general councils of the Church with deliberative power to be held every ten years away from Rome, bringing together the world bishops and elected representative laity and clergy with the pope to debate the key issues facing the Church. These councils would gradually begin to include representatives of the other churches, so that the whole Church could work towards a council that was genuinely ecumenical and represented the whole Christian world. The book also outlined ways in which papal primacy could be exercised in a more collegial way and the possibility of replacing the college of cardinals (the title 'cardinal' is merely an honorary one) with a world synod or representative gathering of bishops and elected Catholics. This is not a new suggestion; it was made by several bishops at Vatican II. Fundamentally, the book was about power and how it is used in the Church.

Clearly for the slightly precious clerics who already had ecclesiastical power, it was somewhat threatening. *Papal Power* is also highly critical of the Roman Curia generally and of the CDF specifically. It presents the Church's central bureaucracy as an incubus that attempts to smother creativity in Catholicism, turning it into a highly centralised monolith. My book is blunt: 'The Holy Office may have changed its name but the ideology underpinning it has survived. It has certainly not changed its methods. It still accepts anonymous accusations, hardly ever deals directly with the person accused, demands retractations and imposes silences, and continues to employ third-rate theologians as its assessors. This body has no place in the contemporary Church. It is irreformable and should be abolished' (p. 7). Certainly, such comments were not likely to win friends and influence people in Rome! But *Papal Power* was not an academic book. It was a piece of popular theology, written for ordinary Catholics. Its bluntness was the product of my conviction that the time had come in the Church for clarity and directness, that the crisis into which we Catholics are now plunged at the end of a long restorationist papacy demands an honest response. The book was also written with Australia specifically and the English-speaking world generally in mind. Our language does not lend itself to the polite evasions, ambiguity and double entendres of the Romance languages. Australians are much more likely to call a spade a spade.

The first I heard of CDF's 'interest' in the book was in January 1998, just ten months after it was published. The whole 'affair' actually began outside a suburban post office in Canberra on the hot Saturday afternoon of 17 January 1998. I had just driven back from Melbourne after visiting my ninety-year-old father. That particular Saturday I had to make it back to Canberra in time for an evening mass at 6.30 in a local parish. On my way to the parish I called in at the post office to check my mailbox. Ironically, it is situated about half a metre from that of the papal nuncio to Australia. Among a number of letters there was an envelope from the general house of the religious order to which I belong, the Missionaries of the Sacred Heart, on the Via Asmara in Rome. Even before I opened it I somehow knew what the letter was about. I had experienced a vague sense of foreboding about the book and its fate for a number of weeks previously. I often joked after the publication of *Papal Power* about 'selling tickets to my burning at the Melbourne Cricket Ground'. While it had of course crossed my mind that the book might well be offensive to the Roman authorities, I never thought that they would take it seriously. It was a work of popular exposition with nothing particularly original in it. It was, as one prominent Australian theologian put it, 'unremarkable'. This was not meant as a put down. It was simply a statement of fact; there was nothing in it that had not been said before, albeit perhaps less forcefully and bluntly.

My view was that even if the officials of the CDF were

personally offended, that did not constitute unorthodoxy. As a bureaucratic structure they were not above criticism and certainly they could not pretend that they had some sort of sacred status that rendered them inviolable to comment. It seemed to me that the Vatican generally and the CDF specifically would have more to do than to waste time on my book. After all, it would only give the book more prominence. In fact, when it became known that the book was being 'examined', that was exactly what happened.

On top of that, it was not as though I was teaching theology in some so-called 'sensitive' area such as a seminary or theology faculty. In fact, I have not been directly employed or paid by the Church for fifteen years. I always tried to keep my pastoral hand in through parish work most weekends, but otherwise I lived from the mid-1980s on a PhD scholarship at the Australian National University, and then on my salary as a broadcaster and editor at the ABC. From 1986 my ministry was exclusively in the broadcast media and writing. Since the latter part of 1996 I have lived as a freelance writer and broadcaster, which gives you maximum freedom on a minimum income. Until you reach the status of a Robert Ludlum, Jackie Collins or John Grisham, most people would be struggling to live on an Australian writer's income – the market for popular theology here is not very large.

I mention this not to complain, but simply to state the facts of the writer's life. Many people imagine the Church pays me a stipend of some sort or generously supports me to play the 'dissident' priest. Except for paying for seminars, workshops and weekend parish work, Church organisations haven't paid me a cent for the past fifteen years. And the fact is that *Papal Power* had sold reasonably, but not extraordinarily well. A little under 4000 copies were purchased in Australia, and 2000 went to HarperCollins in London. It was hardly a bestseller in the popular sense, although it did well in its specific religious market. The CDF 'examination' was to help boost sales and take the book to a fourth reprint.

But back to the contents of the Roman letter. It contained a brief note from the Very Reverend Father Michael Curran, MSC, superior-general of the Missionaries of the Sacred Heart, enclosing a letter from the CDF and a set of Observations on *Papal Power*. In the CDF letter I was asked to 'provide the needed clarifications for submission to the judgment of [the] Congregation'. The letter from the Congregation to Father Curran was signed by Archbishop Tarcisio Bertone, and was dated 12 December 1997. It read:

> Dear Father Curran:
>
> A book written by Fr. Paul Collins, MSC, *Papal Power: A Proposal for Change in Catholicism's Third Millennium* (Fount Paperbacks, 1997), has recently been brought to the attention of this Congregation.
>
> A study of the book has revealed that it contains certain doctrinal problems (cfr. enclosure).
>
> Therefore, this Dicastery entrusts the matter to you, asking that you bring the doctrinal problems presented in the enclosed observations to Fr. Collins' attention, inviting him to provide the needed clarifications for submission to the judgment of this Congregation.
>
> This Dicastery would appreciate being kept informed concerning the progress of your intervention with Fr. Collins.

Two and three-quarter pages of Observations were attached.

There was no mention whatsoever in Bertone's letter of the *Regulations for Doctrinal Examination* issued by the Congregation on 29 June 1997. Fortunately I had a copy of them. At first I misread the *Regulations*, assuming that *Papal Power* was already in the process of an 'ordinary examination' (Arts 8–22). It was only a little later, when I read them more carefully, that I was able to work out exactly where I was in the process. The book was at the stage of an 'office study'. I must say I was surprised that there was no reference to the CDF's processes in Bertone's letter. There seemed to be no reason why the CDF would not refer to their own *Regulations*. An 'office study' is an initial stage of investigation. It presupposed that there were 'doctrinal problems' with *Papal Power* that needed to be clarified. While this is not an accusation of heresy, it certainly places you under a cloud. The CDF claims that its secrecy provision is geared to protecting the accused, but ultimately that is quite specious. The secrecy actually works the other way and places the accused in a vulnerable situation; they are on trial in isolation from their friends and colleagues.

What had already happened without any reference to me was that the book was delated to Rome by an unknown person[s], and after a meeting of the *congresso*, the weekly staff meeting of the CDF, the book was sent out to an anonymous consultor. It was suggested by a letter writer to the *Sydney Morning Herald*, a Sydney priest of well-known conservative leanings, that since the book was on sale at bookshops near the Vatican, it could have been accidentally picked up by a curial employee who discovered my 'deviant' doctrinal views and reported them to the CDF. Perhaps, but that is an unlikely scenario. It is as though the CDF went looking for books to denounce while still complaining of 'overwork' as a result of the amount of material delated to them from all over the world. The evidence, especially the speed with which it happened, points to the fact that the book was brought to the attention of the Congregation soon after its publication by a person well placed enough to be able to pressure them to act quickly.

The book had probably been sent from Australia, even though Bertone's letter refers to the UK Fount edition. There were various 'suspects', including Archbishop George Pell of Melbourne, one of the bishop members of the CDF. The archbishop and I had previously had a very public disagreement one night in the early 1990s on national television. We were involved in a discussion with a group of Catholics that focused on a rather up-market Australian TV miniseries called 'Brides of Christ'. In a series of six hour-long episodes, 'Brides' traced the history of a community of sisters adapting to the changes of Vatican II. In many ways it was quite perceptive. Needless to say, the institutional Church came in for a battering from some of the more alienated Catholic participants in the post-'Brides' TV discussion. We were all seated on indoor studio bleachers, and I found myself sitting directly behind the then auxiliary bishop, George Pell. In the discussion he cast himself in the role of strong defender of all aspects of the institutional Church. In the process he failed to hear what many of the people on the show were saying. Sitting next to him was a well-known actress who, among other things, said that when her marriage broke up she longed for support and pastoral care from the Church, but that she was deeply disappointed because it was not forthcoming. Television is a visual medium, and if Pell had simply moved towards her or touched her arm and said something like, 'I'm so sorry that happened to you', he would have captured the whole show. No matter what he subsequently said, people would have thought, 'He has to say that because he is a bishop, but he is really a kind, thoughtful man, and it's okay.' But he sat ram-rod straight, staring straight ahead. At that moment he lost the audience, which was Australia-wide and numerically very large.

Not long afterwards in the discussion he made a comment to the effect that at the Last Supper Jesus 'had ordained his apostles priests'. It was as though Jesus had donned his alb, chasuble and mitre and uttered the correct Latin sacramental formula. At this point I lost my patience and accused him of 'fundamentalism'. I pointed out that the priesthood as we know it only developed gradually, taking its present form in the third and fourth century. I also said that he simply was not hearing what people were saying. The geography of the studio seating did not help his response: it was difficult for him to argue with someone sitting directly behind him. While he maintained control, his body language said everything. He was understandably very angry.

After I went public with the letter from the CDF, Pell was asked by a TV interviewer if he had reported me to Rome. He commented that, 'Paul Collins certainly has a case to answer'. This all highlights the problem with anonymous denunciation. The procedure of the CDF in accepting and believing anonymous denunciation seems morally irresponsible to me and smacks of fascist or communist regimes.

After all, the Gospel of St Matthew actually sets out a procedure for solving disputes and disagreements within the Church community:

> If another member of the Church sins against you, go and point out the fault when the two of you are alone. If the member listens, you have regained that one. But if you are not listened to, take one or two others along with you ... If the member refuses to listen to them, tell it to the Church; and if the offender refuses to listen even to the Church, let such a one be to you as a gentile and a tax collector (18:15–17).

This involves dealing with contention between Christians at a local level first, through a personal and initial intervention. If people did not want to confront me, the case could have been dealt with through the Australian bishops (who in April 2000 issued a set of norms on 'The Examination of Theological Orthodoxy'), or through the authorities of my religious order. In that way my accusers would not have been able to hide behind anonymity; they would have to be up-front, have the courage of their convictions and ultimately deal with me face to face. It would only be after such a detailed process had been worked through exhaustively in the local Church that anyone would be justified in going to Rome.

I had received very few letters from local Catholics objecting to *Papal Power*, and certainly none from any bishops. Of all the letters I had personally received about the book before the CDF's intervention, nine were negative, several quite violently so. However, no one threatened to delate the book to Rome, nor even to the Australian bishops. In fact, most of the nine letter-writers had only the most rudimentary and inaccurate understanding of the teaching of the Church on infallibility and papal authority. The book also received a reasonable number of reviews, most of which were positive, although a small number were negative. This included one in the *Australian* newspaper where the reviewer was an Anglican clergyman much given to criticising Catholics who he perceives as disagreeing with the pope. I hasten to say again that I have no problem with public criticism. My books are public documents and I accept that you must take what you get in terms of reviews, even if you feel you have been unfairly treated.

Within a couple of days of receiving the letter from Rome I got over my initial shock that the CDF would take an antipodean writer of popular theology seriously. It was then that I began to examine the CDF's concerns and what it was that required 'clarifications for submission to the judgment of [the] Congregation'. At this point I received my second shock. It slowly dawned on me that the Observations that the CDF had sent via Father Curran were quite extraordinary. Not only were the comments of poor quality, but most of them were inferences drawn from quotations from the book taken out of context. In one case a section heading on papal primacy was assumed to be the complete summation of my view of the topic!

So what was the CDF asserting that I was saying in *Papal Power*? Their consultor's view was that the object of the book was 'primarily a critique of papal primacy and the ordinary magisterium'. It was said that I read 'Church history out of context', that I held that 'the primacy of the Roman Pontiff is not rooted in Divine Revelation but in secular political models ... [and that] the book contains not a few historical inaccuracies'. Here it is amusing to note that the consultor himself, who is much given to the use of capitalisation, uses the word 'Pontiff', a word of Roman pagan origin, to describe the pope, and not one drawn from divine revelation or from the Catholic theological tradition. The consultor goes on to make the extraordinary assertion that 'the author's presentation implies that a true and binding Revelation does not exist'.

He then makes seven specific assertions about supposed doctrinal problems contained in the book: 1. 'the author's concept of Tradition is more than nebulous'; 2. 'the author appears to deny the identity of the Church of Christ with the Catholic Church, suggesting a reunion of Christians characterised by indifferentism'; 3. the author holds 'an erroneous concept of infallibility, in as much as he only conceives of it in its solemn and *ex cathedra* manner, thus excluding the infallibility of the ordinary and universal Magisterium'; 4. regarding the doctrine of reception, 'The author maintains that in order for a teaching to become a doctrine of the Church it is first debated by theologians and decided on by Bishops, but then it must be accepted or received by the *congregatio fidelium*'; 5. 'the author failed to understand the true harm of modernism'; 6. 'the author cites the Council of Constance as affirming the notion of conciliarism, when in fact it did not affirm the superiority of the Council over the Pope'; and 7. 'the author appears to reject papal primacy by suggesting that the Council Fathers of Vatican I were not allowed to act freely, and that the required moral unanimity among the minority bishops was lacking ... The author rejects the *plenitudo potestatis* of the Roman Pontiff claiming that it is a juridical term ... and not in divine revelation'. Most of these assertions were illustrated by passages from *Papal Power* taken out of context.

Given that my background was in the media for the previous decade and a half, and I was known in Australia both as a priest and public commentator, I knew there was only one way to go and that was to make the whole affair public. I felt that a public process was the one thing that would protect me, as well as involving the wider Australian Church in the discussion. Years before, Hans Küng had advised me that the only way to keep the Vatican honest in any dispute was to go public immediately. Within a few days I had also made up my mind about two other things. I told my religious superiors that I would not respond to the CDF until they had named my accusers and the Vatican consultor who assessed the book. I said that I also wanted the book publicly assessed by historical and ecclesiological experts who represented a broad cross-section of theological opinion.

So I went public two weeks after first receiving the CDF letter. The release was timed for a Saturday morning in the *Sydney Morning Herald*. I gave the story to the *Herald*'s Chris McGillion, a journalist of integrity. It was treated as front-page news and that led to it being picked up by radio and the evening TV news programs. It was one of the lead stories on the ABC 7 pm news; totally accidentally an old friend and former colleague was executive producer of the news that day. Fortunately, it was a slow news day. The following Saturday there were features in the national broadsheet, the *Australian*, and the *Age*, Melbourne's quality newspaper. Commercial TV also picked up the story and the populist 'A Current Affair' did what turned out to be a very good piece in which they asked Archbishop Pell straight out if he had reported me to Rome. After a brief hesitation he said, 'No, not really.' The media was home territory for me and I hoped that my anonymous delator[s] was/were having second thoughts about providing me with such a great story, and giving *Papal Power* a whole new lease of life.

Throughout the whole media discussion there were many references to a possible 'excommunication'. Tissa Balasuriya's experience was very much in mind. There were a lot of questions as to how I might feel about excommunication or other ecclesiastical penalties. What was interesting was the almost total absence of comment from any bishop or other Catholic religious leader. I say 'almost' because one bishop really put himself out for me. He was Bishop Patrick Power, the auxiliary of the Canberra–Goulburn archdiocese where I live. He wrote to the papal nuncio, then Archbishop Franco Brambilla, on my behalf and received a none-too-friendly response. Brambilla was well known for his lack of tact.

There was also an excellent response from the Australian Conference of Leaders of Religious Institutes (ACLRI), in other words the major superiors of religious orders. The President of ACLRI, Father Kevin Dance, CP, issued a press statement in which he said:

> The Catholic Church is committed to truth, but discovering truth is a process not an accomplishment. Truth is dynamic not static. Dialogue is a better servant of truth than debate or condemnation. Debate is more about winning and encourages rigidity and judgment, whereas dialogue is built on a commitment to listen and to learn ... It is important that we avoid a climate of suspicion within the Australian Church.

Dance's comments were predictably met with a negative response from Cardinal Edward Clancy, the Archbishop of Sydney.

The UK *Tablet* and *Catholic Herald*, as well as the *National Catholic Reporter* in the US also picked up the story. It even eventually rated a couple of paragraphs' mention in a feature article by John Cornwell in the London *Times* on the history of the Inquisition. It also led to a discussion on BBC radio. As the issue faded from the mainstream media in Australia, various religious magazines picked it up and so the story of the antipodean 'heretic' lasted for well on six to eight weeks.

Some months after the first flurry of interviews and features, the ABC program 'Lateline' took up the story. The producers managed to get the Australian Cardinal Edward Cassidy, of the Pontifical Council for Promoting Christian Unity, who was in Washington at the time, to join the famous novelist of Vatican politics, Morris West, author of *The Devil's Advocate*, *Lazarus* and many other novels about power and politics in the Catholic Church, and me in a discussion of the whole 'affair'. I had interviewed Cassidy a couple of times in my own ABC days, and I knew that he was an open-minded and decent man who has done an enormous amount to build bridges with the Jewish faith especially, and to make amends for Catholic participation in the Holocaust.

A number of interesting things came out of our TV discussion. Before we went on air Cassidy asked me what the dispute was all about. I was rather surprised at this question and said: 'You're a member of the CDF. You should know what it is all about.' He replied that my 'case' had never been discussed when he had been at CDF meetings. That confirmed for me that the case was at the stage of an 'office study'. It would only go before the full Congregation if the office study failed. In the course of the TV discussion, Cassidy said that my use of the word 'power' to describe the papacy had given offence in Rome; they much preferred the word 'authority'. At this point both Morris West and I remarked that the popes had used the term *sacra potestas* for a thousand years to describe their primacy. The word *potestas* conveys the nuance of 'power' in the sense of making jurisdictional decisions. It denotes the ability to command and to oblige people to obey, with penalties for those who do not. In contrast, the Latin word *auctoritas* (authority) refers much more to the personal qualities inherent in an individual that persuade rather than command people to do things. For example, it was said of Jesus in the Gospel that, unlike the scribes, 'he spoke with authority'; that is, he was able to persuade people by the sheer quality of his spirituality and personality. Throughout the discussion Cardinal Cassidy was open, friendly and seemed almost to be downplaying the whole affair.

I often talked to Morris West on the phone during this period. His knowledge of the Vatican was encyclopedic and he was most helpful. (He was to die eighteen months later.) There was also support from the majority of the members of my own religious community. In fact, I never felt more part of the Catholic Church. From then on I knew that my sense of belonging to Catholicism would certainly make bearable any unlikely 'excommunication'. I knew that it would only be excommunication by the 'official' Church; I would still be very much part of the Church community in Australia.

Just before I went public I tried to fax a letter to Archbishop Bertone setting out the conditions under which I was prepared to enter into dialogue with the CDF. It proved impossible to get through on the CDF's fax number, despite several days of trying. So I posted the letter to the CDF airmail, and then asked the Canberra papal nunciature to assist by faxing my response directly to the Vatican. I received a terse letter by return mail informing me that 'it is not the policy of this Apostolic Nunciature to forward to the Vatican letters received by fax'. This turned out to be a blessing, because the letter I sent by post to the CDF was lost in the Italian mail, and the nunciature letter served as a confirmation that I had tried to contact Bertone before going public.

In the following two months Michael Curran, the superior-general of my religious order, while offering an honest critique of *Papal Power*, was calm and supportive. He asked me to respond to the CDF's concerns. His view was that if I did so it would be the end of the matter. I was not so sanguine, but given the kindness I had received from the order's superiors, I decided to cooperate. In April I sat down and wrote a detailed, ten-page response to the CDF charges, which was sent to Bertone on 20 April 1998.

I began by again addressing the question of anonymous denunciation. I said that it bred suspicion in the Catholic community. If you do not know whom you are dealing with you can begin to suspect everyone. Also, there is an ethical element in all of this. As I told Bertone: 'Accusers act in the dark and do not have to assume moral responsibility for what they do, so there is an inevitable perception of injustice. I am obliged to answer publicly for my book, but they can act silently, without having to assume any public responsibility for their attacks on me and my perceived opinions.'

There is also the question of the context in which *Papal Power* was written. One of my closest friends, the Anglican theologian Dr Graeme Garrett, commented that the CDF Observations were written as though *Papal Power* was produced in a vacuum and had no real relationship to me. The book was the product of my experience and ministry and some knowledge of that would be needed to make a mature judgment of it. I said that I have also tried to speak to the broader educated community that, perhaps unfairly, often sees the Australian Catholic Church as an outdated rump focused only on the issues of sexuality and social conservatism. Because of the way we Catholics often present ourselves in Australia, the richness and breadth of the tradition of Catholicism has been lost, and we are perceived in public discourse as a Church with a very blinkered vision. Context is also important here and I emphasised that '... my attempt to communicate with the people of today has been through the media – radio, TV and, to an increasing extent, the written word'. I pointed out that the media have their own rhetorical structure and methodology. It is essentially a form of storytelling and requires clarity, simplicity and an element of controversy.

One of the issues that drew criticism both to the book and myself from some reviewers was the perception that I was somehow 'angry' about the papacy. The rather silly review by the Anglican clergyman mentioned earlier even suggested I was suffering from 'thwarted ambition'. Presumably he thought that I was angry that I had missed out on a 'red hat' or election as superior-general. The problem is that some commentators seemingly cannot understand that *Papal Power* is popular writing, not a piece of speculative theology. As such it is subject to all the constraints of the popular genre: the actual size of the book, cost of production, and the use of a journalistic style to maintain general interest. Already a number of readers had complained that the book was 'too complicated'. As I told Bertone:

> *Papal Power* is not, and was never meant to be, an academic treatment of theological issues. It is popular theology written for an intelligent lay audience. In the book I explicitly say that I am not a theologian and I make it clear that my approach is both historical and practical. This, of course, does not excuse me from being doctrinally and historically accurate. Interestingly, if you read them carefully, most of the criticisms of the anonymous consultor are inferences drawn from the book, rather than clear statements of mine that have been found to contain specific doctrinal problems.

Another key issue for me is ecumenism. You cannot have worked in religious media for more than a decade and not become ecumenical. My belief is that there is no future for the churches in the Western world outside the context of intercommunion. As I told the CDF: 'The book is also explicitly ecumenical in intention and is directed to members of the other Christian churches. In *Papal Power* I have tried to explain as openly as possible the Catholic doctrines of ecclesial governance, while remaining true to the tradition, as a gesture of openness toward those Christians separated from us.' I concluded by saying that my approach 'in many ways mirrors the approach taken in official ecumenical dialogues, which are often sponsored by the Holy See'.

I then turned to the substance of the criticisms levelled by CDF Observations. They begin by saying that, 'the book is primarily a critique of papal primacy and ordinary magisterium'. My response to that is that this is simply a completely mistaken reading of the book. It is much broader than that. Fundamentally it attempts to deal with the major structural issues facing the Catholic Church today and makes suggestions as to how we might move as a Church community into the future. One of the things that really annoyed me, and something that was taken up by a number of media commentators, was the absurd assertion that I denied that a 'binding revelation' existed. After pointing out that the CDF consultor uses the word 'implies' and that we are dealing here with an inference, not a fact, I told Bertone:

> At first I could not believe that I was reading this. Excuse my bluntness, but I found that an insulting comment, given that the man making it was hiding behind a mask of anonymity, and that he was a person who clearly knew nothing about me. I have spent much of the last two decades of my life standing up for the Catholic Church in public life in Australia, often having to face hard questions in the media ... There have not been many of us who have stood up and been counted in public as people explicitly committed to the Catholic Church. I am sure you can understand that to have someone chosen by the Holy See imply that I do not believe in the truth of Christianity is rather hard to take.

Talking this over with various people I came to realise that there was a world of difference between the theological attitude of the CDF examiner and my own. It was really the Jesuit theologian, Andrew Hamilton, in an article in the religious magazine *Eureka Street* (April 1998), who first drew it to my attention. For me history is central and embedded in history is the reality of change, whether for good or evil; usually, it is a mixture of both. This includes truth, which is 'dynamic not static' as Kevin Dance had pointed out. But the CDF dwells in a non-historical world of static Truth (with a capital 'T'). Truth is something possessed, not discovered. I told Bertone:

> I am a Catholic believer, indeed a passionate one, but for me faith is always lived out within the context of history. Thus our theological understandings are always determined and limited by the constraints of culture and human experience. We can never exhaust in any one theological approach or statement

the transcendent and mysterious realities that underlie and give context to our beliefs. Among these realities is the Church, whose mystery we are constantly challenged to explore. My belief is that in all of this the Holy Spirit of God is alive and active, constantly guiding the Church. Our understanding of ultimate mystery is always developing ... What I try to do in *Papal Power*, albeit in terms of popular theology, is to examine something of the development of the structure and government of our Church. For me change and development, inspired and guided by the Holy Spirit, is part of the process of belief. However, I would also maintain that there is an organic and continuous development that occurs in, through, and often despite the vagaries of Church history. Your consultor, however, clearly emerges from a different theological perspective. He seemingly proceeds from the assumption that the profound mysteries at the core of faith can be clearly expressed within a specific, established theological tradition, and that the development of doctrine is an almost logical process within that context. The process is largely outside and beyond the realities of history.

John Henry Newman's theory of theological development had influenced me and I told Bertone that 'I would suggest that Cardinal John Henry Newman's notion of the development of doctrine is actually closer to the historical view of faith which I have espoused'. In fact Catholic Christianity has never been a religion of static law and unchanging doctrine, established once and for all in the past and true for ever. Taken to its logical conclusion, this is fundamentalism. Newman argues in his *Essay on the Development of Christian Doctrine* (1845) that the Church's inner life is like an idea that is continually clarified and expanded by development and growth. His profound historical sense led him unerringly to the realisation that the more the Church grows, develops and changes, the more it becomes truly itself. 'Here below to live is to change, and to be perfect is to have changed often.'

One of the things of which I was accused was that I read Church history out of context and that there were 'not a few historical inaccuracies' in the book. I always love these assertions without any examples. It is an argumentative trick whereby you can suggest that there is something essentially untrustworthy about a text without having to do the hard work of describing and arguing against the asserted 'historical inaccuracies'. It is correct that *Papal Power* is incomplete and that it draws examples out of various periods of Church history. Part of my problem was that my most recent book, the more complete papal history, *Upon This Rock: The Popes and Their Changing Role* (2000), was not published until three years after *Papal Power*. This was simply because HarperCollins felt that the more academic treatment of papal history would not sell, and the more populist *Papal Power* was what they wanted. Within their context they were right. However, *Upon This Rock* would have shown that I did have a reasonable grasp of the historical context of papal history.

Interestingly, what the CDF Observations did show was a real lack of acquaintance with more recent historical research. This is especially clear when dealing with issues such as the relationship between council and pope as discussed at the Council of Constance. But the practical problem that my publishers faced is that they had to work within the constraints of size and price when putting out a book such as mine. You cannot say everything in one work.

I must admit I was annoyed that I was accused of the thesis that 'the primacy of the Roman pontiff is not rooted in Divine Revelation but in secular political models' when I had clearly said that papal primacy was 'almost sacramental'. It is hard to win sometimes! I told Bertone in my response:

> I think it is important to get this on the record: I certainly do not deny that the Roman primacy is part of divine revelation. Your consultor does not seem to have read the book carefully. For example, I say unequivocally on page 150: 'The Petrine text is clear that the leadership of the Church was conferred on Peter and it is also demonstrable that there was a strong early tradition of identifying the Bishop of Rome with Peter ... In

fact, as [Father J. M. R.] Tillard points out, the notion of Petrine succession is far more significant than is generally recognised today. He argues that there is an almost sacramental sense in which Peter lives on in his see of Rome.' It is clearly spelled out in the book that I believe in the continuation of Petrine primacy through Roman primacy. Any other reading is a distortion of my position. Certainly, I am critical of the First Vatican Council's definition of primacy precisely because it is couched in canonical, legal terms and has actually neglected the rich theology of primacy that can be found especially in the first millennium of Church history. But criticism of a conciliar text – and I am not alone in this criticism – is not tantamount to rejection. My point about Vatican I is that it did not take Church history sufficiently into account.

Despite this, the problem of primacy did not go away. The CDF's April 1999 reply to my response returned to this issue as though I had said nothing about it.

I then turned to the particular issues that the CDF highlighted. The first issue was that my 'concept of tradition [was] more than nebulous'. Here again I have the feeling that the CDF consultor had not really read the book. I had defined tradition as it was defined in the early Church: there it was seen as a dynamic process of handing on and developing the faith; it was not the static process of merely repeating the past. In *Papal Power* I said:

> Catholics take tradition as a source and norm of faith. God, Catholic theology says, reveals God's self to us through the Bible and through the tradition of the Church. But tradition has never been definitively defined. Probably it cannot be: it is one of those dynamic concepts that defies definition (p. 126).

My argument rejected the idea of tradition that became popular among theologians in the period after the sixteenth-century Council of Trent. This was that tradition was the explicit articulation of the unwritten teachings of Jesus that had not been reported in the Gospels. I then emphasised the creative element in tradition and stressed that tradition is more about process than content. As I told Bertone: 'It is here that we strike again the problem mentioned above: my approach is explicitly historical. My position is that doctrinal truth works itself out in the processes of Church history under the guidance of the Holy Spirit, whereas your consultor seemingly has a more static view. However, all that I have said is in complete harmony with Vatican II's *Dei Verbum*.'

This all led on logically to the CDF's second criticism: that I 'appear to deny the identity of the Church of Christ with the Catholic Church, suggesting a reunion of Christians characterised by indifferentism'. Here again we are dealing with an inference: I 'appear' to deny. But when you read the passage the CDF consultor quotes from page 199 of *Papal Power* I simply talk about 'the richness and diversity of the [other] Christian traditions' and suggest that we work towards intercommunion rather than corporate union, so that the wealth of each of the traditions of faith be preserved. This is hardly a denial of the truth of the Catholic Church. I continued:

> I have said over and over again, both publicly and privately, that I have a deep sense of belonging to the Catholic Church and to its extraordinary tradition. I have no intention of leaving, for it is here that I have found God in the Spirit of Christ. But that does not blind me to the profound Christian truths and tradition embedded within the other Churches. Does your consultor think that the other communities – the Orthodox, for instance – are deficient and second-class Christians? Does he suggest that we Catholics are the only 'true' Christians? If so, he might have difficulty with the 1993 *Ecumenical Directory* (paragraph 17), which I have no doubt your ever-vigilant Congregation would have carefully scrutinised before publication. The *Directory* talks about 'the rich diversity of spirituality, discipline, liturgical rites and *elaborations of revealed truth* [my emphasis] that have grown up among the Churches'. The phrase that I have emphasised

would certainly suggest that a diversity of theological views is also acceptable within the broad ambit of Catholic truth.

This issue was also to recur in the April 1999 response of the CDF. The rhetoric and approach of the consultor give you a further clue to his attitudes. He uses words like 'indifferentism' which have a somewhat dated feel about them. He also says that I fail to understand the 'true harm' of modernism. The consultor seems to have no knowledge of the vast historiographic literature on modernism which would assess the movement in a much more positive light. Second, assessments of historical events are for historians, not the consultors of the CDF. One's view of modernism has nothing to do with the CDF, which is concerned with doctrine. I told the CDF:

> It would seem to me that assessing 'the true harm of modernism' is a matter of historical judgment and has nothing whatsoever to do with doctrine. As a consequence it certainly does not come under the aegis of the Congregation for the Doctrine of the Faith. This statement seems a bit like 'point scoring' to me. In fact, the reality is that the overwhelming weight of historiographic opinion today is against your consultor's view. The best historian of the period, Roger Aubert, says: 'One has to admit that the various measures employed to hold back the tide of modernism must be assessed negatively. Many men loyal to the Church were mercilessly banned ... But more serious than these personal fates were other facts: for a long time the undifferentiated suppression of modernism kept the majority of the clergy from pursuing intellectual investigations ... The gap between the Church and modern culture widened. The solution of fundamental problems was postponed, and by simply ignoring them nothing was won, but, on the contrary, harm was done' (Roger Aubert in Hubert Jedin (editor), *History of the Church: The Church in the Industrial Age* (1981, vol. IX, pp 387–388). Sometimes one is tempted to think that there are

contemporary parallels to the suppression of modernism. And I think I need to ask your Congregation if any consideration is being given to the harm done to the reputations of many loyal and hard-working Catholic lay teachers, theologians, priests and even bishops by reactionaries who constantly call anyone with whom they happen to disagree 'modernists'.

At the core of the CDF criticism is the assertion that I hold 'an erroneous concept of infallibility, in as much as [I] only conceive of it in its solemn and *ex cathedra* manner, thus excluding the infallibility of the ordinary and universal magisterium'. To demonstrate this the consultor quotes four passages from the book which are apparently meant to demonstrate this contention. In fact the passages he cites do not show that I exclude the infallibility of the ordinary and universal magisterium at all. They reveal my concern about the extension at the popular level of the ordinary magisterium to all and every papal teaching. *Papal Power* nowhere suggests that I have any problem with accepting what is universally held by the pope and the bishops. The point that I was trying to make was that the contemporary papacy seems bent on endowing some form of 'infallibility' on a whole range of statements by the pope, which are certainly not infallible.

The theologian, Bernard Häring, is right when he talks about the increasing tendency to cast the net of 'definitively decided' teachings wider and wider, often in the process obfuscating the actual teaching of Vatican I about infallibility (see his *My Hope for the Church*, 1999, pp 75–76). In fact Häring says that we can no longer speak about 'creeping infallibility' but rather what he calls '*galloping* infallibility'. My contention in *Papal Power* is that this extension of the ordinary magisterium to more and more papal utterances is simply not in accord with the teaching of the Church.

In the book I use John Paul II's Apostolic Letter *Ordinatio Sacerdotalis* (22 May 1994) on the ordination of women as an example of ordinary magisterium being 'modulated' into a universal teaching and thus, by implication, into infallible doctrine. The problem that I make reference to is the question of how

Ordinatio Sacerdotalis can be part of the ordinary and universal magisterium when there is no apparent evidence that anyone has asked the bishops their view, and when a sizeable portion of the theological magisterium is seemingly doubtful about how the question should be resolved. I pointed out to the CDF that the highly respected ecclesiologist, Father Francis A. Sullivan, SJ, certainly seemed to back up my concern in the quotation I cite on page 19 of *Papal Power*. He says that for something to be taught infallibly by the ordinary magisterium it has 'to be clearly established that the tradition has remained constant, and that even today the universal body of Catholic bishops is teaching the same doctrine to be definitively held'. It is hard to see how these conditions could be fulfilled when the question has only been around for at most four decades.

The next issue the CDF questioned was my notion of the doctrine of reception. The CDF's consultor said that I maintain 'that in order for a teaching to become a doctrine of the Church it is first debated by theologians and decided on by bishops, but then it must be accepted or received by the *congregatio fidelium*'. He did not say what is wrong with that summary of the notion of reception, although I suspect it is the lack of explicit reference to the pope and the role assigned to the community of the faithful that worried him. Obviously, my text presupposes that the pope participates in this process as head of the college of bishops. Actually, the consultor's summary is a reasonable if abbreviated and simplified statement of my understanding of the doctrine of reception.

I mentioned to the CDF that 'the papal magisterium has a solemn obligation to make sure that what it teaches is in conformity with what the bishops and community of the Church believe. When this is carefully and fully carried out, 'The assent of the Church can never be lacking to such definitions on account of the Holy Spirit's influence' (*Constitution on the Church*, 25). If non-reception occurs those responsible have a serious obligation 'to review their decision in the light of the belief of the faithful'.

A criticism has been made by some theologians that I tend to treat reception as a *post factum* reality; that is, a teaching is ultimately confirmed as true when the Catholic community 'receives' it. I would simply argue in defence of my view that it also seems to be the approach taken by Cardinal Newman. Speaking specifically of the definition of infallibility at Vatican I, he said: 'If the definition is eventually received by the whole body of the faithful ... then too it will claim our assent by the force of the great dictum *securus judicat orbis terrarum*.' He refers to reception by the faithful as 'the ultimate guarantee of revealed truth' (see *The Letters and Diaries of John Henry Newman*, vol. XXV, pp 165, 172).

On conciliarism, the idea that a general council is superior to a pope, the consultor put forward the conventional pro-papal view that the Council of Constance (1414–18), which was called to solve the Great Western Schism when there were three claimants to the papacy, 'did not affirm the superiority of a council over the pope'. In my response I told the CDF that, contrary to their consultor, the superiority of council over pope is the teaching of the Council of Constance.

At the third session on 26 March 1415, led by Cardinal Francesco Zabarella, the Council declared that it had been constituted in a proper way and at the fifth session on 6 April 1415 the fathers confirmed the decree *Haec Sancta* which had already been prepared by Zabarella. The decree is clear about its purpose: 'the eradication of the present schism' and the 'reform of God's Church [in] head and members'. The very directness of the language of *Haec Sancta* conveyed the feeling of the need for action in a time of crisis. The first two points of *Haec Sancta* were the most important theologically: first, Constance claimed that it was 'legitimately assembled', that it represented the whole Church and it had power 'immediately from Christ'. Second, *Haec Sancta* stated: therefore, 'everyone of whatever state or dignity, even papal, is bound to obey it in those matters which pertain to the faith, the eradication of the said schism and the general reform of the ... Church' (The translation is from Norman P. Tanner's *Decrees of the Ecumenical Councils*). Most historians now accept that Constance was ecumenical from the beginning. The idea that it only 'became ecumenical' from the time the legate of Gregory XII staged a reading of the bull of convocation is now largely abandoned. It was not clear who was the pope at the time – there were three candidates – and it is simply an assumption to say that Gregory XII was legitimate pope. Again, we are engaged here in historical issues and it is for historians to decide, not theologians.

Finally the anonymous consultor returned to the question of papal primacy. He said 'The Author appears to reject papal primacy' – another inference – because of lack of freedom of the minority bishops at Vatican I. My response was:

Let's get clear what I actually say. I summarise [the historian] Father Luis Bermejo, SJ, saying: 'There are serious doubts about Vatican I's freedom, but he [Bermejo] emphasises that this is still an open question' (p. 115). 'Open' in English means that the question is still debatable. To say that debate about a possible lack of freedom is an 'open question' is hardly tantamount to rejection of papal primacy. I then went on to examine the question of the required moral unanimity at Vatican I. With Bermejo I think that there are more serious questions to be asked here. I quote Bermejo saying that the required moral unanimity was not reached (p. 116). I have great respect for him as a careful historian who has studied the sources thoroughly. On this issue I neither agree nor disagree with him in my book. And that is still my position. Your consultor also says that I say that 'the place of the Supreme Pontiff in relation to other Bishops is *primus inter pares*' as though this were an absolute statement on my part. But it is qualified in block letters with the phrase 'primacy in the first millennium' (p. 161). The whole section (pp 161–164) simply talks about the theological views held in the period prior to Damasus I (366–384). In this section I am not spelling out what I think, but what the historical situation was. Either the consultor has not read the section, or he misrepresents my position totally. Either way, it is an utterly incorrect assumption to infer – again it is an inference – that this brief saying sums up my view of papal primacy.

The CDF then goes on to accuse me of rejecting 'the *plenitudo potestatis* of the Roman Pontiff claiming it is a juridical term that has its roots in the bull *Unam Sanctam* and not in divine revelation'. Actually, this is a completely incorrect reading of *Papal Power.* In my treatment I tried to show how interest in the revival of Roman law in the Middle Ages influenced ideas about the primacy. However, it was obvious that I would be wasting my time trying to argue this so my response to the accusation was very simple:

> Where in divine revelation can one find the term *plenitudo potestatis?* The historical facts are that the term comes from Roman law. It entered the canonical tradition just before the time of Innocent III. In this period fullness of authority became synonymous in canonical thought with papal primacy. As John A. Watt has pointed out, two historical sources come together to inject meaning into the term *plenitudo potestatis.* The canonists linked the authority granted to Peter in the Petrine text with the notion of imperial or monarchical power which had came into canon law from Roman law. Increasingly, in practice, the popes imitated imperial power. By the time of Innocent III the term *plenitudo potestatis* denoted papal sovereignty. This sovereignty became co-terminus with primacy. Again here we are dealing with historical facts. To infer from this historical discussion that I reject papal primacy is totally incorrect.

As I said at the beginning I was surprised at the superficiality of the CDF Observations. Perhaps they are right; they really *are* overworked! Certainly, that would be the most charitable explanation for the poor quality of the work they produce. I tried to indicate something of this in the final comment in my response: 'In conclusion, Archbishop, I have to say that in general I found your consultor's Observations quite extraordinary. With the exception of the issue of the ordinary and universal magisterium, the criticisms are nothing more than inferences drawn from quotations taken out of context from my book.'

This response was sent on 20 April 1998. Some people felt that the whole thing would now go away; this was not a view I shared. I sent a copy of the response to Morris West and he told me that he felt that I had said far too much. His view was that all of the detail in the response simply gave the CDF more ammunition, or more areas to examine. He was right in a sense because it did lead to a CDF response focusing on the question of the ordination of women, as well as on primacy and ecumenism. But first there was silence for twelve months. Then on 10 April 1999 Father Curran received another letter concerning me from the CDF. A number of people interpreted this letter as taking a more 'softly, softly' approach. This may or may not be true. If it is, it is probably the result of the fact that I had gone public and was publishing everything on the Internet and in whatever media outlets I could.

I was not the slightest bit surprised to hear from them again. The CDF is persistent, no matter how long it takes, no matter how drawn out the affair. The 1999 letter came to me by the usual roundabout route: Bertone wrote to Curran, whose assistant faxed it to the Australian provincial of the order, who then posted it to me. The good part of it was that since they did not mention four of the topics from the first letter (tradition, magisterium, conciliarism and reception), I have assumed that they have accepted that my views are entirely orthodox on these issues. However, despite the slightly conciliatory tone of the 1999 letter, they made it clear that the 'dialogue' stage was now over and that the time for submission had come.

I was to write an article which set out what they wanted. It was to be submitted to them for prior vetting before being published. So, as I told both the provincial and general, I now decided to return to my original position: I would not respond to letters that came to me third or fourth hand, nor would I condone anonymous denunciation and assessment. This remains my position and, in a way, this chapter and book is my response.

The first topic mentioned in the letter was papal primacy. It conceded that 'the Rev. Collins asserts that he does not deny the primacy of the Pope. Rather, he says that there are serious questions to be asked concerning the moral unanimity of the Bishops at the First Vatican Council. Apart from this historical discussion, it must be noted that the post-conciliar adherence to *Pastor Aeternus* by the Bishops of the time constituted, at least after the Council, moral unanimity.' Now, that's an interesting concession; one could conclude from that statement that the CDF admits the possibility that Vatican I actually lacked moral unanimity, which was precisely the point that Luis Bermejo, the historian to whom I referred in *Papal Power*, was making. Bermejo is a Spanish Jesuit who taught theology at Pune in India for many years. His very interesting 1992 book is *Infallibility on Trial*; it is worth reading. Bermejo also addresses the question of post-conciliar unanimity and he questions whether, in fact, it was present. Despite problems with Vatican I, obviously the clincher for the CDF is in the next sentence: 'Above all, the Second Vatican Council confirmed the validity of the First Vatican Council in general, and the doctrine of the primacy of the Pope in particular.'

Sure, but so what? This whole discussion arose from the CDF consultor's inference that I do not accept papal primacy. I do, and it is hard to see how anyone could maintain that I did not when, drawing on the work of Tillard, I had argued that primacy is 'almost sacramental' in the sense that St Peter (and St Paul) live on in the See of Rome. *Papal Power* clearly argues that Roman primacy goes right back to the early Church, and that it has been constantly accepted in varying degrees both in the West and in the East. What I argued in *Papal Power* was that from an ecumenical perspective the way in which the Vatican I definition of primacy is worded is problematic, especially for the Orthodox, most of whom consider it to be heresy. My point was that this has to be taken seriously. This is precisely what John Paul II seems to mean when he says that he has 'to find a way of exercising the primacy which, while in no way renouncing what is essential to its mission, is nonetheless open to a new situation' (*Ut Unum Sint*, 95).

Second, the 1999 letter turned to the question of ecumenism. The view it expresses is surprising and probably reflects the real approach to this question taken by conservatives in Rome. Bertone says: 'While it cannot be denied that the other Christian churches and ecclesial communities possess many elements of sanctification and of truth, it must be acknowledged that the Catholic Church *alone* [my emphasis] offers the fullness of the means of salvation.' I think there are some real problems here, especially with the language used and the attitudes that it betrays. This CDF interpretation is not new. The same restrictive approach was taken in the CDF's Notification in the mid-1980s on Leonardo Boff's book *Church, Charism and Power*. Certainly Vatican II said that Christ's Church 'subsists' in the Catholic Church. But this word has to be taken in context. From the debates at the Council it is clear that 'subsists' was used precisely to indicate that elements of sanctification and truth can be found in churches outside the Catholic Church. Further, the whole context of Vatican II was profoundly ecumenical. It was essentially about reaching out to other Christians and to the wider world. Any other interpretation of the Council is a distortion. The word 'subsists' was Vatican II's attempt to express its belief in the truth of Catholicism and in the fact that it believed it had held on to Christ's teaching in its integrity, while at the same time not excluding the truth to be found in the other churches. The non-exclusive word 'subsists' allowed it to maintain its own position while respecting the Christian faith and practice of the other churches.

The use of the word 'alone' in the CDF's phrase 'it must be acknowledged that the Catholic Church *alone* offers the fullness of the means of salvation' is particularly worrying. It seems to me to go well beyond the concern of Vatican II and it certainly sounds like a claim that the Catholic Church is 'the one, true Church' in an exclusivist sense. My view remains that while these kinds of concerns may keep the staff of the CDF awake at night, I am much more concerned with achieving one of the primary goals of Vatican II: Christian unity.

The third issue raised in the Bertone letter was the question of the ordination of women. Morris West was right. This is something that was not explicitly raised in the CDF's first letter and really only came to the surface in the second. This is actually a reply to issues raised in my 1998 response. Substantially Bertone argued that the teaching contained in *Ordinatio Sacerdotalis* on the ordination of women has been confirmed by the pope and that it 'belongs to the deposit of faith, and that it requires definitive assent by all the faithful'. In other words 'it has been set forth infallibly by the ordinary and universal magisterium'. In my view there are quite a number of problems in this statement. (In my response I have drawn on the work of Francis A. Sullivan, *Creative Fidelity: Weighing and Interpreting the Documents of the Magisterium* (1996), and Klaus Schatz's *Papal Primacy: From its Origins to the Present* (English trans. 1996).)

First of all, the problem with the exclusion of the possibility of the ordination of women is the papacy's premature rush to judgment on this issue and the attempt to stifle any further discussion. Connected to this is the question of reception. In this regard Sullivan quotes an interesting statement of the then Father Josef Ratzinger in 1969: 'When neither the consensus of the whole Church is had, nor clear evidence from the sources is available an ultimately binding decision is not possible' (p. 89). If a pope attempted a definition in these circumstances Ratzinger says 'the question would have to be raised concerning its legitimacy'. It is within this context that many Catholics find it hard to see how the discussion on women's ordination can be definitively closed. The question has only been debated for four decades at most. It took the Church more than 400 years to reach consensus on the trinitarian nature of God, and even then it was not accepted entirely by all. Even papal infallibility, depending where you place the historical origin of the doctrine, has been debated since at least the late Middle Ages. It is hard to see how any definitive consensus could be reached about women's ordination in forty years.

In an interesting afterword in *Creative Fidelity* (pp 181–4) Sullivan discusses the CDF's 18 November 1995 statement which claimed that the doctrine excluding the ordination of women pertained to the deposit of faith and that it had been infallibly taught by the ordinary and universal magisterium. (This is what Bertone is referring to in his letter to Curran.) Sullivan says that for something to be taught infallibly by the ordinary and universal magisterium, it has to be 'clearly established' that 'the tradition has remained constant and that even today the universal body of Catholic bishops are teaching the same doctrine as definitively to be held'. To establish this tradition there has to be some form of consultation. There is no evidence that this happened in the case of *Ordinatio Sacerdotalis*.

In terms of the development of doctrine, a doctrine is hardly a 'constant tradition' after only forty years of theological debate. Sullivan says that unless there is consultation of all Catholic bishops, a consensus among Catholic theologians and common adherence of the faithful, 'I do not see how it can be certain that this doctrine has been taught by the ordinary and universal magisterium'. He also notes that we can be certain that the 'statement of the CDF is not infallible'. Infallibility is a gift with which the dicasteries of the Roman Curia are not endowed. Thank God for small mercies!

Here it needs to be noted that very solemn papal teaching, sometimes couched in ever stronger terms than *Ordinatio Sacerdotalis*, has been changed, or quietly jettisoned. For instance Boniface VIII's bull *Unam Sanctam* (1302) which proclaimed the extreme hierocratic notion that the temporal was completely subject to the spiritual and, as a consequence, 'it is altogether necessary for salvation for every human creature to be subject to the Roman pontiff'. No sane person holds this today. Another example is that many of the propositions from the 1864 *Syllabus of Errors* of Pius IX have now been completely abandoned. Introducing Hans Küng's piece, I referred to the complete turnaround on the question of freedom of religion and conscience from the teaching of the Encyclical *Mirari Vos* of 1832 to the teaching of Vatican II. I mention these because it is important to keep in mind when one examines one's attitude to ordinary magisterium that past papal teaching has been changed. While respect should be shown to the magisterium, without consultation and clear evidence of reception you cannot pretend that this teaching is 'definitive', no matter how solemn the pope's language is. Also you have to take into account how alienating *Ordinatio Sacerdotalis* has been for many Catholic women, and you cannot escape the fact that a majority of Catholics in the Western world, including theologians and bishops, do not accept the pope's teaching on this issue. They are part of the receiving faithful and, as such, must be taken seriously.

As I write this, nothing more has been heard from the CDF. I may be wrong, but I am certain that they will not go away. However, this is no longer the central issue for me. Their case against me is completely minor and of no real long-term theological significance whatsoever. In fact, from my perspective, what has happened now is that the whole game has turned right around: what is important for the whole Church now is the urgent task of either the radical reform of the CDF, or its complete abolition. My own view is that history shows that reform has proved impossible on several previous occasions when it has been tried. Therefore, the Church's only recourse is abolition.

There are many other much more creative ways in which a Catholic's orthodoxy can be established and the truth of the Gospel and the Church's teaching maintained than the use of such a blunt instrument as the CDF. For the first 1500 years of its existence, Catholicism was maintained in truth without the existence of the CDF, or the Holy Office, or the Roman Inquisition. Whatever the demands of the Counter-Reformation may have been, the new millennium calls for a whole new approach: one that is open, transparent and in accord with human dignity and rights.

The seven of us here have told our stories hoping that they may contribute, in however small a way, to the building of a more humble Christ-like Catholic Church, dedicated to ecumenism, and to the building up of a renewed and free community. The transition we face is from inquisition to freedom.

Author's Note

*In March 2001, just after this book had been published in Australia, I
made the decision to resign from the active priesthood of the Catholic
church. As I was reasonably well known in my own country I thought it
was necessary to explain my action. So I put out a statement which will
not only explain my action, but also provide a conclusion to this piece. Here
are my reasons for resignation:*

After thirty-three years I have decided to resign as an 'active' priest
to return to being an ordinary Catholic believer. Many people will
justifiably ask: why? The reason is simple: I can no longer
conscientiously subscribe to the policies and theological emphases
coming from the Vatican and other official church sources.

While the reason is straight-forward, the decision to resign is the
result of a personal and theological process. This, of course, is not a
step that I have taken lightly and I have been considering it for
some time. I will try to outline the reasons in detail.

The core of the problem is that, in my view, many in ecclesiastical
leadership at the highest level are actually moving in an increasingly
sectarian direction and watering down the catholicity of the church
and even unconsciously neglecting elements of it's teaching. Since
this word 'catholicity' will recur often I will define it. It is derived
from the Greek word 'katholikos' which means 'general', 'broad' or
'universal'. The Shorter Oxford Dictionary defines 'catholicity' as
'the quality of having sympathies with or being all-embracing;
broad-mindedness; tolerance'.

But 'catholicity' also has a profound theological meaning. The American Cardinal Avery Dulles, SJ has a fine book entitled *The Catholicity of the Church* (1988). Catholicity, he says, is characterised by (1) inclusiveness, which means openness to various cultures and opposition to sectarianism and religious individualism; (2) by an ability to bridge generations and historical periods; (3) by an openness to truth and value wherever it exists; (4) by a recognition that it is the Holy Spirit who creates the unity of the church through whose indwelling we participate in the life of God.

This is the kind of Catholicism that I, and many others, have embraced throughout our lives. Its foundations, which are deeply embedded in church history, were given modern expression in the vision of the church articulated at the Second Vatican Council in the 1960s. For Catholics like myself our benchmark is a church that is defined as the living sacrament of God's presence and the place where God's sovereignty is acknowledged, expressed through a participative community of people dedicated to the service of the world and characterised by collegiality and ecumenism. It is precisely this image of Catholicism which I think is being distorted by many at the highest level in the contemporary church. I increasingly feel that being a priest places me in the position of co-operating with structures that are destructive of that open vision of Catholicism and of the faith of the people who have embraced it. If I am to be true to my conscience, resignation seems the only option.

The fact that we are retreating from the Vatican II vision of Catholicism may not be everyone's view of what is actually taking place in the church. I accept that, and I also accept that the tension between a broad, open vision of Catholicism rooted in living experience, and a narrower, static, hierarchical view of faith, runs right through church history. It is my perception that at present many in the hierarchy and some laity are moving increasingly in this narrow, elitist direction. Over the last few years I have watched with escalating concern as a series of documents have been published by the Vatican, the last of which was the declaration of the Congregation for the Doctrine of the Faith, *Dominus Jesus* (DJ), issued on 6 August 2000. DJ, which claims to protect the uniqueness of Christ, in fact expresses a profoundly anti-ecumenical spirit at odds with the sense of God's grace permeating the whole cosmos. DJ gives voice to a wider movement that is slowly but pervasively turning the Catholic church inward in an increasingly sectarian direction. It is this which concerns me most.

Sectarianism is incompatible with genuine catholicity. It is the antithesis of the kind of openness to the world, tolerant acceptance of others and a sense of religious pluralism that most thinking Catholics have been formed in and have embraced over the last three or four decades. Thus many Catholics find themselves involved in a corrosive disjunction between what they believe and have experienced, and the views expressed at the highest levels of the church. The reason is because those who claim to articulate Catholic belief seem to be abandoning their 'catholic' spirit. As a result there is a turning away from the other Christian churches, and a rejection of the search for common ground with the other great religious traditions. Thus more and more thinking Catholics who have been educated and live in pluralist, democratic and tolerant societies, find themselves in conflict with church hierarchs who seem to be moving in an ever-more sectarian direction.

Sometimes there is a hankering after a more genuinely Catholic approach - as you find in John Paul II's encyclical *Ut unum sint* (1995), where he went so far as to ask the other churches for advice on papal primacy. But ecclesiastical reality indicates that this hankering is, in fact, merely ecumenical wishful-thinking, while the hierarchical reality is exclusivist.

There have also been regular attempts to 'muzzle' and condemn the discussion of issues such as the ordination of women through the use of a new category of doctrine. This has received its clearest expression in the apostolic letter *Ad Tuendam Fidem* (30 June 1998). The letter argues that there is an intermediary, 'second-level' of revealed doctrine between the established and defined teaching that all Catholics believe, and what up until now has been called the 'ordinary magisterium'. Before the introduction of this so-called 'second-level', all non-infallible or non-defined teaching was exactly that: doctrine that should be respected and offered various levels of submission of mind and will, but still ultimately open to debate, discussion and development within the Church community.

What *Ad Tuendam Fidem* has done is to introduce formally through this 'second-level' a category of 'definitive' but non-infallibly-defined doctrine. Cardinal Josef Ratzinger says that this second-level teaching is, in fact, infallible. He says that it includes '... all those teachings in the dogmatic or moral area which are necessary for faithfully keeping and expounding the deposit of faith, even if they have not been proposed by the magisterium as formally revealed'. As examples of second-level definitive teaching he includes the condemnation of euthanasia, the validity of the canonization of a particular saint, the legitimacy of a papal election, and even the invalidity of Anglican orders. The gratuitous reference to 'Anglican orders' is astonishingly maladroit and insulting; it reveals a real lack of ecumenical sensitivity.

There is also an emerging unspoken assumption among some very senior church leaders that the contemporary western world is so far gone in individualism, permissiveness and consumerism that it is totally impervious to church teaching. Claiming to assume the broader historical perspective, these churchmen have virtually abandoned the secularised masses, to nurture elitist enclaves which will carry the true faith through to future, more 'receptive' generations. This is why the New Religious Movements (NRMs) have received so much favour and patronage in this papacy. The NRMs have embraced an essentially sectarian vision of Catholicism, are very hierarchical in structure and theologically reactionary. This is true of some elements in the Catholic charismatic movement, and also outfits like Opus Dei, Communion and Liberation, the Neo-Catechuminate and the Legionaries of Christ, as well as a number of other smaller, less significant groupings.

Over the years my public disquiet with increasing papal centralism and the erosion of the vision of a more ecumenical Catholicism is well known, especially in Australia. I have often been critical of the church's leadership, perhaps too harshly at times, in books, broadcasts, talks and articles. I have been concerned with ecclesiastical narrowness and the de facto denial of catholicity. But

I also constantly argued that it was only by 'staying in' the priesthood that someone like myself could influence things and bring about change. But it was always an every-day decision to continue the struggle through the internal structures of the church. And there can come a moment when you decide that both conscientiously and strategically 'staying in' no longer remains a viable or honest option. You realise that you can no longer collude in what is happening by remaining in the official priesthood.

While important, life-changing decisions may seem sudden to outsiders, and even some times to the person who makes them, that is rarely the case. Such conclusions are more likely to be the product of long unconscious reflection on an issue. Slowly the connections, inferences and directional movement in which the internal and unarticulated argument has been progressing comes into consciousness. Often it will be a single event that focusses your thought and impels you toward a decision. Suddenly you realise that, in conscience, you can no longer allow your name to be associated with what is happening. Of course, your judgement may be wrong, frighteningly so, but the Catholic tradition has always been that you must follow even an erroneous conscience. Certainly you must do everything you can to ascertain what is really happening and what your obligations are, but in the end you must be true to conscience.

What helped to focus my mind was the article 'Catholic Fundamentalism. Some Implications of *Dominus Jesus* for Dialogue and Peacemaking' by my friend, John D'Arcy May. [The article is one of a series of essays in the book, *Dominus Jesus. Anstoessige Wahrheit oder anstoessige Kirche* edited by Michael Rainer]. DJ is primarily directed against those Catholics involved in the 'wider ecumenism' who have been trying to find common ground with the great non-Christian religious traditions. But DJ also managed to offend many Anglicans and Protestants through an awkwardly-worded passage that was so obscure that many journalists incorrectly took it to mean that only Catholics could be saved. The passage actually says that Anglicanism and the various forms of Protestantism 'are not churches in the proper sense'(DJ, Paragraph 17).

It was the opening sentences of May's commentary that struck me between the eyes. 'There is no reason, in principle, why the Roman Catholic church, despite its enormous size and global presence, could not become a sect. Sectarianism is a matter of mentality, not size ... The deep shock *Dominus Jesus* caused in ecumenical circles consisted precisely in their exposure to the specifically Roman Catholic form of fundamentalism'. This put into words what I had unconsciously concluded but had not articulated.

It is precisely this movement in a sectarian and fundamentalist direction with which I profoundly disagree. A person with a public commitment like a priest is bound in conscience to ask: 'Can I continue to co-operate with this kind of regime in the church?' I feel bound in all honesty to say now: 'No. I cannot'. But I emphasise this does not mean that I have the slightest intention of leaving the community of the Catholic church, nor of abandoning my work in writing and media, as long as that is available to me.

But there is also a second constellation of reasons that have led to my resignation. They centre around the book *Papal Power* (1997) which is currently being examined by the Congregation for the Doctrine of the Faith (CDF), that part of the papal bureaucracy that deals with Catholic belief. I have consistently tried to keep this so-called 'examination' in perspective and have not treated it too seriously. However, it is clear to me that the CDF is moving toward an escalation of the issue. This inevitably involves other people. The CDF demands that all correspondence with me pass through a third party, the Superior General of my religious order, the Missionaries of the Sacred Heart (MSCs). This means that my superiors and the order will be caught in any cross-fire between the CDF and myself. I do not wish to put them in this position.

On 14 December 2000 the current Superior General of the MSCs, Father Michael Curran, was summoned to a meeting in the Palazzo of the Holy Office in the Vatican. This meeting happened totally without my knowledge and I only found out about it five weeks later. At the meeting Father Curran was asked why I had not responded to three issues raised in a letter from the CDF sent to me via Curran and my Australian superior in April 1999. He responded by providing the CDF with an article I had written in a theological magazine called *Compass* responding to the CDF's concerns. He felt the article 'would go a long way to answering' the CDF's questions. In the course of the discussion reference was also made to a mildly critical media statement about the CDF that I had made, which was briefly reported in the US *National Catholic Reporter* (16 July 1999).

Ratzinger claimed in a subsequent letter to Curran (18 December 2000) that my critical comments 'may put [my] alleged adherence to magisterial teaching in question'. In other words, even if my theological answers in the *Compass* article were found to be satisfactory, the comments in the *NCR* would show that I had not really repented because I was still criticising the CDF after writing the *Compass* article.

However, the Cardinal's chronology was wrong. His comments make it clear that he believes that the *NCR* interview was published after the *Compass* article. In fact, the 16 July, 1999 *NCR* interview was published several months before the spring 1999 edition of *Compass*. I suppose you could forgive the Cardinal for not remembering that spring in the southern hemisphere comes in September–October, and not in April–May as in the northern hemisphere. The *Compass* interview was published in the southern spring of 1999, which was October–November. That is some three or four months after the July *NCR* article.

Be that as it may, the whole tone of Ratzinger's letter to Curran makes it obvious that the CDF is preparing to censure me because the Cardinal's comments clearly prejudge the issue. The constant difficulty in dealing with the CDF is that your accusers are also your judges. An accused person is not even allowed to choose their own defence counsel; they are not even permitted to know the counsel's name.

This situation with the CDF will be exacerbated even more when a new book that I have edited is published in 2002 in the United States. It is entitled *The Modern Inquisition*. It consists of interviews that I put together with six people who have also been 'investigated' by the CDF. Those participating in it are Tissa

Balasuriya, Hans Küng, Charles Curran, Lavinia Byrne, Jeannine Gramick, and Robert Nugent, as well as myself. I have contributed two other essays, the first outlining the history of how the Roman Inquisition eventually evolved into the CDF, and a second describing and critiquing the details of the Congregation's procedures. While the tone of the book is respectful and moderate, I don't think it will win friends and influence people in Rome. I foresee considerable problems. The most important of these are that the book will eventually place Father Curran particularly, and the MSCs generally, in the likely position of being forced by the CDF to take some form of punitive action against me.

I have no doubt that the Congregation will not go away, and that they will not let this matter rest. As the experience of the six other people in the new book makes abundantly clear, there is never any form of dialogue. The Congregation simply demands that a person not only submit to what they define as 'doctrine', but they are determined that you actually use the words that they dictate. I knew exactly what I was doing when I edited *The Modern Inquisition*, but I thought it was important these stories be told for they expose the injustice of the CDF's procedures and their persecution of people who are clearly concerned to live a truly Catholic life and to give ministerial and theological leadership to others. But there is also no doubt that the book will lead to a further exacerbation of my relationship with the CDF, and that the order and Father Curran will be caught in the middle. My resignation will to some extent save them from that.

Finally, I want to make it absolutely clear that my resignation does not mean that I have any intention whatsoever of leaving the Catholic church. I am just changing status in the family. Catholicism is my home and I have no intention of leaving - come what may.

Paul Collins, March 1, 2001

Glossary

Anthropocentrism: the assumption that humankind constitutes the essential purpose and meaning of the whole universe. It includes the notion that the world was created primarily for human beings and that all other species are subservient to us.

Apologetics: the technique of defensive argumentation on behalf of religious belief. Within the Catholic context it refers specifically to that part of theology which explains what Catholics believe and why they believe it.

Apostasy/apostate: the total and deliberate abandonment of one's religion. Technically, it refers to a person who has publicly and completely rejected the faith into which they were baptised.

Aristotelian–Thomistic synthesis: the attempt by the great medieval theologians, particularly St Thomas Aquinas (1225–74), to integrate their theology with the philosophy of Aristotle (384–22 BC).

Base communities: in Spanish, *communidad de base*. These are small groups of usually poor Christians, mainly in Latin America, who gather together to reflect on their experience of life in the light of the Bible and Church teaching. They are usually lay-led and it is from this matrix that liberation theology has developed.

Burghers: a term of presumably Dutch origin, used to describe people of mixed-race origin in Sri Lanka.

Catechetics/catechist: the process of formation of a person in Christian faith. It is related to the word 'catechism', but nowadays refers to the systematic study of the belief of the Church and to basic initiation into the Christian community.

Christology: the theology of Christ. The word refers to critical theological reflection on a series of interconnected questions about the relationship between Jesus of Nazareth and Christ, and the relationship between Christ and God.

Collegiality: the word refers to the worldwide college of bishops in their cooperation with the Bishop of Rome in the government of the Catholic church. It re-emphasises the traditional notion that a bishop by his ordination is not just responsible for his own diocese, but also shares in a universal responsibility with the pope for the whole church.

Congregation: the term refers to the most important bureaucratic departments of the Roman Curia, the central government of the church. The word is derived from the Latin *congregatio*, meaning committee.

Consequentialism: a theory of ethical reasoning that is generally derived from utilitarianism. It emphasises that the morality of an action – that is, the rightness or wrongness of the action – is primarily constituted by the results or consequences of the action.

Delation/delate: derived from a Latin legal term referring to the action of reporting, accusing or denouncing someone to a legal authority for a presumed crime or misdemeanour. In the ecclesiastical sense it refers to reporting someone to the CDF for presumed unorthodoxy.

Diaconal: derived from the word 'deacon', it refers to the act of service or ministry.

Dicastery: the technical term used to describe a bureaucratic subdivision of the Roman curia.

Dominican: a member of the Order of Preachers (OP) founded by St Dominic Guzman in 1216.

Ecclesiology/ecclesiologist: that part of theological reflection which focuses on the nature of the Church, its structure and constitution.

Encyclical: a formal letter, usually concerned with a theological or pastoral topic, addressed by the pope to all the bishops of the world.

Episcopate: this word refers to the office and dignity of a bishop.

Faculties: authorisation granted to a priest which is derived from either canon law itself or through explicit delegation from a bishop or his approved delegate (e.g. his chancellor) to preach, celebrate the sacraments publicly and hear confessions in a specific diocese. These faculties are good until they are explicitly revoked.

Fascicle: a part of a printed work bound together as an instalment to facilitate publication.

Formation: the word refers generically to the training given to a person in a religious order. Fundamental formation is given in the novitiate. The person then advances to further studies in theology and other areas of expertise.

Habilitation: in Germany, the post-doctoral lecturing qualification, usually required before a person can become a lecturer in a university.

Homunculus: literally, 'little human being'. It refers here to the ancient medical belief that sperm contained tiny fully formed humans that only needed a womb in which to develop.

Infallible/infallibility: the gift of the Spirit that ensures that official church teaching is immune from error. It is the pope who normally gives voice to the accepted universal belief of the bishops and the church community.

Institute of the Blessed Virgin Mary: a religious order of sisters, also some times known as the 'English Ladies' (*Englische Fraulein*) founded in 1609 by Mary Ward.

The order was modelled on the Jesuits. Nowadays the sisters are engaged largely in education in the broadest sense of the word.

Jansenism/Jansenist: a religious reform movement in the Catholic church which originated with Cornelius Jansen (1585–1638). Its influence spread across Europe. Deeply pessimistic about human nature, it demanded a strict asceticism and moral rigorism. It was opposed to the centralising tendencies of the papacy and the absolutism of the French monarchy.

Jesuit (SJ): The Jesuit order of priests and brothers is the most well known in the Catholic church. Its proper title is the Society of Jesus. Founded by the Spaniard Ignatius Loyola in 1540, the Jesuits undertake an extraordinarily wide variety of ministries and the order is found in many countries of the world.

Liberation theology: a theological reflection that emerges from an oppressed group's attempts to articulate Christian faith from within the context of injustice and political and economic exploitation. It is intimately related to the base community movement.

Magisterium: teaching authority in the Church. It is exercised by the pope and the bishops. There is also a sense in which theologians also have a magisterium.

Manualist: one who writes textbooks. In this context one of the writers of moral theology textbooks, produced largely from the late seventeenth to the early twentieth centuries which were used in seminaries in the days before the Vatican Council II (1962–5).

Mariology: the theology of the role and function of the Blessed Virgin Mary.

Missionaries of the Sacred Heart (MSC): a religious order of priests and brothers founded in France in 1854. Nowadays they carry on a wide range of ministries, especially in developing countries.

Monsignor: an ecclesiastical title given by the pope to a senior priest. It is purely honorary.

Oblates of Mary Immaculate (OMI): a religious order of priests and brothers founded in 1816 in France. Nowadays they conduct missions in parishes and retreats and are involved with the poor and the most disadvantaged.

Obsequium religiosum: a Latin term which can mean either 'religious respect' or 'religious submission'. It specifically refers to the attitude that a theologian or Catholic ought take to teachings of the ordinary, non-definitive papal magisterium. It connotes willingness to submit loyally to the teachings of the magisterium.

Opus Dei: literally 'the work of God'. Here it refers to an organisation of lay people and priests founded in 1928 in Madrid, Spain by the priest Jose Maria Escriva de Balaguer (1902–75). Its lay and priestly members work largely is educational ministries, and the organisation is characterised by alleged secrecy, theological conservatism and rigorous spirituality.

Patristics: the study of the fathers or ancient theologians of the Church.

Physicalism: the identification of a moral act with the physical structure of the act.

Plentiudo potestatem: a Latin tag meaning 'the fullness of power'. It comes from Roman Law and in the medieval period became gradually identified with papal primacy. Thus the pope is seen as exercising the fullness of power and authority in the church.

Popular religion: characterises the peripheral but often colourful beliefs, rites and practices that almost always accompany mainstream religion.

Praxis: literally 'practice' as opposed to theory. In theology it refers to the expression of discipleship through ministry.

Primacy (papal): the jurisdictional authority of the pope over the whole Church and every person in the Church. It was defined at Vatican Council I (1870) and further clarified at Vatican Council II (1962–5).

Proportionalism: strictly speaking it is the moral theory that says that you can commit a physical evil if there is a proportionate reason. In more general terms it refers to the fact that no moral judgment can be made about an action without taking into consideration all of the circumstances that constitute and are part of that action. It is only by weighing all of these circumstances that one is able to make an ethical judgment about that act.

Proselytism: seeking to make converts; persuading people to change from one religion to another.

Provincial: religious orders are divided into geographical areas called provinces. A provincial-superior is the person in charge of the province.

Redemptorists (CSsR): the Congregation of the Most Holy Redeemer, a religious order of priests and brothers, commonly known as the Redemptorists. Founded in Naples in 1732 by St Alphonsus Liguori, their main ministries are retreats, parish missions and education.

Rigorism: the theory in moral theology that the ethical law must always be applied in the fullness of its rigour. It is based on a notion of God as a severe judge who demands total obedience.

Roman Curia: the central bureaucracy of the Catholic Church.

Salesians of Don Bosco (SDB): a religious order of priests and brothers founded by St John Bosco in Turin, Italy in 1859. Today numerically one of the largest orders in the Church. Their primary ministry is helping poor youth and offering them education.

Salvatorians (SDS): The Society of the Divine Saviour, a religious order of priests and brothers founded in Rome in 1881. They minister through education, parishes and give retreats.

Schism/schismatic: a formal breach of church unity when a group breaks off from a Church or religious body over doctrinal or disciplinary differences.

School Sisters of Notre Dame (SSND): a religious order of sisters founded in

Munich, Germany, in 1833. They came to the United States in 1847 with German immigrants. They are now spread across the world with over 6000 sisters, mainly engaged in the ministry of education.

Silentium obsequiosem: a Latin tag meaning respectful or submissive silence. It refers to the attitude that should be taken by a theologian who does not accept a teaching of the ordinary and non-definitive magisterium.

Superior: a person who exercises leadership in religious order.

Superior-general: Sometimes referred to as general-superior. A person who exercises the highest level of leadership in a religious order.

Teilhard de Chardin, Pierre (1881–1955): French Jesuit priest and scientist whose theories on biological and human evolution have had tremendous influence on contemporary theology.

Thomism: the theology of St Thomas Aquinas (1225–74).

Ultramontanism: the word is derived from *ultra montes* (beyond the mountains) and it refers to the tendency of Catholics to look beyond the Alps to papal Rome as the source and fountain of all theological wisdom, power and teaching in the church. Generically, it means an attitude of papo-centrism.

Young Christian Workers (YCW): a lay movement of young Catholics founded in Belgium after WWI by the priest (later cardinal) Joseph Cardijn. They are also known as 'Jocists'. They tried to incorporate their Catholic values into their work environment.

Bibliography

Allen, John 2000, *Cardinal Ratzinger: The Vatican's Enforcer of the Faith*, Continuum, New York.

Balasuriya, Tissa 1976, *Jesus Christ and Human Liberation*, Centre for Society and Religion, Colombo.

Balasuriya, Tissa 1977, *The Eucharist and Human Liberation*, Centre for Society and Religion, Colombo.

Balasuriya, Tissa 1990, *Mary and Human Liberation*, Centre for Society and Religion, Colombo.

Bermejo, Luis 1992, *Infallibility on Trial: Church, Conciliarity and Communion*, Christian Classics Inc., Westminster, MD.

Boff, Leonardo 1985, *Church, Charism and Power*, English translation, Crossroad, New York.

Byrne, Lavinia 1988, *Women Before God*, SPCK, London, and Twenty Third Publications, Mystic CN.

Byrne, Lavinia (ed.) 1991, *The Hidden Tradition*, SPCK, London, and Crossroad, New York.

Byrne, Lavinia (ed.) 1993, *The Hidden Journey*, SPCK, London.

Byrne, Lavinia (ed.) 1994, *Woman at the Altar*, Mowbrays, London.

Byrne, Lavinia (ed.) 1995, *The Hidden Voice*, SPCK, London.

Byrne, Lavinia 1999, *The Dome of Heaven*, Hodder Headline, London.

Byrne, Lavinia 2000, *The Journey is My Home*, Hodder Headline, London.

Cahill, Lisa Sowle 1999, 'Silencing of Nugent, Gramick, Sets a Novel Standard of Orthodoxy', *America*, August 14, pp 6–10.

Chadwick, Owen 1981, *The Popes and European Revolution*, Oxford University Press, Oxford.

Collins, Paul 1986, *Mixed Blessings: John Paul II and the Church of the Eighties*, Penguin, Melbourne.

BIBLIOGRAPHY

Collins, Paul 1995, *God's Earth: Religion as if Matter Really Mattered*, HarperCollins Religious, Melbourne.

Collins, Paul 1997, *Papal Power: A Proposal for Change in Catholicism's Third Millennium*, HarperCollins Religious, Melbourne.

Collins, Paul 2000, *Upon this Rock: The Popes and their Changing Role*, Melbourne University Press, Melbourne.

Cornwell, John 1989, *A Thief in the Night*, Penguin, London.

Curran, Charles & Hunt, Robert 1970, *Dissent in and for the Church: Theologians and Humanae Vitae*, Sheed & Ward, New York.

Curran, Charles (ed.) 1962, *Contraception, Authority and Dissent*, Herder & Herder, New York.

Curran, Charles 1986, *Faithful Dissent*, Sheed & Ward, Kansas City.

Dessain, Charles Stephen (ed.) 1974, *The Letters and Diaries of John Henry Newman*, vol. 25, Oxford University Press, Oxford.

Dupuis, Jacques 1999, *Toward a Christian Theology of Religious Pluralism*, Orbis, Maryknoll, NY.

Fuchs, Josef 1984, *Ethics in a Secular Arena*, Gill & Macmillan, Dublin.

Gramick, Jeannine & Nugent, Robert (eds) 1995, *Voices of Hope: A Collection of Positive Catholic Writings on Gay and Lesbian Issues*, New York: Center for Homophobia Education, New York.

Häring, Bernard 1963 (vols 1 & 2), 1967 (vol. 3), *The Law of Christ*, English translation, Mercier Press, Cork.

Häring, Bernard 1999, *My Hope for the Church: Engagement for the Twenty-First Century*, Triumph, Liguori, Missouri.

Hasler, August Bernhard 1981, *How the Pope Became Infallible: Pius IX and the Politics of Persuasion*, English translation, Doubleday, New York.

Hunt, John F. & Connolly, Terrence R. 1970, *The Responsibility of Dissent: The Church and Academic Freedom*, Sheed & Ward, New York.

Jedin, Hubert (ed.) 1981, *History of the Church: The Church in the Industrial Age*, vol. 9, Crossroad, New York.

Kaiser, Robert Blair 1985, *The Politics of Sex and Religion*, Leaven Press, Kansas City.

Kosnick, Anthony & Modras, Ronald 1977, *Human Sexuality: New Directions in American Catholic Thought*, Paulist, New York.

Küng, Hans 1961, *The Council and Reunion*, Sheed & Ward, London.

Küng, Hans 1964, *Structures of the Church*, Thomas Nelson, New York.

Küng, Hans 1964, *Justification: The Doctrine of Karl Barth and a Catholic Reflection*, Thomas Nelson, New York.

Küng, Hans 1967, *The Church*, Burns & Oates, London.

Küng, Hans 1971, *Infallible? An Inquiry*, Collins, London.

Küng, Hans 1977, *On Being a Christian*, Collins, London.

Küng, Hans 1978, *Truthfulness: The Future of the Church*, Sheed & Ward, London & New York.

Küng, Hans 1980, *Does God Exist? An Answer for Today*, Collins, London.

Küng, Hans 1984, *Eternal Life?* Collins, London.

Messori, Vittorio 1985, *The Ratzinger Report: An Exclusive Interview on the State of the Church*, Ignatius, San Francisco.

McCormick, Richard 1987, 'Notes on Moral Theology, 1986', *Theological Studies*, 48 (1987), pp 8 – 105.

Nugent, Robert, Gramick, Jeannine & Oddo, Thomas 1976, *Homosexual Catholics: A Primer for Discussion*, Dignity, Washington.

Nugent, Robert (ed.) 1983, *A Challenge to Love: Lesbian and Gay Catholics in the Church*, Crossroad, New York.

Nugent, Robert & Gramick, Jeannine (eds) 1992, *Building Bridges: Gay and Lesbian Reality and the Catholic Church*, Twenty-Third Publications, Mystic CT.

Örsy, Ladislas 1998, 'Are Church Investigation Procedures Really Just?', *Doctrine and Life*, 48 (1998), pp 453–65.

Reese, Thomas 1996, *Inside the Vatican: The Politics and Organization of the Catholic Church*, Harvard University Press, Cambridge, Mass.

Rock, John A. 1962, *The Time Has Come: A Catholic Doctor's Proposal to End the Battle for Birth Control*, Knopf, New York.

Rynne, Xavier 1963, *Letters from Vatican City*, Farrer, Straus, New York.

Schatz, Klaus 1996, *Papal Primacy: From its Origins to the Present*, English translation, Liturgical Press, Collegeville, Minn.

Schillebeeckx, Edward 1981, *Ministry: Leadership in the Community of Jesus Christ*, English translation, Crossroad, New York.

Shannon, James Patrick 1998, *The Reluctant Dissenter*, Crossroad, New York.

Sullivan, Francis A. 1996, *Creative Fidelity: Weighing and Interpreting the Documents of the Magisterium*, Paulist, New York 1981.

Swidler, Leonard (ed.) 1981, *Küng in Conflict*, Doubleday, New York.

Tadeschi, John 1991, *The Prosecution of Heresy: Collected Studies on the Inquisition in Early Modern Italy*, Medieval and Renaissance Texts and Studies, Binghampton, NY.

Witham, Larry 1991, *Curran v. the Catholic University: A Study of Authority and Freedom in Conflict*, Edington-Rand, Riverdale, MD.